PLAYS AND PROGRAMS
for
BOYS AND GIRLS

Plays and Programs for Boys and Girls

*A collection of thirty royalty-free,
one-act plays for young players*

By
CLAIRE BOIKO

Publishers   **PLAYS, INC.**   *Boston*

U.S. Library of Congress Cataloging in Publication Data

Boiko, Claire.
    Plays and programs for boys and girls.

    SUMMARY: Among other topics includes plays on ecology and various holidays as well as those that dramatize science fiction, fairy tales, and American Indian legends.

    1. Children's plays. [1. Plays. 2. One-act plays]
I. Title.
PN6120.A5B6444   812'.5'4   72-75324
ISBN 0-8238-0134-9

MANUFACTURED IN THE UNITED STATES OF AMERICA

Contents

PLAYS AND PROGRAMS
for
BOYS AND GIRLS

Take Me to Your Marshal

Characters

MR. REED   ZANTHUS
MRS. REED   1ST TV VOICE, *Martian Giant Angleworm*
ROBBIE   2ND TV VOICE, *Commander Smash Borden*
JIM   3RD TV VOICE, *announcer*
LORI   4TH TV VOICE, *Dr. Cynthia Cyborg*

TIME: *A summer evening.*
SETTING: *The Reed living room.*
AT RISE: ROBBIE, JIM, *and* LORI *sit on floor crosslegged, looking at television, which faces away from audience.* MRS. REED *sits on sofa, center, and* MR. REED *on chair, right, reading newspaper. As children watch program,* TV VOICES *are heard.*

1ST TV VOICE: So, earthlings, you have invaded our planet Mars.
2ND TV VOICE: Yes, and we were hardly prepared for what we found. But listen, Giant Angleworm—people and worms can coexist.
ROBBIE: Yeah—people and worms get along fine on Earth.
1ST TV VOICE: Never! You have too many arms and legs. You are unsightly. Ugh! I will expedite you.
2ND TV VOICE: Very well. Expedite me. But let my trusty technician, the girl scientist and cook, Dr. Cynthia Cyborg, go free.

3

LORI (*Excited*): Oh, yes, let the girl go free!

4TH TV VOICE (*A woman*): No. No, Smash Borden, Commander of the Mars Exploration Module. I must stay with you. Duty calls. Loud and clear!

2ND TV VOICE: R-r-roger, Dr. Cynthia Cyborg. You are . . . you are all heart. By Jupiter, you're a real *girl!*

4TH TV VOICE: Oh, Smash. You never called me "girl" before. Giant Angleworm, we are prepared to meet our doom.

1ST TV VOICE: Splendid! Line up single file. Perhaps you have noticed my highly efficient corkscrew nose, which is actually a lethal weapon? Stand still, earthlings. I am going to *bore* you to death! (*Dramatic music, fading out*)

3RD TV VOICE: Well, junior spacemen! Will Commander Smash Borden and his trusty technician, Dr. Cynthia Cyborg, girl scientist and cook, actually be *bored* to death? What a way to go! Tune in next week and find out what ghastly future awaits our dauntless duo in the episode entitled, "The Giant Angleworm Meets the Mighty Mole!" (ROBBIE *turns TV set off.*)

LORI: That was scary. Imagine—a giant angleworm. I can't even stand little earthworms!

ROBBIE: Dad, do you think there are such things as giant angleworms on other planets?

MR. REED (*Putting down paper*): There certainly could be. Somewhere in the galaxy there are bound to be other forms of life.

MRS. REED: Of course. Look at the range of life here on Earth: everything from human beings to giant squid.

JIM: If there are giant angleworms in outer space, I hope they stay there and don't decide to start a real estate development on Earth.

LORI: Real estate—that's nothing, Jim. I'd gladly give them a few acres of land. But what if we're the main dish on some outer-space menu?

ROBBIE (*Walking to* LORI, *stiff-legged*): Ah, here is my appetizer. (*He takes her hand and pretends to nibble her fingers.*) Knuckles of earth-girl in mud pie sauce. Very tasty, but next time, go easy on the mud.

LORI (*Pulling hand away; nervously*): Now stop that, Robbie. It's not funny. All kinds of things could be flying around up there.

JIM (*Soberly*): Yeah. We've been making a lot of noise in space lately. Maybe we've been attracting attention.

MRS. REED: Funny you should say that. I heard that the airport has been reporting strange blips on the radar. They can't account for them.

MR. REED (*Impatiently*): Now, Janet. There are hundreds of reasons for unidentified radar blips, including an unscheduled flight of sea gulls. (*Lights flash on and off.*)

LORI (*Gasping*): Wh-what was that? (ROBBIE *goes to window, right, and peers out.*)

ROBBIE: The whole sky is lighted up.

MR. REED: Heat lightning. That's all. (*Lights flash again.*)

ROBBIE (*Looking out window; excitedly*): Dad—come here! (MR. REED *joins* ROBBIE *at window, and rest of family crowds in behind them.*)

JIM: Holy smoke! What is that?

MR. REED: Say—it's a fireball. A real fireball zooming around over our house.

MRS. REED: A fireball! Is it dangerous?

MR. REED: Of course not. It's a kind of static lightning. It's quite harmless, but rather rare. I never expected to see it this close.

JIM: Hey—look! What a neat fireball. It has little windows in it and an antenna!

MRS. REED: Harry—should a fireball have little windows and an antenna?

MR. REED: Of course not! You're imagining things. (*He takes closer look out window, then draws back.*) Good heavens!

Listen, everybody. Don't panic. Do exactly what I tell you to do. Come away from the windows slowly—as if everything were normal. (*All back away slowly, frightened.*) Children—sit down by the television set, just as you were. (*They sit down, exchanging puzzled glances.*) Janet—you knit or whatever. I'll sit here and read the paper. (MRS. REED *sits, knitting with trembling hands.* MR. REED *sits in chair, reading paper upside down.*)

MRS. REED (*Whispering*): Harry, for goodness' sake! What did you see? (MR. REED *puts down paper.*)

MR. REED: That fireball has little windows and an antenna. I think it's a flying saucer.

ALL (*Loudly*): Oh!

MR. REED: Sh-h-h. It's important that we don't attract the attention of whoever or whatever is inside those windows.

LORI (*Whispering tearfully*): Oh, Daddy. I don't want to be anybody's blue-plate special.

MR. REED: We have to have a plan now. Listen . . . This is Plan A. . . . If anything comes through that door, I will simply pick up a poker from the fireplace and hit it on the—on whatever it uses for a head.

JIM: But, Dad, we don't have a fireplace.

MR. REED: Then we'll use Plan B. . . . I'll tackle it as it comes through the door. Robbie, you sit on its feet. Janet, you call the police, and Jim, you stand by your sister.

ROBBIE (*Softly*): But, Dad, suppose it doesn't have any feet? Suppose it has slimy tentacles.

MR. REED: In that case, Plan C goes into effect. . . . We try diplomacy. I will greet it in the name of Earth. Robbie, you bow very low. Janet, you call the State Department. And, Lori, you bring out the ladyfingers and the ginger ale.

LORI: But suppose it'd rather have *real* ladyfingers.

MR. REED: Oh, for heaven's sake! We don't know what

kind of creature it is. It might be nothing more than a giant carrot.

MRS. REED (*Wailing*): Oh, no!

MR. REED: What's wrong, Janet?

MRS. REED (*Breaking down*): We had carrots for dinner. Maybe it's offended!

MR. REED (*Exploding*): You can't offend a carrot! Now listen, everybody. Keep cool. Chances are that it's looking for the power lines to refuel. (*Lights go out.*)

ALL (*Ad lib*): Oh! It's dark. What happened? (*Etc.*)

MR. REED (*At the top of his lungs*): Quiet! Quiet! (*Whispering*) Pretend that nobody's home. (*After moment of total silence, lights come on dim. Approaching footsteps are heard.*)

MRS. REED: Harry—something's coming toward the house.

MR. REED: Sh-h-h. I'm trying to hear how many feet it has. (*Sound of footsteps climbing stairs.*)

ROBBIE: It's on the porch. (*Sound of doorknob rattling.*)

JIM: Dad, it's at the front door.

ROBBIE: Which plan, Dad? Which plan?

MR. REED: Get behind the door with me, boys. (*They cross to door upstage.*) Janet and Lori, crouch down behind the sofa. (*They do so.*) When it comes through the door, we'll tackle it.

ROBBIE: What signals, Dad?

MR. REED: Six-twenty-forty-two-hike. (*Sound of doorknob rattling.*)

MRS. REED: It's coming in! (ZANTHUS, *wearing space suit and cap with antennae, cautiously opens door and enters.*)

MR. REED: Six-twenty-forty-two-hike! (ROBBIE, JIM *and* MR. REED *tackle* ZANTHUS. *All land in heap upstage.* MRS. REED *and* LORI *cover their faces with hands and scream. Lights go on full.*)

ZANTHUS (*From bottom of heap*): H-e-e-lp!

ROBBIE (*Rising, astonished*): It said "help"!

JIM: Hey, let's see what kind of thing the thing is. (*He rises and peers at* ZANTHUS.)

MR. REED (*Getting up*): Get away, boys. He may have a weapon that could evaporate you. (*Doubling his fists and moving toward* ZANTHUS) Don't reach for anything or I'll pound you to a pulp.

ZANTHUS (*Sitting up, putting his hands above his head*): Don't hit me! Don't hit me!

JIM: Hey, what do you know? It's an English-speaking thing.

ROBBIE: With one head, two arms and two legs. (*He walks around the cowering* ZANTHUS.) And no tail. (MRS. REED *and* LORI *slowly raise their heads and look at* ZANTHUS.)

MR. REED (*Cautiously*): We're not out of danger yet. He may have strange powers beyond those of mortals. Smile, everybody. Show your teeth. (*To* ZANTHUS) We friends. (*Indicating family*) We no hurt spaceman. Understand?

ZANTHUS (*In a pronounced Western accent*): Sure I understand. (*He rubs his head.*) You're the kind of friends that ambush a feller in the dark and set on him when he's paying a social call. (*He stands and dusts himself off.*) I come down all the way from the back of the moon to ask you a favor, and you push me down and set on me! By dogies, that ain't nice!

ROBBIE: Dad, I think we goofed.

JIM: It's an English-speaking cowboy-creature.

MRS. REED: Oh, dear. Harry—do you suppose he's an ambassador from another planet? Have we caused an incident?

MR. REED (*Rubbing his head*): Probably. It'd be just our luck. I'll do what I can to pacify him. (*To* ZANTHUS) Ah—sir. Sir, we apologize for our rough reception. We've never had a spaceship land in our backyard. We didn't know what to expect.

MRS. REED: Invite him to sit down, Harry. That is, if he
sits.

MR. REED: Would you like to sit down? You do sit down,
don't you?

ZANTHUS (*Relieved*): Why, sure. That sounds more like it.
(*They all take seats.* ZANTHUS *sits in chair right;* ROBBIE *and*
JIM *sit on arms of chair.* MR. REED, MRS. REED *and* LORI *sit
on sofa. There is an awkward pause, as they stare at each other.*)

MR. REED: Well!

ZANTHUS: Well! So, this here is the planet Earth.

MRS. REED (*Brightly*): That's right. That's absolutely right.
Did you have a long trip?

ZANTHUS: Mighty long. Yes, ma'am. (*They all look at each
other expectantly.*) Well. So this here is the planet Earth.

MR. REED: Oh, yes. This is definitely Earth.

MRS. REED: Have you visited us before?

ZANTHUS: No. This is my first trip down to the surface.

MRS. REED: Imagine that, Harry. This is his first trip down
to the surface. (*Silence falls again.*)

ROBBIE: Boy-oh-boy. A guy from outer space lands in our
backyard. It must be the most historic moment since the
discovery of fire, and nobody can think of a thing to say!

MR. REED: We're dumbfounded, just dumbfounded. (*To*
ZANTHUS) Are you a little dumbfounded, too?

ZANTHUS: Yes sirree, dumbfounded.

JIM: What's your name?

MRS. REED: Sh-h-h, Jim. It might not be polite. Perhaps
he'd rather not disclose his name.

ZANTHUS: Shucks, I don't mind. My name is Zanthus—
Zanthus Amanthus from the planet Radamanthus in the
constellation Orion. But you can call me Buck.

MR. REED: This is fantastic. I don't know exactly how to
proceed. Is there someone you'd like to make contact
with? Somebody official? Would you like to meet our
President?

ZANTHUS: Shucks, I'm not here on an official mission. Matter of fact, I sneaked off for a visit. My boss doesn't even know I'm here—I hope.

MRS. REED: Your . . . boss. Oh, dear. Are there more of you—just waiting to invade us?

ZANTHUS: No, ma'am. Just me. I'm your friendly Pry in the Sky.

ROBBIE: What's a Pry in the Sky?

ZANTHUS: A monitor. A sky-jockey. A feller who sits up on a rocky pasture up on the far side of the moon and watches and listens.

MRS. REED (*Sighing with relief*): Then you're not going to invade us?

ZANTHUS: Shucks, no. We have a nice planet of our own. We're keeping an eye out to see that *you* don't invade *us.* Matter of fact, this is my last tour of duty. Tonight I go back to Orion for good. (*Rapid beeping sound is heard from offstage.*)

MR. REED: What's that?

ZANTHUS: My boss is calling. I knew it was too good to last. He's sent a probe, and he wants to know what I'm doing down yonder. He's telling me to get going right away. (*He takes out slide whistle and blows it.*) There. That ought to hold him for a while.

JIM: Say, Buck. Why do you talk like a cowpoke? Where'd you learn English?

ZANTHUS: From your television. We tap your frequencies. I've been studying your lingo for nigh onto five years, day and night. If you don't mind my saying so—you Earth folks are mighty strange!

MR. REED: Wait a minute. I'm beginning to understand. What particular frequency have you tapped?

ZANTHUS: It's called Channel Seven.

MR. REED: Channel Seven! No wonder he sounds like a cowboy, Jim. Channel Seven runs nothing but Westerns!

ZANTHUS: Say, now, I've been forgetting my manners. You folks go right ahead. I know all about your customs. Go right ahead. Break.

LORI (*Bewildered*): Break? Break what?

ZANTHUS: Break for a commercial.

LORI (*Laughing*): We don't break for commercials. We'd never get anything done. (*Sound of louder and more insistent beeping is heard from offstage.*)

ZANTHUS: There he goes again. Never gives me a minute's peace. (*He blows whistle again.*) I swear, I'm not going back until I've shaken the hand of the mighty man from Dodge.

JIM: Who's the mighty man from Dodge?

ZANTHUS: Why, that's the favor I was going to ask you. There's one feller above all the others who sticks in my mind as I watch the posses come and go on my receiver up there. A feller who walks six-and-a-half feet tall. Quick on the draw. Honest and strong. My hero. Marshal Dillon. Take me to your Marshal!

ROBBIE: Oh, boy, are we in trouble!

JIM: But, Buck. You don't understand . . . (MR. REED *stops him.*)

MR. REED (*Taking* JIM *aside*): Not now, Jim. . . . It's Zanthus's last night on Earth. You can't tell him there's no real Marshal Dillon. It's too cruel. Let me handle this. Do what I say. (*He whispers into* JIM's *ear.* JIM *nods and exits left.*)

ZANTHUS: Marshal Matt Dillon. I sure admire that man.

MR. REED: Zanthus—uh—Buck. I'm sorry to have to tell you this. You're about a thousand miles away from Dodge City.

ZANTHUS (*Regretfully*): I am? Why I thought, sure as shooting, I was right on target, on the outskirts of Dodge. (*Sound of very rapid beeping is heard from offstage.*)

MR. REED: Your boss sounds angry. We don't want you to

get into trouble with him, Zanthus. I'll tell you what we'll do. When we next see Marshal Dillon, we'll give him your regards. (*Turning*) Won't we, everybody? (*They all nod vigorously.*)

ZANTHUS: Why, that's mighty fine of you folks, mighty fine! Just tell Marshal Dillon that somebody up there likes him. (*He blows on whistle.*) I'm coming. Hold your horses! (*He starts to cross to upstage door.*) I'm coming.

JIM (*Running in from left carrying cowboy belt, two six-guns, and a Stetson with two holes*): Wait, Buck! We can't let you go back to your planet without official souvenirs of Earth. (*He holds out gifts.* ZANTHUS, *overcome with delight, takes them, buckles on belt and puts on Stetson over his antennae.*) See—I even cut two holes in the Stetson for your antennae.

ZANTHUS: There's nothing on Earth I'd rather have. (*He draws gun quickly.*) Draw! Say—that was pretty good for a foreigner, wasn't it? (*All applaud warmly.*) Thank you kindly, folks. I sure am sorry I can't return the favor. But I'll tell you this: We've been monitoring you for quite a spell. Some of the reports haven't been so good. We put you on the intergalactic blacklist for tourists. But you folks here have been so nice that I'm going to put four stars after my report on you.

MRS. REED: Four stars? What does that mean?

ZANTHUS: It means approved for tourists from outer space. (*Curtains begin to close.*) You just wait, ma'am. You're goin' to be the luckiest lady in your territory. In thirty days, spaceships from just about everywhere are going to be landing in your backyard!

JIM, ROBBIE, *and* LORI: Hooray!

MR. *and* MRS. REED (*Holding their heads*): Oh, no! Not again! (*Curtains close quickly.*)

THE END

How to Choose a Boy

Characters

WOOFINGTON T. BOWSER, *a dog*
MADAME FIDEAUX ⎫
FIFI FIDEAUX ⎬ *poodles*
NANCY
EMILY OGLEBY VON BLUESTOCKING
MAJOR BEAGLE, *a dog*
BILL
MR. ROVER ⎫
MRS. ROVER ⎬ *dogs*
SPORTY ROVER, *a pup*
HUNTER
BOXER
GREYHOUND DRIVER
HUSKY BOY

SETTING: *Woofington T. Bowser's People Shop.*
AT RISE: WOOFINGTON T. BOWSER *is writing on order form at counter, up center. Signs on curtain or counter read:* PEDIGREED PEOPLE SOLD HERE. A DOG'S BEST FRIEND IS A MAN. THIS IS BE KIND TO HUMANS WEEK. *Telephone on counter rings.*

BOWSER (*Answering phone*): Hello? Woofington T. Bowser's People Shop. Our people are guaranteed free from fleas. May I help you? . . . You say your pet is listless, pale,

13

and won't eat? . . . What kind of pet, and how old is it, please? . . . A teen-age boy? I see. What have you been feeding him, ma'am? . . . Hamburgers three times a day? You'll have to stop that, ma'am. That's too much hamburger even for a teen-age boy. Try hot dogs for the next week or two—well-done, and be sure to use mustard. Human beings need lots of mustard. . . . Thank you, ma'am. (*He hangs up, shaking his head.*) Honestly, dogs are so careless about people these days! (MADAME FIDEAUX *and* FIFI, *who holds* NANCY *by collar of her dress, enter from right.* NANCY *carries jump rope.*) Ah, Madame Fideaux and little Fifi. What brings you back to my shop so soon?

MADAME: Monsieur Bow-sair, this little girl you sold us— she will not do. When Fifi first saw her in your window, gamboling with all the other little girls, she thought this girl was perfect. But now—

FIFI (*Fussily*): She's spoiled. She's too, too dull. She doesn't know how to play with me. I want her to chase balls on the lawn, and dig for bones in the garden with me. But this girl—all she wants to do is stand on her silly hind legs and jump over that silly old rope she has. (NANCY *jumps rope.*) See? What kind of a companion is that?

BOWSER: Down, Nancy. Good girl. (NANCY *stops jumping.*) Why, she's just a child. It takes time and patience to teach a human being to dig for bones. Some never learn.

FIFI: Take her back. I want a smarter human being.

BOWSER: All right, all right. Back to your kennel, Nancy. There's a good little person. (NANCY *exits left.*)

MADAME: I myself would like someone much showier. Someone with a pedigree that we could enter in the People Show. Have you anyone like that, perhaps?

BOWSER (*Bowing*): Of course, Madame. (*Calling off left*) Emily! Here, Emily! (EMILY *enters left, wearing party dress and an elaborate hair-do. She walks over to* BOWSER.)

FIFI: Well, that's more like it.

BOWSER: This is Emily Ogleby Von Bluestocking, a direct descendant of the Bluestockings who came over on the *Mayflower* with the English Bulls. A pedigreed poodle like yourself would never be ashamed to walk down the street with Emily. She's a real conversation piece.

MADAME: Has she had obedience training?

BOWSER: The best. Let me demonstrate. (*He fastens clip end of leash to his collar, and places end of leash in* EMILY's *hand. Then he leads her down right. She walks in haughty fashion.*) Heel, Emily. (*She trips daintily beside him.*) Sit, Emily. (EMILY *sits in chair. She folds her hands in her lap and crosses her ankles.* BOWSER *unfastens leash from his collar.*)

FIFI: Does she do tricks? I want a girl who can do tricks.

BOWSER: Of course. Speak, Emily.

EMILY (*In cultured voice*): How do you do? I am delighted to make your acquaintance.

MADAME: *Charmante!* A real blue-blood. We'll take her. Just charge her to my account and send along a diamond-studded leash for her. Come, Fifi. *Au revoir*, monsieur. (BOWSER *clips* EMILY's *leash to* FIFI's *collar.* FIFI *and* EMILY *walk haughtily off right, followed by* MADAME.)

BOWSER (*Calling off right*): Goodbye, Madame Fideaux. I hope she works out for you. (*To audience*) That's their fourth child in a month. Those poodles are never satisfied. Tricks! Shows! Why don't they get a toy that winds up? It seems that dogs don't want human beings for friendship any more. (MAJOR BEAGLE *storms in right, dragging* BILL *by the arm.* BILL *is crying.*) Why, it's Major Beagle, and Bill. What's the matter, Major?

MAJOR (*Sputtering*): Matter, sir, matter? False representation. That's what. You sold me this miserable boy yesterday. You assured me he was in perfect shape—intelligent, reliable—

BOWSER: He is. At least, he was in perfect shape when I sold him to you.

MAJOR: Then why can't he hunt ducks, tell me that? He can't point. He can't retrieve. He just sits and looks at me. The ninny!

BOWSER: But, I thought you wanted a friend—somebody to sit by your side. Somebody to tell your troubles to.

MAJOR: Fiddle-faddle. I want a hunting boy, sir, someone I can treat like a well-oiled machine. I don't need a friend. I need a hunter, sir.

BOWSER: All right. All right. (*He pats* BILL *on head and feels his brow.*) Hm-m. Your head is hot. Emotionally upset, that's what you are. Never mind, Bill, we'll find a good home for you. (BILL *sits in chair down right.*) Here, Major, I'll call a hunter for you. (*Takes whistle from his pocket and pretends to blow it.*) Did you hear that whistle?

MAJOR: No, sir. I heard nothing.

BOWSER: It's a new low-pitch whistle. Only humans can hear it. (HUNTER, *a boy in pith helmet, with a toy gun slung on his back, runs on from left.*) There you are, Major Beagle. A real hunter.

MAJOR: Does he point? That's the important thing.

BOWSER: Point, boy, point. (HUNTER *shades his eyes, looks off right, and slowly extends his arm, pointing his finger toward ceiling.*)

MAJOR: Splendid. By Jove, that's just what I want. Sold! (*He whistles.*) Come along, boy. (*They exit right.*)

BOWSER (*Shaking his head*): A well-oiled machine! That's all a human being means to him. Sometimes I think I ought to close up shop and go back to being a bloodhound. Dogs! Never satisfied. Dogs! Why, dogs are going to the people these days. (MR. *and* MRS. ROVER *and* SPORTY *enter right.*)

MR. ROVER: Good afternoon. We're looking for a person for our pup, Sporty, here.

SPORTY: Every pup on the block has a boy, and I want one, too.

BOWSER: Right you are, tail-wagger. Nothing like a boy to teach a pup responsibility. I'll show you a few of my best people. (*He blows whistle.* BOXER, *a boy wearing trunks and boxing gloves, enters from left. He shadow-boxes to center, then holds pose.*) There you are, folks, my very best watchman and protector. A Boxer.

MRS. ROVER: Oh, we weren't looking for protection. (SPORTY *goes to* BILL, *who is still sitting in chair, and pats his head.* BILL *perks up and smiles at him.* BOXER *exits left, still shadow-boxing.*)

BOWSER: Well, then, how about a really speedy fellow? You can enter this one in the races. (*He blows whistle.* GREYHOUND DRIVER, *wearing bus driver's uniform and carrying an auto horn, enters left. He pantomimes driving to center stage.*)

GREYHOUND: . . . and leave the driving to us!

BOWSER: How do you like that one? A genuine Greyhound!

MR. ROVER: Oh, we didn't want to race our boy. We wanted somebody more—friendly. (SPORTY *pats* BILL *again, as* GREYHOUND *exits left.*)

BOWSER: Then how about a good work person? Somebody to help around the yard. (*He blows whistle.* HUSKY BOY *enters left, wearing sweatshirt stuffed with "muscles," and dungarees. He carries large barbells across stage, pauses at center, lifts them above his head, and holds them there.*) There he is. He'll pull, push, shovel, and carry. A genuine Alaskan Husky!

SPORTY: I don't want a boy just for working. I want a pal, a two-legged pal like this fellow right here. (*He pats* BILL'*s head.*) He has a nice head of hair and understanding eyes. (BILL *nods and smiles.*) See? He likes me, too.

BOWSER: Well, well, well. Young tail-wagger, you've restored my faith in the canine race. But before I let you take this boy, you have to repeat the oath of allegiance to people. Are you ready? (SPORTY *nods.*) Do you, Sporty Rover, take Bill to be your best friend? Will you see that he gets sunshine and fresh air, and plenty of romping in the fields? Will you feed him three square meals a day, not forgetting his orange juice? Will you give him a friendly bark from time to time and wag your tail to let him know you're pleased with him? Will you give him a place of his own by the fire, and once in a while give him a chocolate bar for good behavior?

SPORTY (*Solemnly*): I will.

BOWSER (*Handing end of leash to* BILL *and fastening clip to* SPORTY'*s collar*): Then, I now pronounce you dog and boy! (*Smiling*) Well, now, maybe I won't go back to being a bloodhound after all. You know, if there's anything that encourages a People Shop owner like me, it's getting the right dog and the right boy together! (SPORTY *barks,* MR. *and* MRS. ROVER *howl in approval, and* BILL *cheers, as curtains close.*)

THE END

Lady Moon and the Thief

Characters

BOW-LOW, *the storyteller*

WONG ⎫
LING ⎬ *fishermen*
MING ⎭

NID-NOD, *the sage*

AH ME, *his servant*

CHOW, *the farmer*

LORD SUN

LADY MOON

CHANG, *the thief*

GONG HO, *the gong player*

DING, *the xylophonist*

VILLAGERS

TWO PROPERTY BOYS

TIME: *Long ago in China.*

SETTING: *Ting-A-Ling, a village in ancient China.*

AT RISE: *At center on platform there is blue pagoda. On top of pagoda stands* LORD SUN, *holding golden shield downward.* VILLAGERS *are seated around pagoda, holding fans. At left, sitting on a bridge over a pond, are* WONG, LING, *and* MING, *fishing with long poles. Up right,* CHOW *kneels at edge of rice paddy. There is a basket of rice shoots beside him. Down right, under pine tree,* NID-NOD *sits at a low tea table, while* AH ME *holds long-handled fan over him. At left,* GONG HO, *with his gong, sits cross-legged on a silk pillow, and* DING, *with his xylophone, sits on pillow at right. At the back on each side of the pagoda, are Day Screens painted with trees, sky, birds, etc., and next to each screen stands* PROPERTY BOY. *All hold their poses. Oriental music is heard as* BOW-LOW *enters, and bows to audience. He carries a scroll from which he reads.*

19

Bow-Low: Honorable ladies and gentlemen, please observe before your eyes the humble village of Ting-a-ling. It is not Ting-a-ling now; it is Ting-a-ling of a thousand years ago. Before electric light, before candlelight, before—yes, even before moonlight. Why did the lovely moon decide to shine upon such a small, insignificant place as Ting-a-ling? Please turn your ears to me, and I will bring this picture to life, so you will know why the moon came to Ting-a-ling. (GONG HO *rings gong once softly.*) Here, upon the topmost ridge of the blue pagoda, is the ruler of the sky (*Gong sounds again.*), Lord Sun. (LORD SUN *lifts his shield half-way up.*) It is morning. Chow, the farmer, is planting shoots of rice. (CHOW *begins to move, taking rice shoots from basket and putting them in ground.*) Nid-Nod, the resident sage, has begun to think. (NID-NOD *smiles and nods slowly.*) His servant, Ah Me, fans him. (AH ME *slowly fans his master.*) The three fishermen, Wong, Ling, and Ming, cast their lines for glittering carp. (*They bob their poles up and down slowly.*) The villagers sit in the shade of the blue pagoda and gossip.

VILLAGERS (*Fluttering fans slowly and chanting rhythmically in unison*): Chitter-chatter-talk-talk. Chitter-chatter-talk-talk. Talk-talk-chitter-chatter. Chitter-chatter-talk-talk.

Bow-Low (*Wiping his brow*): Whew, Lord Sun is strong today. (LORD SUN *raises shield above his head. All wipe their brows.*)

ALL: Whew!

Bow-Low: But is this not excellent? With a strong sun the rice will grow faster (CHOW *plants faster.*), the fish will leap higher (*Fishermen bob their poles more rapidly.*), the sage will be wiser (NID-NOD *nods quickly.*), the servant will work harder (AH ME *fans faster.*), and the villagers will have lively conversations in the shadow of the pagoda.

VILLAGERS (*Fanning rapidly and chanting very fast*): Chitter-chatter-talk-talk. Chitter-chatter-talk-talk. Talk-talk-chitter-chatter. Chitter-chatter-talk-talk.

Bow-Low: Afternoon comes. Lord Sun grows weary. (LORD SUN *puts shield down slowly. As he does so, all work slower and slower and finally stop.*) It is the time of the darkening of the sky. (GONG HO *sounds gong once.* PROPERTY BOYS *take dark cloak from behind screen and put it around* LORD SUN, *who puts shield under the cloak*) It is the time of the going-down of Lord Sun. (GONG HO *sounds his gong again. All stand and bow toward* LORD SUN. PROPERTY BOYS *assist him down from pagoda. He stands behind it.* PROPERTY BOYS *slide Day Screens off, revealing the Night Screens in place behind them.* GONG HO *sounds his gong a third time.*) It is night. Deep, dark night. (*All face front again, sit, and put their hands to their faces, closing their eyes. They hold the pose while slow Oriental music is played. After a few bars,* CHANG *peers from behind pagoda.* GONG HO *beats gong softly and steadily like a warning.* CHANG *sidles to center and looks about with satisfaction.*) Ah . . . who is this? Who is this who slithers and sidles and slinks in the darkness? (Bow-Low *stands down left.*)

CHANG (*Bowing to audience*): I am Chang. Chang the dishonorable. Chang the thief. Please to watch Chang's nimble fingers like darting minnows. (*He swiftly plucks fans from laps of sleeping* VILLAGERS.) Please to notice Chang's fancy footwork, soft as kitten in the snow. (CHANG *dances over to* CHOW *and takes his basket, slipping fans into it; then runs to bridge.*) Please to enjoy Chang's artistic pole-snatching. (*He takes poles from sleeping fishermen, then steals large fan from* AH ME *and teacups from* NID-NOD. *He puts everything into basket, then goes down center and bows.*) Was that not first-class thievery? Please do not applaud. It might wake up the villagers. Did you see how the darkness helped me? (*He bows to Night Screens.*) Thank you, friend darkness, for making me the shadow of a shadow. May you always keep midnight over the eyes of the people so that Chang may become the number one thief of China. (*He looks left and right, then darts to pool, dips his hand into it and pulls out large gold carp, putting it, too, into basket. He then runs off right, as* PROPERTY BOYS *push in Day Screens and* LORD SUN, *without cloak, his shield raised, mounts to top of pagoda.* GONG HO *rings gong urgently. All except* NID-NOD, *who remains sound asleep, rub their eyes and stretch, then discover their losses.*)

ALL (*Waving hands in air; ad lib*): Help! Help! Help! A thief! A thief! (*Etc.*)

WONG: Help! The fishing poles are gone!

LING: Quite gone.

MING: Help! The golden carp is gone!

LING: Quite gone.

CHOW: What shall we do?

WONG: Ask Nid-Nod—

VILLAGERS (*Ad lib*): Yes, ask the sage. Ask Nid-Nod. (*Etc.*)

AH ME: I am sorry. Nid-Nod cannot help you. Look for yourselves.

VILLAGERS (*Shading eyes and looking at* NID-NOD): Asleep!

CHOW: Asleep! In the middle of the day. Wake up, Nid-Nod.

AH ME: Nid-Nod is not here. He is enjoying a voyage to the back of his mind. He will return to the front of his mind when the leaves are falling.

1ST VILLAGER: Oh! Who will help us? Who?

AH ME: I will help you.

CHOW: You? Are you an ancient sage?

WONG: You? Are you a wise man?

AH ME: I am not ancient. I am not wise. But I have a head on my shoulders and it thinks sometimes. Listen—

VILLAGERS (*Putting hands to right ear; together*): We listen.

AH ME: This wicked thief who stole our treasures comes covered from head to toe in darkness. Therefore, we cannot see him. Therefore, we cannot catch him.

VILLAGERS: Therefore—

AH ME: Therefore, we need a light. A light at night.

VILLAGERS (*Together*): A light at night!

CHOW: A welcome sight.

LING: Where shall we find this light at night?

AH ME: The Lord Sun has light and light to spare. Ask him to send you a little globe of glow. A little ball of bright-ness. (*All turn to* LORD SUN *and chant.*)

ALL (*Together*):

> Great Lord Sun, burnished bright,
>
> Send to us a light at night.

(GONG HO *strikes gong softly.* PROPERTY BOYS *put the dark robe on* LORD SUN. *He covers his shield and goes behind pagoda.* PROPERTY BOYS *remove Day Screens.*)

CHOW: Did he hear us?

MING: Did he listen?

VILLAGERS (*Together*): Did he heed our plea?

AH ME: Look up. (*All look at pagoda.*) Look higher, higher. Look up. Look up and see. (DING *plays gentle arpeggio on xy-lophone, as* LADY MOON, *dressed in silver with two silver fans, appears on top of pagoda.*)

WONG (*Bowing*): Ah, how beautiful. A silver maiden.

LADY MOON (*Motioning with fan*): Good evening.

CHOW (*In awe*): What shall we call you, silver lady of the sky?

LADY MOON: You may call me Lady Moon. I am the con-sort of the great Lord Sun. (*She bows and gestures with fans.*) I shine in his reflected glory. Great Lord Sun has heard your plea. He has sent me to watch over you, a light in the night. (*She holds fans above her head.*)

1ST VILLAGER: Ah, how bright she is.

LADY MOON: I will not always be so bright. Listen, I must tell you something important about my light—(CHANG *enters right, from behind pagoda, carrying fishnet on pole.*)

WONG (*Interrupting her*): Oh. Look there. A stranger. A sly, skulking stranger! (GONG HO *beats same insistent soft gong music as before.*)

CHANG (*To audience*): Chang has returned. Chang will steal the rest of the fish from the pool while the village sleeps. Perhaps Chang will even steal the blue pagoda! And then Chang will be the number one thief in China.

2ND VILLAGER (*Putting finger to lips*): Sh-h-h! We will watch this stranger. Sh-h-h! (*They shade their eyes and watch him. CHANG tiptoes over to pool and dips net. LADY MOON points fan at him.*)

LADY MOON: No, no, Chang. (CHANG *straightens up, startled, and looks around.*)

CHANG: Who said that? Who sees me in the dark?

LADY MOON: Lady Moon sees you, Chang. Up here. (CHANG *turns and looks up at her, astonished.*)

CHANG: Oh, there you are. In the sky, of all places. This is none of your business. (*He turns back to pool and slides fishnet into it again.*)

LADY MOON: Don't do that, Chang.

CHANG: Oh, bother. (*He waves her away.*) Go away. Stop watching me. (LADY MOON *turns slightly. The back of her kimono is black. She turns one fan so that its dark side is to audience.*)

LADY MOON: Dishonorable Chang, I am not the only one who is watching you. Look around you.

CHANG: Ha! How can I look around me when the darkness covers me from tip to toe. (*He points at his head and feet, and suddenly becomes aware that he can see his finger. He looks at it for a moment.*) Ho! What is this? I can see my finger, and my feet, and—and—(*He suddenly sees the others, who are watching him*)—everybody. (*Bowing embarrassedly.*) Good evening, honorable everybody.

VILLAGERS (*Pointing at him; together*): Shame. Shame. Bad Chang. Bad Chang. (LADY MOON *turns so that half of her dark side shows.*)

CHANG (*To* LADY MOON): You, up there. You spy-in-the-sky. You have caused all my troubles. (*He raises fishnet and begins to climb up pagoda, left.*) What a prize you are. A great silver prize. (*He is halfway up.*) I will end my troubles and become number one thief in all the world. (*Just as he attempts to clap net over* LADY MOON'*s head, she turns her dark side and dark fans toward audience. He does not catch her.*) I will steal *you!*

WONG: Oh, wicked Chang!

CHOW: Lady Moon is gone! You have stolen her!

CHANG (*Climbing down and putting fishnet under his cloak, as he gloats*): Chang the Greatest has stolen Lady Moon. She is here. In my fishnet, under my cloak. (*To others*) I will not give her back unless you promise to let me go free and until you proclaim in a loud voice, "Chang is the number one thief in all the world."

1ST VILLAGER: Woe. Woe. Give us back our moon.

CHANG: Say it.

ALL (*Hanging their heads and repeating together in subdued voices*): Chang is—Chang is—(LADY MOON *turns and reveals her silver side. She holds her fans high again. Xylophone ripples.*)

LADY MOON: Chang is a silly fool!

WONG: Lady Moon! (*All gaze up at her.*)

LADY MOON: I did not finish telling you. Once every moon-time I must turn my dark side to your village. But I promise you I shall always return my light side for your protection and delight. (CHANG *takes out fishnet and shakes it out.*)

CHANG (*Mournfully*): Empty.

LADY MOON: Empty as your head. And now, Chang, bring back all the things you have stolen. But before you do, you must proclaim in a loud voice, "Chang will steal no more."

CHANG: Oh, woe!

LADY MOON: Say it.

CHANG (*Sighing*): Chang will steal no more.

LADY MOON: Now—bring back the stolen goods. (CHANG *goes left, and gazes longingly into pool. He turns his back to pool and slyly slides his hand into water. All point at him and shout.*)

VILLAGERS (*Together*): Chang will steal no more! (CHANG *takes his hand out of pool and shakes water off, then goes left behind pagoda, as* LADY MOON *steps down, and* LORD SUN *mounts pagoda and holds up shield.* PROPERTY BOYS *bring in Day Screens.* BOW-LOW *comes to center.* GONG HO *strikes gong three times.*)

BOW-LOW: It was so from that time until now. (CHANG *returns with basket and fishing poles.*) Chang brought back the fans to the villagers, and they resumed their conversations. (CHANG *gives fans back.*)

VILLAGERS (*Fluttering fans*): Chitter-chatter-talk-talk. Chitter-chatter-talk-talk. Talk-talk-chitter-chatter. Chitter-chatter-talk-talk.

BOW-LOW: Wong, Ling, and Ming received their fishing poles and their beloved golden carp. (CHANG *returns fishing poles and throws carp into pond.*) And as the sun rose higher (LORD SUN *raises shield above his head.*), Ah Me fanned his sleeping master, Nid-Nod. (CHANG *returns fan to* AH ME, *and tea cups to table.*) And Chow, the farmer, began to plant rice shoots again from his rattan basket. (CHANG *returns basket to* CHOW. *Curtains slowly begin to close.*) It is all the same in the village of Ting-a-ling as it had been before, and as it will be tomorrow, except for Nid-Nod. When he wakens at the time of the falling of the leaves—will there not be a wonderful story to tell him about Lady Moon and the thief?

AH ME (*Bowing low with* BOW-LOW): A wonderful story to tell! (NID-NOD *smiles gently and nods in his sleep. All bow. Curtain.*)

THE END

The Book That Saved the Earth

Characters

Historian
Great and Mighty Think-Tank
Apprentice Noodle
Captain Omega
Lieutenant Iota
Sergeant Oop
Offstage Voice

Before Rise: *Spotlight shines on* Historian, *who is sitting at table down right, on which there is a movie projector. A sign on an easel beside him reads:* museum of ancient history: department of the twentieth century. *He stands and bows to audience.*

Historian: Good afternoon. Welcome to our Museum of Ancient History, and to my department—curiosities of the good old, far-off twentieth century. The twentieth century was often called the Era of the Book. In those days, there were books about everything from anteaters to Zulus. Books taught people how to, and when to, and where to, and why to. They illustrated, educated, punctuated and even decorated. But the strangest thing a book ever did was to save the Earth. You haven't heard about the Martian invasion of 1980? Tsk, tsk. What *do* they

27

teach children nowadays? Well, you know, the invasion never really happened, because a single book stopped it. What was that book, you ask? A noble encyclopedia? A tome about rockets and missiles? A secret file from outer space? No, it was none of these. It was—but here, let me turn on the historiscope and show you what happened many, many centuries ago, in 1980. (*He turns on projector, and points it left. Spotlight on* HISTORIAN *goes out, and comes up down left on* THINK-TANK, *who is seated on raised box, arms folded. He has huge, egg-shaped head, and he wears long robe decorated with stars and circles.* APPRENTICE NOODLE *stands beside him at an elaborate switchboard. A sign on an easel reads:* MARS SPACE CONTROL. GREAT AND MIGHTY THINK-TANK, COMMANDER-IN-CHIEF. BOW LOW BEFORE ENTERING.)

NOODLE (*Bowing*): O Great and Mighty Think-Tank, most powerful and intelligent creature in the whole universe, what are your orders?

THINK-TANK (*Peevishly*): You left out part of my salutation, Apprentice Noodle. Go over the whole thing again.

NOODLE: It shall be done, sir. (*In singsong*) O Great and Mighty Think-Tank, Ruler of Mars and her two moons, most powerful and intelligent creature in the whole universe—(*Out of breath*) what-are-your-orders?

THINK-TANK: That's better, Noodle. I wish to be placed in communication with our manned space probe to that ridiculous little planet we are going to put under our generous rulership. What do they call it again?

NOODLE: Earth, Your Intelligence.

THINK-TANK: Earth—of course. You see how insignificant the place is? But first, something important. My mirror. I wish to consult my mirror.

NOODLE: It shall be done, sir. (*He hands* THINK-TANK *hand mirror.*)

THINK-TANK: Mirror, mirror, in my hand, who is the most fantastically intellectually gifted being in the land?

OFFSTAGE VOICE (*After a pause*): You, sir.

THINK-TANK (*Striking mirror*): Quicker. Answer quicker next time. I hate a slow mirror. (*He admires himself.*) Ah, there I am. Are we Martians not a handsome race? So much more attractive than those ugly earthlings with their tiny heads. Noodle, you keep on exercising your mind, and some day you'll have a balloon brain just like mine.

NOODLE: Oh, I hope so, Mighty Think-Tank. I hope so.

THINK-TANK: Now, contact the space probe. I want to invade that primitive ball of mud called Earth before lunch.

NOODLE: It shall be done, sir. (*He twists knobs and adjusts levers on switchboard. Electronic buzzes and beeps are heard.* NOODLE *and* THINK-TANK *remain at controls, as curtains open.*)

*   *   *

SETTING: *The Centerville Public Library.*

AT RISE: CAPTAIN OMEGA *stands at center, opening and closing card catalogue drawers, looking puzzled.* LIEUTENANT IOTA *is up left, counting books in bookcase.* SERGEANT OOP *is at right, opening and closing book, turning it upside down, shaking it, and then riffling pages and shaking his head.*

NOODLE (*Adjusting knobs*): I have a close sighting of the space crew, sir. (THINK-TANK *puts on pair of huge goggles and turns toward stage to watch.*) They seem to have entered some sort of Earth structure.

THINK-TANK: Excellent. Make voice contact.

NOODLE (*Speaking into a microphone*): Mars Space Control calling the crew of Probe One. Mars Space Control calling the crew of Probe One. Come in, Captain Omega. Give us your location.

CAPTAIN OMEGA (*Speaking into disc which is on chain around his neck*): Captain Omega to Mars Space Control. Lieutenant Iota, Sergeant Oop and I have landed on Earth without incident. We have taken shelter in this (*Indicates room*)—this square place. Have you any idea where we are, Lieutenant Iota?

IOTA: I can't figure it out, Captain. (*Holding up book*) I've counted two thousand of these peculiar things. This place must be some sort of storage barn. What do you think, Sergeant Oop?

OOP: I haven't a clue. I've been to seven galaxies, but I've never seen anything like this. Maybe they're hats. (*He opens book and puts it on his head.*) Say, maybe this is a haberdasher's store!

OMEGA (*Bowing low*): Perhaps the Great and Mighty Think-Tank will give us the benefit of his thought on the matter.

THINK-TANK: Elementary, my dear Omega. Hold one of the items up so that I may view it closely. (OMEGA *holds book on palm of his hand.*) Yes, yes, I understand now. Since Earth creatures are always eating, the place in which you find yourselves is undoubtedly a crude refreshment stand.

OMEGA (*To* IOTA *and* OOP): He says we're in a refreshment stand.

OOP: Well, the Earthlings certainly have a strange diet.

THINK-TANK: That item in your hand is called a "sandwich."

OMEGA (*Nodding*): A sandwich.

IOTA (*Nodding*): A sandwich.

OOP (*Taking book from his head*): A sandwich?

THINK-TANK: Sandwiches are the main staple of Earth diet. Look at it closely. (OMEGA *squints at book.*) There are two slices of what is called "bread," and between them there is some sort of filling.

OMEGA: That is correct, sir.

THINK-TANK: To confirm my opinion, I order you to eat it.

OMEGA (*Gulping*): Eat it?

THINK-TANK: Do you doubt the Mighty Think-Tank?

OMEGA: Oh, no, no. But poor Lieutenant Iota has not had

his breakfast. Lieutenant Iota, I order you to eat this—this sandwich.

IOTA (*Dubiously*): Eat it? Oh, Captain! It's a very great honor to be the first Martian to eat a sandwich, I'm sure, but—but how can I be so impolite as to eat before my Sergeant? (*Handing Oop book; brightly*) Sergeant Oop, I order you to eat the sandwich.

OOP (*Making a face*): Who, sir? Me, sir?

IOTA *and* OMEGA (*Slapping their chests in a salute*): For the glory of Mars, Oop!

OOP: Yes, sirs. (*Unhappily*) Immediately, sirs. (*He opens his mouth wide. OMEGA and IOTA watch him breathlessly. He bites down on corner of book, and pantomimes chewing and swallowing, while making terrible faces.*)

OMEGA: Well, Oop?

IOTA: Well, Oop? (*OOP coughs. OMEGA and IOTA pound him on back.*)

THINK-TANK: Was it not delicious, Sergeant Oop?

OOP (*Slapping his chest in salute*): That is correct, sir. It was *not* delicious. I don't know how the Earthlings can get those sandwiches down without water. They're dry as Martian dust.

NOODLE: Sir—O Great and Mighty Think-Tank. I beg your pardon, but an insignificant bit of data floated into my mind about those sandwiches.

THINK-TANK: It can't be worth much, but go ahead. Give us your trifling bit of data.

NOODLE: Well, sir, I have seen surveyor films of those sandwiches. I noticed that the Earthlings did not *eat* them. They used them as some sort of communication device.

THINK-TANK (*Haughtily*): Naturally. That was my next point. These are actually communication sandwiches. Think-Tank is never wrong. Who is never wrong?

ALL (*Saluting*): Great and Mighty Think-Tank is never wrong.

THINK-TANK: Therefore, I order you to listen to them.

OMEGA: Listen to them?

IOTA *and* OOP (*To each other; puzzled*): Listen to them?

THINK-TANK: Do you have marbles in your ears? I said, listen to them. (*Martians bow very low.*)

OMEGA: It shall be done, sir. (*They each take two books from case, and hold them to their ears, listening intently.*)

IOTA (*Whispering to* OMEGA): Do you hear anything?

OMEGA (*Whispering back*): Nothing. Do you hear anything, Oop?

OOP (*Loudly*): Not a thing! (OMEGA *and* IOTA *jump in fright.*)

OMEGA *and* IOTA: Sh-h-h! (*They listen intently again.*)

THINK-TANK: Well? Well? Report to me. What do you hear?

OMEGA: Nothing, sir. Perhaps we are not on the correct frequency.

IOTA: Nothing, sir. Perhaps the Earthlings have sharper ears than we do.

OOP: I don't hear a thing. Maybe these sandwiches don't make sounds.

THINK-TANK: What? What? Does someone suggest the Mighty Think-Tank has made a mistake?

OMEGA: Oh, no, sir. No, sir. We'll keep listening.

NOODLE: Please excuse me, Your Brilliance, but a cloudy piece of information is rolling around in my head.

THINK-TANK: Well, roll it out, Noodle, and I will clarify it for you.

NOODLE: I seem to recall that the Earthlings did not *listen* to the sandwiches. They opened them, and watched them.

THINK-TANK: Yes, that is quite correct. I will clarify that for you, Captain Omega. Those sandwiches are not for ear communication, they are for eye communication. Now, Captain Omega, take that large, bright-colored sandwich over there. It appears to be important. Tell me what you observe. (OMEGA *picks up very large copy of "Mother Goose," holding it so that the audience can see title.* IOTA *looks over* OMEGA's *left shoulder, and* OOP *squints over his right shoulder.*)

OMEGA: It appears to contain pictures of Earthlings.

IOTA: There seems to be some sort of code.

THINK-TANK (*Sharply interested*): Code? Code? I told you this was important. Describe the code.

OOP: It's little lines and squiggles and dots. Thousands of them, next to the pictures.

THINK-TANK: Code. Perhaps the Earthlings are not so primitive as we have thought. We must break the code. We must.

NOODLE: Forgive me, Your Cleverness, but did not the chemical department give our spacemen a supply of Vitamin X to increase their intelligence?

THINK-TANK: Stop! A thought of magnificent brilliance has come to me. Spacemen, our chemical department has given you a supply of Vitamin X to increase your intelligence. Take it immediately and then watch the sandwich. The meaning of the code will slowly unfold before you.

OMEGA: It shall be done, sir. Remove pill. (*Crew take vitamins from boxes on their belts.*) Present Vitamin X. (*They hold vitamins out in front of them, stiffly.*) Swallow. (*They put vitamins into their mouths and gulp simultaneously. They open their eyes wide, shake their heads, and they put their hands to their foreheads.*) The cotangent of a given angle in a right triangle is equal to the adjacent side divided by the hypotenuse.

IOTA: *Habeas corpus ad faciendum et recipiendum!*

OOP: There is change of pressure along a radius in curvilinear motion.

THINK-TANK: Excellent. Now, decipher that code.

ALL: It shall be done, sir. (*They frown over book, turning pages.*)

OMEGA (*Brightly*): Aha!

IOTA (*Brightly*): Oho!

OOP (*Bursting into laughter*): Ha, ha, ha!

THINK-TANK: What does it say? Tell me this instant. Transcribe, Omega.

OMEGA: Yes, sir. (*He reads with great seriousness.*)
  "Mistress Mary, quite contrary,
  How does your garden grow?
  With cockle shells and silver bells
  And pretty maids all in a row."

OOP: Ha, ha, ha. Imagine that. Pretty maids growing in a garden.

THINK-TANK (*Alarmed*): Stop! This is no time for levity. Don't you realize the seriousness of this discovery? The Earthlings have discovered how to combine agriculture and mining. They can actually *grow* crops of rare metals such as silver. And cockle shells. They can grow high explosives, too. Noodle, contact our invasion fleet.

NOODLE: They are ready to go down and take over Earth, sir.

THINK-TANK: Tell them to hold. Tell them new information has come to us about Earth. Iota, continue transcribing.

IOTA: Yes, sir. (*He reads very gravely.*)
  "Hey diddle diddle! The cat and the fiddle,
  The cow jumped over the moon,
  The little dog laughed to see such sport,
  And the dish ran away with the spoon."

OOP (*Laughing*): The dish ran away with the spoon!

THINK-TANK: Cease laughter. Desist. This is more and more alarming. The Earthlings have reached a high level of civilization. Didn't you hear? They have taught their domesticated animals musical culture and space techniques. Even their dogs have a sense of humor. Why, at this very moment, they may be launching an interplanetary attack of millions of *cows!* Notify the invasion fleet. No invasion today. Oop, transcribe the next code.

OOP: Yes, sir. (*Reading*)

"Humpty Dumpty sat on the wall,
Humpty Dumpty had a great fall;
All the King's horses and all the King's men,
Couldn't put Humpty Dumpty together again."

Oh, look, sir. Here's a picture of Humpty Dumpty. Why, sir, he looks like—he looks like—(*Turns large picture of Humpty Dumpty toward* THINK-TANK *and audience.*)

THINK-TANK (*Screaming and holding his head*): It's me! It's my Great and Mighty Balloon Brain. The Earthlings have seen me. They're after me. "Had a great fall!" That means they plan to capture Mars Central Control and me! It's an invasion of Mars! Noodle, prepare a space capsule for me. I must escape without delay. Spacemen, you must leave Earth at once, but be sure to remove all traces of your visit. The Earthlings must not know that I know—(OMEGA, IOTA *and* OOP *rush about, putting books back on shelves.*)

NOODLE: Where shall we go, sir?

THINK-TANK: A hundred million miles away from Mars. Order the invasion fleet to evacuate the entire planet of Mars. We are heading for Alpha Centauri, a hundred million miles away. (OMEGA, IOTA, *and* OOP *run off right, as* NOODLE *helps* THINK-TANK *off left and curtain closes. Spotlight shines on* HISTORIAN *down right.*)

HISTORIAN (*Chuckling*): And that's how one dusty old book of nursery rhymes saved the world from a Martian invasion. As you all know, in the twenty-fifth century, five hundred years after all this happened, we Earthlings resumed contact with Mars, and we even became very chummy with the Martians. By that time, Great and Mighty Think-Tank had been replaced by a very clever Martian—the Wise and Wonderful Noodle! Oh, yes, we taught the Martians the difference between sandwiches and books. We taught them how to read, too, and we established a model library in their capital city of Marsopolis. But, as you might expect, there is still one book that the Martians can never bring themselves to read. You've guessed it—*Mother Goose!* (*He bows and exits right.*)

THE END

Beware the Genies!

Characters

DAN	CAVE BOY
LUCY	UNDERGROUND MOTHER
WENDY	UNDERGROUND FATHER
GENIE-OF-THE-AIR	UNDERGROUND GIRL
GENIE-OF-THE-WATER	DUSTERS
GENIE-OF-THE-EARTH	SWABBERS
CAVE MOTHER	PAPER PICKERS
CAVE FATHER	

TIME: *The present.*

SETTING: *The city dump. Backdrop shows city skyline, with smoking chimneys. Down right is a sign reading,* CITY DUMP, *and beside it are overflowing trash cans. Large brass bottle of Oriental design with locket around its neck is on pile at center. Down left is large rock, and beside it, sign reading,* SWEETWATER RIVER— CONTAMINATED.

AT RISE: DAN *is sitting on rock, dangling his fishing line in river. Suddenly he pulls up line excitedly.*

DAN: I've caught one. I've caught a real, live (*He pulls rubber boot into view.*)—rubber boot. That's three rubber boots and two inner tubes, and the only fish I've caught was in a rusty can of sardines. (LUCY *and* WENDY *enter right.* LUCY *is crying.* WENDY *consoles her.*)

LUCY: I'll never find my locket, never!

WENDY: Yes, you will, Lucy. We know it accidentally fell into the wastebasket. This is where all wastebaskets end up, isn't it? The city dump.

LUCY: But look at it. Mountains of rubbish. Acres of trash. It would take a month to go through all of this.

DAN (*Crossing right*): Hello, Wendy. What's up? What's the matter with Lucy?

WENDY: Hi, Dan. Lucy lost her locket. A solid gold locket with a picture in it.

DAN: A solid gold locket. That's too bad. I'll help you look for it. (*He shakes his head.*) And, boy, will you need help! Lucy, you look around in those bottles over there. (LUCY *crosses to center and goes down on her hands and knees. She picks up brass bottle and examines it curiously.*) Wendy, you and I will look through these trash cans.

LUCY (*Seeing locket around neck of bottle*): My locket! I found it! It's caught on the bottle.

WENDY: You found it already?

DAN (*As they all come down center in front of curtain*): Here, let me see the bottle. I'll help you get the locket off. (*He takes bottle and tries to remove locket. Curtains close behind them.*) It's all tangled up. There! (*Hands locket to* LUCY, *who puts it on*)

WENDY: What a funny old bottle. It looks like the one in the Arabian Nights.

DAN (*Pulling out cork*): I pulled out the cork! I didn't mean to do that. Oh! (*Lights flash on and off. There is a short blackout.* GENIES *rush onstage through center of curtain.* WENDY *and* LUCY *draw back frightened, and* DAN *steps away.*)

GENIES (*Together*): Salaam, O slaves. Salaam.

DAN: G-g-genies!

WENDY: Three real genies!

LUCY: In one bottle.

GENIE-OF-THE-AIR: It is so, children. Three genies for the price of one. I am the Genie-of-the-Air. (*Bows*)

GENIE-OF-THE-WATER (*Bowing*): I am the Genie-of-the-

Water. We have been the servants of men for a thousand years.

GENIE-OF-THE-EARTH (*Bowing*): I am the Genie-of-the-Earth. Now it is our turn. We shall be your masters!

DAN: Our masters? But, I thought genies were the slaves of whoever opened the bottle.

GENIE-OF-THE-AIR: It was so in the ancient days.

GENIE-OF-THE-WATER: But it is so no longer.

GENIE-OF-THE-EARTH: It must not be so in the future. Men have been bad masters to us genies.

GENIE-OF-THE-AIR: What have you done to the air? It is not fit for man or genie.

GENIE-OF-THE-WATER: What have you done to the water? Even the crocodiles do not wish to swim in the rivers.

GENIE-OF-THE-EARTH: What have you done to the earth? There are rusty tin cans from the North Pole to the South Pole.

DAN: But—but *we* didn't do all those things, did we?

GENIE-OF-THE-AIR: Silence! We will show you the past. We will show you what happened in the ancient days when man was permitted to be master of the air, and the water, and the earth. (*Curtains open.*)

GENIES: Behold! (*City backdrop and dump scene have been removed.* CAVE FATHER *and* CAVE BOY *are sitting beside fire, down right.* BOY *is carving bow and arrow with sharp flint. Down left,* CAVE MOTHER *is beating hide on rock. She has large wooden bowl beside her.* GENIES *go to center and stand with arms folded, as* LUCY, WENDY, *and* DAN *watch from down right.*)

CAVE FATHER: Look, boy. Fire. See the fire burn. Look, boy. Leaves. I put in leaves. Make much smoke in air. Funny, funny smoke. Ha ha. (*He throws handfuls of leaves on fire.*)

GENIE-OF-THE-AIR (*Raising his hand in alarm*): Please. Please, O master, do not put smoke in the air. Trouble will begin.

CAVE FATHER: Never mind, Genie. Plenty of air. Always plenty of air.

CAVE MOTHER: Nice and clean. I wash leopard skin nice and clean. But soaproot makes bubbles. Oh, well. River will take care of bubbles. (*She empties wooden bowl into river.*) Here, river. Nice bubbles for you.

GENIE-OF-THE-WATER (*Raising hand*): Please. Please, oh, mistress, do not put bubbles into the river. Trouble will begin.

CAVE MOTHER: Never mind, Genie. There are many rivers. There is much water. Much, much water.

CAVE BOY (*Holding up bow and arrow*): Look, Father. Look, Mother. I have made a bow and arrow. But I have also made many chips and much sawdust. What shall I do with the chips and sawdust?

CAVE FATHER: Just put them anywhere, my son.

CAVE MOTHER: Just put them anywhere—outside the cave, my son. (BOY *scatters his chips.*)

GENIE-OF-THE-EARTH (*Raising his hand*): Please. Please, little master. Do not scatter litter everywhere. Trouble will begin.

CAVE BOY: Never mind, Genie. There are many miles of land. Miles and miles of land. (*Curtains begin to close.*)

CAVE FATHER (*Piling leaves on fire*): Plenty of air.

CAVE MOTHER (*Throwing bubbles into river*): Much, much water.

CAVE BOY (*Scattering litter*): Miles and miles of land. (GENIES *join* LUCY, WENDY, *and* DAN, *as curtains close behind them.*)

LUCY: But that isn't true any more. There are thousands of factories now. There isn't plenty of air.

WENDY: And there are so many people that the rivers are full of junk.

DAN: And the city dumps keep creeping toward the cities.

GENIE-OF-THE-AIR: Now do you see why humans can no longer be masters of the air, the water, and the earth?

Observe. We will show you another picture. A picture of the future.

GENIE-OF-THE-WATER: In this picture, there will be no genies to serve you.

GENIE-OF-THE-EARTH: In this picture, it is too late. Too late. (GENIES *and children stand down right, as lights dim and curtains open, revealing dingy, underground dwelling. A sign reads,* UNDERGROUND APARTMENT—2B. UNDERGROUND GIRL *is sitting at table center, reading.* UNDERGROUND FATHER *is beside rock at left, digging. They wear coveralls and miners' hats with lights.*)

GIRL: Father, look at this picture in my geography book. It's a picture of a strange world. I see dark skies, ugly yellow rivers. I see mountains of ashes and barren lands. Is it Mars, Father? (FATHER *crosses to her and looks at book.*)

FATHER: No, my child. This is our planet, Earth. You are looking at a picture of the way the Earth looks above ground.

GIRL: Is that why we have to live underground, Father? Is that why we live like moles and earthworms, far beneath the surface of Earth?

FATHER: Yes. For generation after generation, people didn't take care of the world. Time after time, people said, "Oh, let the next generation worry about the pollution of the air, and the water, and the earth." Finally, we ran out of generations, so this generation lives underground, because the earth has been poisoned by those who lived there before us. (*He goes back to his digging.*)

UNDERGROUND MOTHER (*Entering with basket filled with cans*): See what I have in the basket, child. The store gave us a bonus ration today. (*Puts basket on table and takes out cans*) "Powdered Fresh Air." "Essence of Rainbow." Oh, let's open this one—"Condensed Sunshine." (*She opens can.* GIRL *takes it and looks into it.*)

GIRL: Look how it shines! It's so toasty, goldeny warm. I could let it shine on my face all day long. Oh! It went out. I wish I had more.

MOTHER (*Sadly*): That's all the condensed sunshine for this month. But I remember when we used to play in the sun for hours and hours. And the sun used to shine down on the earth for whole days at a time.

FATHER: Mother! Child! Come here. I've struck water! (MOTHER *and* GIRL *cross left and stoop down to taste water.*)

MOTHER: Is it good? Is it pure, safe water? Remember how water used to taste cold and silvery. How clear it was in the old days.

FATHER: It tastes like— It tastes like—(*He makes a face.*)

GIRL (*Grimacing*): Soap.

MOTHER: Sulphur.

FATHER (*Sighing*): Well, I'll keep trying. Somewhere on this ugly earth there must be one pure, clean stream left.

GIRL: Is it so bad down here, Mother? Is it awful to live underground, Father? I don't know any other way of living.

MOTHER: It *is* awful when you remember better things, my child. Like the sky that was blue and went up and on and out forever.

FATHER: And the waterfalls, like ribbons of white lace.

MOTHER: And green meadows covered with buttercups. Oh, well—you can get used to anything.

FATHER *and* GIRL (*Sadly, as curtains begin to close*): You can get used to anything. (*Curtains close.*)

LUCY: Oh, no! I don't want to get used to "anything." Let me serve you, Genies.

WENDY: Please, oh, please, Genies. No sunshine in a can. Tell me what to do.

DAN: I won't live underground. I won't. I'll be your slave, Genies.

GENIE-OF-THE-AIR: Then, hasten. Undo the mischief that has been done to the air.

GENIE-OF-THE-WATER: Be quick. Turn back the tide of pollution in your waters.

GENIE-OF-THE-EARTH: Bestir yourselves. Make your lands fit for living again.

GENIE-OF-THE-AIR (*Pointing to* LUCY's *locket*): To catch another glimpse of the future, look into the locket.

GENIES (*As they bow and exit through the curtain, center*): Look into the locket. Look into the locket. (LUCY *removes locket, and all three gather around. Curtains open, revealing city dump scene, as it was at the beginning. Across stage, near backdrop, are* DUSTERS, *wearing mop caps and aprons. They flourish dust rags. As they dust air, they also erase smoke from chimneys on backdrop, revealing blue sky and sun.*)

DUSTERS (*Singing to tune of* "London Bridge Is Falling Down"):
Lend a hand, and shake a rag,
Shake the dust into the bag.
Flick the flecks and snatch the specks;
Clean up, ladies!

Brush the breeze and whisk the smoke,
Strain the soot that makes you choke,
Dust with care and make the air,
More fair, ladies!

(DUSTERS *hold pose, shaking dustcloths.* SWABBERS *enter, pushing their mops back and forth.*)

SWABBERS (*Singing to tune of* "Row, Row, Row Your Boat"):
Swab, swab, swab the scum,
Scrub away the slough.
Separate; filtrate;
Aerate; percolate,
Till it's clean enough.

Mop, mop, mop the mud,
Gently to the sea,
Renew it, shampoo it,
Whatever you do, it
Crystal clear must be!

(*One* SWABBER *removes contamination sign, while another puts up beach umbrella, with sign,* SWEETWATER RIVER—SWIMMING, FISHING, BOATING AND ALL SUMMER SPORTS. *They hold pose, leaning on mops, while* PAPER PICKERS *enter, bending down and pantomiming picking up papers. Some* PAPER PICKERS *remove trash cans and* CITY DUMP *sign, while others bring in border and flowers, and finally sign reading,* CITY PARK.)

PAPER PICKERS (*Singing to tune of "Pick a Bale of Cotton"*):
Bend down, turn around, pick a piece of paper,
Bend down, turn around, scout around for scraps.
Shake down, rake down, shovel down the rubbish.
Hoe away, throw away, cans and bottle caps.

1ST PAPER PICKER:
Even Peter Piper picks a peck of paper pieces.
Even Peter Piper puts the paper in the pack!

(PAPER PICKERS *hold pose.* LUCY, WENDY *and* DAN *walk about park, admiring it.*)

DAN: They've changed it from a dump to a park. Now that's more like it. (*He joins* SWABBERS.) I'm going to work at keeping this water pure.

WENDY: I want to be part of the picture, too. (*She joins* DUSTERS.) I'll help keep the air clean.

LUCY (*Joining* PAPER PICKERS): I'll help keep the earth free from litter. (*To audience*) We can all be part of the picture. We can all help the genies of the air and the water and the Earth. (GENIES *enter and stand at center with arms folded.*)

DUSTERS: Clean up the air—right now.

ALL: Before it is too late.

SWABBERS: Clean up the water—right now.

ALL: Before it is too late.

PAPER PICKERS: Clean up the land—right now.

GENIES (*Bowing*): Before it is too late.

ALL: Before it is too late. (*Curtain*)

THE END

A Roman Romance

Characters

POMONA   SEPTIMUS
MARCUS   THREE MAIDENS
QUINTUS   VENUS
GALBA

SETTING: *Pomona's orchard. There is backdrop of trees bearing fruit. Down right there is an elm tree, around which is twined grapevine. Down left is an apple tree, beneath which stand bench, and bucket with dipper. Across downstage area is a low fence with gate, upon which is nailed scroll reading:* POMONA'S ORCHARD. . . . ABSOLUTELY NO ADMITTANCE.

AT RISE: POMONA *dances onstage, carrying basket full of fruit. She pauses down left to examine apple tree.*

POMONA: Good morning, all you juicy little apples. How beautiful you are. (THREE MAIDENS *enter left, bearing jars on their shoulders.*)

MAIDENS: Pomona, Pomona! Come with us.

POMONA (*Crossing to gate*): Where are you going in such a hurry?

1ST MAIDEN: To the well. (*They giggle.*)

2ND MAIDEN: We have heard that the shepherds and reapers and herdsmen are coming to the well.

3RD MAIDEN: We might meet them there.

46

Pomona: I have no use for shepherds and reapers and herdsmen.

1st Maiden: Don't you want to find a husband?

Pomona (*Scornfully*): A *husband?* Why should I give up my lovely orchard for a husband?

1st Maiden: A husband would take care of you, Pomona.

Pomona (*Haughtily*): I can take care of myself.

2nd Maiden: A husband would keep you company, Pomona.

Pomona: My trees keep me company. They never order me around or answer back, and they never make me scrub floors. A husband? No, thank you! (*Turns away*)

3rd Maiden: But when will you want a husband, Pomona?

Pomona: When the moon is blue, dear friends. (*She drops apple from her basket and kneels behind fence to pick it up. Maidens exit right. Quintus and Septimus enter left, followed by Galba, pulling the protesting Marcus with him.*)

Quintus: Come on, Marcus, you old woman-hater.

Galba: Come to the well and meet the maidens.

Quintus: We'll find you a sweet, helpless little wife.

Marcus: I don't want a wife.

Galba: We're going to find wives. You don't think we'll let you remain the only bachelor, do you?

Septimus: Think, Marcus. A wife would fetch and carry for you. A wife would fix your dinner and mend those rags you call clothes.

Marcus: And nag, and beg, and demand, and wheedle. Oh, no. I'm a simple shepherd. (*He drops his crook and bends to pick it up.*)

Quintus: You're simple, that's true enough. (*As Marcus picks up crook, his eyes meet Pomona's. They stare at each other. Pomona rises and turns away and goes to bench left.*)

Pomona: Rude fellow. Why do you stare at me so? (*She arranges fruit in basket. Marcus staggers back into arms of his friends.*)

MARCUS (*Clutching heart*): Oh, oh.

QUINTUS: What happened? Speak! Are you ill?

MARCUS: Ill? I think I'm dying!

GALBA: Wicked Pomona! Did she cast a spell over you?

MARCUS (*Speaking name with relish*): Pomona. What a heavenly name!

QUINTUS (*Feeling* MARCUS' *pulse and frowning*): Tsk-tsk. What a shame.

SEPTIMUS: Is he dying?

QUINTUS: Worse. He's in love.

GALBA: In love? With *her*? (*He points to* POMONA.)

SEPTIMUS (*Earnestly*): Marcus, dear old chum. You don't want to be in love with Pomona. Why, she's aloof and stuck-up. Apollo himself wouldn't suit that one.

MARCUS (*Moaning*): Pomona.

GALBA: What can we do for him?

QUINTUS: Perhaps if we took him to the well, he might see someone even more choice than Pomona. Come on, Marcus. She's not the only pebble on the shore.

MARCUS (*Waving them away*): Leave me to my delicious misery.

SEPTIMUS (*Shaking his head*): Oh, he's far gone. Hear me—let us go to the well and bring the maidens back to him.

QUINTUS: That's a good notion. (QUINTUS, SEPTIMUS, *and* GALBA *exit right.*)

POMONA (*Crossing to gate, as* MARCUS *stands openmouthed*): Are you still here, shepherd? What do you want?

MARCUS (*Dramatically*): Oh, Pomona, I did but gaze upon you once. Now I am yours forever.

POMONA: Mine? But whatever shall I do with you? I don't need a shepherd.

MARCUS: Be my wife. (*Aside*) Did *my* mouth utter those words?

POMONA (*Indignantly*): Your *wife*! This is really too much! I am not in the market for a husband.

MARCUS (*Wringing his hands*): Let me through the gate. Please. I cannot whisper sweet things to you out here.

POMONA: Oh, no. If I let you through that gate, the next thing I know, you'll be taking over my orchard, ordering me around and telling me to scrub floors.

MARCUS: What is it about me you object to? Would you like me better if I were someone else?

POMONA: How can I tell? You are *you*. Until you are someone else, I cannot tell. (*She crosses to bench, and arranges basket of fruit.* QUINTUS, SEPTIMUS, GALBA *and* MAIDENS *enter right.*)

QUINTUS: Pssst—Marcus. (MARCUS, *sighing deeply, crosses to them.*)

GALBA: We have found a maiden for you! (*He points to* MAIDENS, *who fold their hands and bow, then giggle.*)

MARCUS (*Covering eyes, waving them away*): My heart is taken.

SEPTIMUS: Just take a peek.

MARCUS: Take them away. (GALBA *shrugs.* MAIDENS *exit right.*)

QUINTUS: You are completely mad, Marcus. I ask you—did Pomona even give you the time of day?

MARCUS: Not exactly. I don't think she cares much for shepherds. (*Pauses*) Perhaps, if I were a reaper . . . Quintus, give me your reaper's smock and your hat. (QUINTUS *removes smock and hat.* MARCUS *dons them and, carrying* QUINTUS' *basket of barley ears, crosses to gate. He assumes deep, growling voice.*) Greetings, fair Pomona. I bring a gift from a friend. May I come through the gate?

POMONA: You bring a gift? Enter, reaper. (MARCUS *enters, crossing to bench. He falls on his knees.*)

MARCUS (*Declaiming*): Oh, beautiful Pomona. Upon bended knee I beg you . . . hear me. (POMONA *stands, angrily snatches off* MARCUS' *hat, scrutinizes his face, then pulls hat over his eyes, pointing to gate.*)

POMONA: I hear you. And I see you. You are that impossible

shepherd. Out, I say. (MARCUS *scrambles to his feet, picking up basket.*)

MARCUS: I'm going.

POMONA (*Grabbing basket*): I'll keep the barley ears. You said they were a gift. (MARCUS *slinks back to his friends.*)

QUINTUS: She kept my barley ears!

GALBA: You see how shamefully she treats you?

MARCUS: The more she rejects me, the more my heart is inflamed with love for her. Perhaps if she pitied me—(*He takes off* GALBA's *leather apron and headband.*)

GALBA: Here, what are you doing?

MARCUS (*Donning apron, and putting headband low over his eyes*): Put your pruning shears in my hand. (GALBA *gives him shears.* MARCUS *stumbles to gate, calling out in a whining voice.*) Pruning! Expert pruning! Give a poor old blind man a chance. (POMONA *crosses to gate.*)

POMONA: Pray, enter, poor fellow. Can you prune my apple tree? (MARCUS *staggers to grapevine, right. He feels grapes.*)

MARCUS: Ah, what a fine crop of apples! (*Snaps shears*)

POMONA (*Crossing behind him*): What is this? This blind man doesn't know an apple from a grape. (*She pulls off his headband.*) Just as I thought. The shepherd.

MARCUS: Pomona . . . if you would but listen.

POMONA (*Taking shears*): Go away.

MARCUS: My shears, please.

POMONA (*Hiding them behind her back*): A blind man shouldn't have shears. I will keep them. (MARCUS *returns to his friends, and hands* GALBA *his apron and headband.*)

GALBA (*Angrily*): You gave her my shears.

QUINTUS: And my barley ears. (*He shakes fist at* MARCUS.)

MARCUS: All right. I'll get them back for you.

SEPTIMUS: Do you know what you need, Marcus? You need someone to plead your cause.

MARCUS (*Thoughtfully*): Someone to plead my cause, eh? (*Pauses*) Give me your cloak and staff, Septimus.

SEPTIMUS (*Handing him cloak and staff*): What are you going to do?

MARCUS (*Laughing*): My dear old grandmother is going to plead my cause. (*He puts on cloak, and leaning heavily on staff, crosses to gate. He speaks in an old, quavery voice.*) Dearie, oh, dearie. Can you spare some water for an old woman?

POMONA (*Crossing to bucket, and drawing dipper of water*): Why, of course. Come through the gate, old mother. (*She holds out dipper to* MARCUS, *who sips it daintily.*)

MARCUS: My, my, what a pretty little thing you are.

POMONA: Thank you, old mother. But why is an old one like you traveling this dusty road so far from town?

MARCUS: I am searching for a certain shepherd named Marcus. He is my dear, devoted grandson. Have you seen a handsome shepherd on the road today?

POMONA: Strange that you should ask. There was a bothersome shepherd here today. He wouldn't leave me alone.

MARCUS: That must have been my Marcus. What a wonderful fellow.

POMONA: Wonderful?

MARCUS: A prince. Ah, they don't make shepherds like Marcus any more. He's looking for a wife, you know.

POMONA (*Sarcastically*): I know.

MARCUS: A girl couldn't do better than my Marcus. So generous, gentle, wise—his sheep adore him.

POMONA (*Sitting on bench, annoyed*): I am *not* looking for a husband.

MARCUS (*Looking around in mock caution*): Sh-h-h. Heaven will hear you. You know what Venus does to hardhearted maidens, don't you? (*He sits next to her.*)

POMONA: What?

MARCUS: I have heard that she seeks out maidens who will not wed and she turns them into cold, hard statues.

POMONA: But surely, you wouldn't consider me—hardhearted?

MARCUS: No? How did you treat poor Marcus?

POMONA: I told him to get out. Nicely.

MARCUS (*Moaning*): Oh, you didn't. You have crushed him. (*He rises, watching* POMONA *out of the corner of his eye.*) I must find him, before—

POMONA (*Rising*): Before what, old mother?

MARCUS: Do you remember the tale of Anaxarete? (POMONA *shakes her head.*) It was dreadful. The maiden, Iphis, disdained him. He—he—I cannot tell you the rest. It's not for your tender ears.

POMONA (*Alarmed*): But Marcus wouldn't do anything foolish, would he?

MARCUS: He's very sensitive.

POMONA: I didn't mean to hurt him, truly. I—I wish he would come back.

MARCUS: You do? Then you care, just a little.

POMONA (*Sniffling*): Just a little.

MARCUS (*Dramatically*): If he should return—perhaps from the very grave . . .

POMONA: From the grave!

MARCUS: Even now, the poor fellow may be a shade in Hades, finding no rest until Pomona consents to become his wife. I think I hear him calling—"Po-mo-na."

POMONA: Ah me! (*Calling out in great agitation.*) Marcus, hear me, wherever you may be . . . I will be your wife. (*Despairingly*) Oh, do you think I am too late? (*She buries her head on* MARCUS'S *shoulder.* QUINTUS, GALBA, *and* SEPTIMUS *cross to gate, pantomiming joy at sight of* POMONA *and* MARCUS *together.* MARCUS *waves them away. They tiptoe off right, grinning.*) Do you think I am too late? (*She raises head to look at him.*)

MARCUS (*Slowly pulling down hood of cloak, and speaking in his natural voice*): I think you are just in time.

POMONA (*Astonished*): Marcus! What a trick! I despise trickery. Are you going to hold me to my promise?

MARCUS: Yes.

POMONA: I suppose now you will take over my orchard?

MARCUS: That was the farthest thing from my mind. I don't know an apple from a grape. But—you could teach me.

POMONA (*Faltering*): I suppose you are going to order me around—do this, do that?

MARCUS: I never order maidens around. I invite them. *Please* do this. *Please* do that.

POMONA (*Dubiously*): And what about your floors? Must I scrub your floors?

MARCUS: Alas, I don't have a floor for you to scrub. But, if you could find it in your heart to toss together a little cottage cheese and curds for a lunch, now and then . . .

POMONA (*Relenting*): This is a very large orchard. It needs two gardeners. Welcome, Marcus. (*She takes his hands. They hold pose, as* VENUS *enters up center. She crosses to the elm.* QUINTUS, GALBA, *and* SEPTIMUS *enter, each with a* MAIDEN, *and take positions across stage to form a chorus.*)

VENUS (*Commandingly*):

Fair Pomona. Virtuous Marcus.

I am the sovereign of all hearts, Venus.

From far Olympus I have watched your comedy of court-
ship.

You have won my favor. Henceforward you shall be together.

You shall be as yonder elm tree, vine-entwined.

You, Marcus, are the elm, alone and strong.

Pomona, you the vine, which cannot stand alone.

Together you shall rule the orchards and the seasons.

And when each summer ends, Marcus, you

Shall blow the trump of winds, and bring forth autumn.

Pomona, you, with bounteous fruits and flowers,

Shall fill the horn of plenty for mankind.

QUINTUS, GALBA, SEPTIMUS, *and* MAIDENS:

Here ends the legend of the simple shepherd,

Who dared to woo the haughty nymph of autumn.
Remember, when cool winds sweep through the orchards,
When leaves of gold and russet tumble downward,
And ruby-laden boughs of fruit bend earthward.
Remember, oh, remember fair Pomona.
Remember, oh, remember bold Marcus.
(*They bow, and the curtains close.*)

THE END

The Long Table

Characters

NARRATOR
MRS. SARAH JOSEPHA HALE
DR. ANTIQUARIUS
HENRY GIDEON
ADELAIDE PRUITT
SECRETARY
TWO GUARDS
PRESIDENT LINCOLN
PILGRIM FAMILY   ⎫
INDIAN
NORTHERN FAMILY
SOUTHERN FAMILY   ⎬   *tableau characters*
PLANTATION FAMILY
MESSENGERS FROM THE
   FUTURE   ⎭
ASTRONAUT
CHORUS
TWO PROPERTY BOYS

SCENE 1

SETTING: *President Lincoln's waiting room. There is a long bench in front of curtain. This scene is played before curtain.*

BEFORE CURTAIN: NARRATOR, *dressed as a Pilgrim, enters and stands at one side.*

NARRATOR: Once upon a time, there was no Thanksgiving Day in America. Oh, here and there a few people held their own local celebrations. But nobody said, "This whole great country ought to sit down and count its blessings." Nobody even thought of such a holiday—until somebody remarkable arrived upon the scene. . . . (MRS. HALE *enters down right, wearing bonnet and shawl. In one hand, she carries sheaf of letters. In her other hand, she carries parasol. She stands down right.*) Somebody with a bee in her bonnet.

MRS. HALE: Letters. I have written thousands of letters. We must—nay, we *shall* have a national day of Thanksgiving. Such a holiday would bring the whole country together.

NARRATOR: Ah, yes. This is a most determined lady. Mrs. Sarah Josepha Hale. She has written to governors and high officials—but she won't stop there. Listen. That bee is buzzing in her bonnet again.

MRS. HALE (*Folding letters*): There. So much for the letters. Now, I shall spread my ideas about Thanksgiving with an editorial. If that does not bring results, I shall pay a visit to the President of the United States *himself!* (*Raps her parasol smartly on floor, then opens it and exits right.*)

NARRATOR: Now, that is the kind of lady I should like to have on my side. She never gives up. (DR. ANTIQUARIUS *enters left, peering into crystal ball.*) But who is this odd gentleman, poring so intently over his crystal ball?

DR. ANTIQUARIUS (*Bowing*): Dr. Antiquarius. Collector of cobwebs and promises. Dealer in rare trappings from old times and new times and sometimes. Drop in to my antique shop, off a little side street somewhere in your town. But, now, pray excuse me. I must keep my eyes upon the crystal ball. I am following the flight of a bee—a bee I have sent to bother a lady of great determination, Mrs. Sarah Josepha Hale. Ah, yes. We have business together, Mrs. Hale and I—business which will take us to Washington. . . . (*Blackout.* Narrator *and* Dr. Antiquarius *exit.* "*The Battle Hymn of the Republic*" *begins to play offstage. In a moment,* Two Guards *enter and stand right and left of center of curtain, at ease.* Henry Gideon, Adelaide Pruitt *and* Mrs. Hale, *carrying her parasol, enter and sit on bench. Music fades out. Lights come up full, and* Secretary, *carrying appointment book, enters through curtain, center.*)

Secretary: You people, there. Are you Mr. Lincoln's afternoon appointments?

Gideon (*Eagerly*): Oh, yes indeed, sir.

Adelaide: I've been waiting ever so long to see Mr. Lincoln, sir.

Mrs. Hale: Would you be kind enough to inform Mr. Lincoln that Mrs. Sarah Josepha Hale is present in his antechamber?

Secretary: Humph. I am Mr. Lincoln's personal secretary. You will pay close attention to my instructions. Mr. Lincoln is not to be bothered with cigar smoking, lobbying, buttonholing, sniveling or idle gossip. You will proceed according to my list. You will be given exactly five minutes per capita to conduct your business. (*Reads first name on list in appointment book.*) Henry Gideon? State your business.

Gideon: Why—I'm from President Lincoln's home town. I knew him when he was a little lad no higher than this. Look here, this letter says to come see him if I'm ever in Washington. (*He unfolds tattered letter.* Secretary *glances at it.*)

Secretary: This letter was written five years ago. Go along with you now. The President hasn't time to lollygag with every Tom, Dick and Harry in Illinois. (*He dismisses* Gideon *with a wave of his hand.* Gideon *exits sadly.*) Miss Adelaide Pruitt? State your business.

Adelaide: Oh, please, sir. It's so very important. It's about my brother Tom. He's been in a Yankee prison for years and years. (*She begins to weep.*) President Lincoln must pardon him. He must!

SECRETARY: Here, here. Don't snivel. The President hates sniveling women. Well—go on. Go in. (ADELAIDE *goes through curtain hesitantly.* DR. ANTIQUARIUS *enters from right, consulting his watch. He sits next to* MRS. HALE.)

MRS. HALE (*Thumping parasol; to* SECRETARY): Upon my soul! You are the rudest secretary I have ever encountered. Surely President Lincoln could have spared a moment for poor Mr. Gideon. Surely President Lincoln would not begrudge that unhappy girl her tears. I tell you, sir, if you were my secretary, I'd have you fired this instant! (*She pounds parasol again.*)

SECRETARY: Indeed, madam. And who might you be? (*He consults list.*) Mrs. Sarah Josepha Hale. Well, Mrs. Sarah Josepha Hale, let me tell you that if I were not here to protect him, President Lincoln would be besieged by every lunatic from here to Canada. Just what is your business, Mrs. Hale—eh?

MRS. HALE (*Crisply*): My business is *my* business. I shall disclose it when I meet the President and not before.

SECRETARY (*Pompously*): Very well, Mrs. Hale. But I shall have to look up your correspondence with the President to be sure you have fitting business with him. That will take considerable time.

MRS. HALE: I will wait.

SECRETARY: As you wish. (*He exits through curtain*)

DR. ANTIQUARIUS (*Consulting pocket watch*): Three-fifteen. The President must see me soon. My train for Baltimore leaves in twenty minutes. Who knows when I shall be able to make another appointment?

MRS. HALE: Perhaps I can help you. My appointment is for three-fifteen. Take my appointment—for that rude secretary is bound to make me wait forever.

DR. ANTIQUARIUS: Thank you. That is really most kind of you. My mission is urgent. Now, where is that secretary?

MRS. HALE (*Impishly*): I'll bring him out here flying! (*She thumps parasol vigorously.* SECRETARY *rushes in through curtain, center, agitated.*)

SECRETARY: Sh-h-h! Stop that infernal racket!

MRS. HALE: This gentleman has an urgent mission. I said he might have my appointment time.

SECRETARY: Oh, very well. Very well. (*He beckons to* DR. ANTIQUARIUS.) You may go directly to the President.

DR. ANTIQUARIUS (*Rising*): Thank you. (*To* MRS. HALE) May I know your name, madam? I should like to put in a good word for you when I speak with the President.

MRS. HALE: I am Mrs. Sarah Josepha Hale. You might tell the President that I am here to promote the cause of Thanksgiving. The Union needs such a day of rejoicing and homecoming. Yes, you must mention Thanksgiving.

SECRETARY (*Impatiently*): Hurry along now.

DR. ANTIQUARIUS (*Bowing*): I'll do my best, Mrs. Hale. (*Blackout. A reprise of "Battle Hymn of the Republic" is heard. Waiting-room bench is removed, and* MRS. HALE, GUARDS, *and* SECRETARY *exit. As music fades out, curtains open and lights come up full.*)

* * *

SCENE 2

SETTING: *President Lincoln's office. Chorus stands to one side.*

AT RISE: PRESIDENT LINCOLN, *absorbed in signing a document, does not look up as* DR. ANTIQUARIUS, *standing at right, looks about uncertainly.*

PRESIDENT LINCOLN: I'll be with you presently. Sit down, please. Make yourself comfortable.

DR. ANTIQUARIUS (*Sitting in chair, right*): Thank you, Mr. President.

PRESIDENT LINCOLN (*Looking up, as he blots document*): There. Another pardon signed. Well, sir, how may I help you?

DR. ANTIQUARIUS: My card, Mr. President. (*He hands card to* PRESIDENT LINCOLN, *who reads it aloud, with interest.*)

PRESIDENT LINCOLN: "Dr. Antiquarius. Dealer in curios. Special furnishings for state occasions." What sort of furnishings, Dr. Antiquarius?

DR. ANTIQUARIUS (*Eagerly*): A table, Mr. President. A table so unique that it is fit only for the White House. A table of rare dimensions and beauty. An infinitely flexible table, seating thousands. Moreover, this is a table which has leaves extending into the past and into the future. A long, long table, Mr. President. May I show it to you?

PRESIDENT LINCOLN (*Interested*): Why, that sounds remarkable. Yes. I should like to see that table. (DR. ANTIQUARIUS *sounds a clicker.* TWO PROPERTY BOYS *bring on first section of table. Table is bare, but has centerpiece: a wooden bowl of apples and nuts.* PROPERTY BOYS *exit.* DR. ANTIQUARIUS *rises and stands down right of table.* PRESIDENT LINCOLN *also rises and stands left of table.*)

PRESIDENT LINCOLN: Well, now, this doesn't appear to be such a long table.

DR. ANTIQUARIUS: Wait. This is only one leaf of the table— the leaf called the Past. Watch the table closely, Mr. President, for it brings with it shapes and presences—the spirits of those who first dined at the Long Table. (*He sounds clicker again. "Come, Ye Thankful People, Come" is played or hummed as background for entrance of* PILGRIM FAMILY, *who enter slowly, accompanied by an* INDIAN. *Family members take their places around table, leaving right side free so that another section may be joined to table.* PILGRIM FAMILY *fold their hands and bow their heads.*)

CHORUS (*Speaking in unison*):

"As one small candle may light a thousand,
So the light here kindled,
Hath shone unto many,
Yea, in some sort to our whole nation . . ." *
(CHORUS *sings first verse of "Come, Ye Thankful People, Come."*
At conclusion of song, members of tableau hold their poses.)

DR. ANTIQUARIUS: Now we shall see the center of the Long
Table. For the heart of the table is the Present. The moment. The everyday, mundane, now. (*He sounds clicker.*
PROPERTY BOYS *enter with long center section of table, bearing a*
floral centerpiece. They set it next to Pilgrim table. PRESIDENT
LINCOLN *crosses down left of table.*) This is a perfect table for
homecomings. All kinds of homecomings. From every
part of the country—North and South. (*"When Johnny*
Comes Marching Home" is heard in background. NORTHERN
FAMILY, *with Father in Union uniform, enters from up right,*
crossing to the upstage side of the table. SOUTHERN FAMILY, *with*
Father in Confederate uniform, enters from down left, crossing to
the table end, left.)

CHORUS (*Unison or solos*):
"With malice toward none:
With charity for all:
With firmness in the right,
As God gives us to see the right,
Let us strive on to finish the work we are in.
To bind up the nation's wounds,
To care for him who shall have borne the battle,
. . . To do all which may achieve and cherish
A just and lasting peace among ourselves,
And with all nations." †
(CHORUS *sings "When Johnny Comes Marching Home," first*
verse.)

PRESIDENT LINCOLN (*Noticing downstage side of table is empty*):

---

* Governor William Bradford.
† Abraham Lincoln's Second Inaugural Address.

Why, that's mighty fine. But look—there's still room at the table.

DR. ANTIQUARIUS: Plenty of room. Plenty of room for another kind of homecoming. A homecoming from bondage. (PLANTATION FAMILY *enters left, taking its place at downstage side of table. "Let My People Go" is played in background.*)

CHORUS:

". . . And by the virtue of the power,

And for the purpose aforesaid,

I do order and declare

That all persons held as slaves,

. . . Henceforward shall be free!" *

(CHORUS *sings first verse of "Let My People Go."*)

DR. ANTIQUARIUS: But the past and the present are only parts of this ingenious table. (*He sounds clicker.* PROPERTY BOYS *bring on third section.* SOUTHERN FAMILY *joins* NORTHERN FAMILY *on upstage side of table. Third section contains silver tray, empty, as centerpiece.*) For look, Mr. President. The table expands in yet another direction—into the future. Here are the early, gathering ghosts of the Things Which Are to Be.

PRESIDENT LINCOLN: The things which are to be . . . (MESSENGERS FROM THE FUTURE *enter, carrying lamp, telephone, atom model, toy auto, and airplane, which they place on rim of silver tray.*)

CHORUS:

"Not only will atomic power be released

But someday we will harness the rise and fall of the tides,

And imprison the rays of the sun . . ." †

(ASTRONAUT *enters left, bringing globe model of moon, which he places on table.*)

EAGLE SOLO: "Houston, Tranquility Base here. The Eagle has landed."

CHORUS: The Eagle has landed!

* The Emancipation Proclamation, Abraham Lincoln.
† Thomas Alva Edison, August 22, 1921.

EAGLE SOLO: "I'm at the foot of the ladder. The LM foot beds are only depressed in the surface about one or two inches. It's almost like a powder. It's very fine. I'm going to step off the LM now. (*Pauses*) That's one small step for man, one giant leap for mankind. . . ." *

CHORUS: One small step for man, one giant leap for mankind! (CHORUS *sings first and second verses of "These Things Shall Be."* † *Lights begin to dim on second line of song. At conclusion of second verse, there is a blackout. All characters of tableau and* DR. ANTIQUARIUS *exit.* PROPERTY BOYS *remove table. Lights come up.*)

PRESIDENT LINCOLN: Dr. Antiquarius? Why—he's gone. And he's taken that remarkable table with him. Perhaps it's just as well. It was truly a table of State—but what national celebration would do it justice? (SECRETARY *enters.*)

SECRETARY: The appointments are finished for the afternoon, Mr. President. Right on schedule. (*From offstage,* MRS. HALE *pounds furiously on floor with her parasol.*)

PRESIDENT LINCOLN (*Chuckling*): What's that? A disappointed woodpecker?

SECRETARY (*Fuming*): It's that impossible Mrs. Hale. I'll send her packing immediately. The woman's a menace, with her folderol about a "national Thanksgiving."

PRESIDENT LINCOLN: Mrs. Hale? Mrs. Sarah Josepha Hale? Thanksgiving—of course. (*He crosses down right.*) Please come in, Mrs. Hale. (*He shakes hands with* MRS. HALE *as she enters. They cross to center.*)

SECRETARY (*Objecting*): But, Mr. President—

PRESIDENT LINCOLN (*Dismissing him with wave of his hand*): You may leave us alone now. Surely there is something for you to file in the outer office. (SECRETARY *bows stiffly*

---

* Neil Armstrong, July 20, 1969.

† From *Sing Together:* A Girl Scout Handbook, 1957 Edition.

and exits down right.) Mrs. Hale, I have read your editorials in *Godey's Lady's Book* with the greatest interest.

MRS. HALE (*Eagerly*): Then you know of my proposal for a national Thanksgiving Day? Oh, Mr. President, I know it would bring us together. (*She takes documents from her reticule.*) Look—here is what George Washington had to say —and here—President Madison's Thanksgiving for peace.

PRESIDENT LINCOLN: Now, now. You need go no further. (*Thoughtfully*) For I have just been convinced that this country needs a day set apart. A day when all may sit down at a long table and remember the stirring incidents of national history. A day of rejoining and rejoicing in the progress of the Union. Yes, Mrs. Hale. You and I and the people of this commonwealth shall have a Thanksgiving Day!

MRS. HALE: Oh, thank you, Mr. President. Thank you. (*Curtains close. "America, the Beautiful" is played behind* CHORUS.)

CHORUS:

> "We are grateful for the plentiful yield of our soil . . .
> We rejoice in the beauty of our land . . .
> We deeply appreciate the preservation
> Of those ideals of liberty and justice
> Which form the basis of our national life
> And the hope of international peace . . ." *

NARRATOR (*Entering down right*): We are grateful. . . . We rejoice. . . . We appreciate. . . . These are words which all Americans should use at Thanksgiving time. Although part of the story you have seen was imaginary, in your history book you will find a real Mrs. Sarah Josepha Hale. As for the mysterious Dr. Antiquarius—who knows? Perhaps someday, somewhere, you will find that

---

* Thanksgiving Day Proclamation, 1958, Dwight D. Eisenhower.

little side street where he keeps a curio shop. And who knows? Perhaps he will take you into a back room of that curio shop and show you the Long Table. (*He bows and exits.*)

THE END

Jack Jouette's Ride

Characters

JOHN FIFER	COLONEL TARLETON
ROBBIE FIFER	TWO AIDES
MOLLY FIFER	MRS. WALKER
JACK JOUETTE	LIZZIE
LORD CORNWALLIS	TWO SOLDIERS
GEORGE WILSON	CHORUS

SCENE 1

TIME: *June, 1781.*

SETTING: *The Cuckoo Tavern in Louisa County, Virginia. There is a brick fireplace up center, with skillets and pots hanging from mantel. Fire tools are on the hearth. A sign reading* THE CUCKOO TAVERN *hangs above fireplace. Up left and right are mullioned French windows covered with closed curtains. There are two tables with benches downstage left and right. Exits are right and left.*

AT RISE: JOHN FIFER, *the old tavern keeper, and his granddaughter,* MOLLY, *are polishing mugs on a tray at left table. Tray also holds a teapot.* ROBBIE FIFER *pokes the fire with poker.*

JOHN FIFER: The fire's burned low, Robbie. You'd best fetch another armload of logs.

ROBBIE: Yes, Grandpa. While I fetch them, I'll keep a sharp lookout for Redcoats.

FIFER: Redcoats, eh? You'll look long and hard for Redcoats in this county, Robbie. They're all down at York-town, plotting wicked doings.

ROBBIE: But you never know what Redcoats are up to, Grandpa. I'll spy out the land—just in case. (*He exits left.*)

MOLLY (*Yawning and stretching*): 'Tis almost time to close the tavern, Grandpa. Hasn't it been a quiet night? Hardly a soul stopped by.

FIFER: Everybody with two good legs has gone North to fight with General Washington. (JACK JOUETTE *enters down right, in full Continental officer's uniform.*) If they'd any use for an old graybeard like me, I'd go, too.

JACK JOUETTE: We need you here, John Fifer. You're a man who knows how to keep his ears open and his mouth shut.

FIFER (*Crossing to shake hands with* JACK JOUETTE): Why, bless me, it's Captain Jack Jouette home again. What's the news from the war, Captain?

JOUETTE: I wish I knew. The British are landing by the thousands at Yorktown. And yet, Lord Cornwallis does nothing, and moves nowhere. He's like a great lion, ready to pounce. But where? When? (ROBBIE *runs on at left.*)

ROBBIE (*Breathlessly*): Grandpa, they're coming! A million of them. Run!

JOUETTE: Get hold of yourself, Robbie. Who is coming?

ROBBIE: Redcoats, Captain Jouette. Hide, everybody, hide!

MOLLY: Redcoats—here? What shall we do?

JOUETTE: So . . . the lion has pounced. (*Urgently*) Think carefully, Robbie. How many are there?

ROBBIE: There are thirty, maybe forty lines of foot soldiers. Half that many on horses. Guess that's not quite a million.

JOUETTE: No, but it's more than I'd expect. What can those lobsterbacks be up to? (*He crosses to French window up right, looks out cautiously.*) They're not in sight yet. What can they be doing here? I must find out.

FIFER: You'd best stay, Captain Jouette. They'll hang you soon as they see you in that uniform.

JOUETTE: Then I will make certain they don't see the uniform.

MOLLY: I've a perfect disguise for you. It will take me but one minute. (*She runs off left.*)

JOUETTE (*Crossing to* ROBBIE): Robbie, will you be a good soldier again? (ROBBIE *nods.*) You must catch the Redcoats before they turn off the road. Take the reins of the commander's horse and beseech him to come for supper at your grandfather's tavern.

ROBBIE: Me? Speak to a Redcoat general?

JOUETTE: You must do it, boy. It's the only chance to find out their plans.

ROBBIE: I reckon that's so. (*Slowly*) I always wanted to be a spy, but not so soon. (*He exits down right, as* MOLLY *returns with ragged coat and floppy hat.*)

MOLLY: Here you are, Captain Jouette. A present from the scarecrow in Grandpa's back field. (*She helps him into coat and hat. He leaves his officer's hat on the table. Drumbeats are heard from off.*)

FIFER: Drums! They're almost here. (JOUETTE *crosses to window and peers out.*)

JOUETTE: I'm heartily glad there's a full moon. I can see the road as clear as at midday. Ah, there's Robbie running out. Now he's seized the reins of the commander's horse. He's gabbing like a trooper. The commander is looking this way. By my sword, it's Cornwallis himself!

FIFER *and* MOLLY (*Together*): Cornwallis!

JOUETTE: And riding beside him is that wily fellow, George Wilson. The third officer is Colonel Tarleton. This is no merry fox hunt, I'll tell you that.

MOLLY: What shall we do? I'm shaking from head to toe.

JOUETTE: Calm yourself, Molly. We must go on as usual. John, you bring yonder table closer, so it's within earshot.

(FIFER *moves tables closer.* JOUETTE *sits on bench at right table, and rests his head on his arms. Loud drum roll is heard, then silence.*)

MOLLY: Grandpa, they're here!

FIFER: Hush, lass. Polish those mugs as if your very life depended upon it. (MOLLY *starts to polish mugs.* ROBBIE *enters.*)

ROBBIE: I've brought you some soldiers, Grandpa. (CORNWALLIS, *followed by* GEORGE WILSON *and* COLONEL TARLETON, *enters.*)

CORNWALLIS: You will address us as British officers, boy.

COLONEL TARLETON: What can you expect of Colonial bumpkins, my lord?

CORNWALLIS (*To* FIFER): You, tavern keeper—fetch us a light, quick supper.

TARLETON: The boy here says your waffles and sweet syrup are exceptional. We are very hungry. Bring us some waffles at once.

FIFER: Yes, sir. Robbie, fetch more wood. (FIFER *and* ROBBIE *exit left.*)

WILSON (*Spotting* JOUETTE's *hat on table and pointing to it*): Girl, to whom does this hat belong?

MOLLY (*Frightened*): Hat? I see no hat.

TARLETON: Egad, 'tis there in front of your nose, on the table.

MOLLY (*Pointing to hat*): That? Is that what you call a hat? Indeed, you British gentlemen need Mr. Franklin to make you new spectacles. That is no hat. It is a tea cozy. (*She puts hat over teapot on tray and marches off left, carrying tray.*)

CORNWALLIS: Enough of this, gentlemen. We have an errand of high importance to discuss.

WILSON (*Indicating* JOUETTE, *who still sits at right table, snoring*): My lord, we may be overheard.

TARLETON: Egad, Wilson, you see spies everywhere. Why, that fellow's a simpleton and fast asleep to boot.

CORNWALLIS: You overrate the dangers of these rustics, Wilson. (*Takes map from pocket and unrolls it.*) Examine this section of Virginia. When we have finished here, Wilson and I will ride to Petersburg. But you, Tarleton, will continue to the West with the army. You must capture this hill.

TARLETON: This hill? What is the importance of this hill?

CORNWALLIS: One word will tell you: Monticello.

TARLETON: Egad, what a bold stroke! Capture Monticello and take Governor Thomas Jefferson prisoner.

CORNWALLIS: That is not the end of the matter. You must then proceed to Charlottesville, arrest the Virginia legislature and take three hostages, Richard Henry Lee, Thomas Nelson, and Benjamin Harrison.

WILSON: You must understand, Colonel Tarleton, that the Colonials set great hopes upon those three, and Governor Jefferson, of course. They all signed that infamous Declaration of Independence. (*Turning to* CORNWALLIS) What will you do with those traitors, my lord? (ROBBIE *peers in at door, then hastily withdraws.*)

CORNWALLIS: I will hang them from the tallest tree in Virginia.

TARLETON: And then?

CORNWALLIS: Then, the Colonials will beg our humble pardon, and on bended knee they will ask His Majesty for his forgiveness. (JOUETTE *snores loudly.*) Gentlemen, God Save the King!

TARLETON *and* WILSON: God Save the King. (1ST AIDE *enters.*)

1ST AIDE: My Lord Cornwallis, you asked me to inform you when the horses arrived. The dragoons have taken all the horses from the plantations hereabouts.

CORNWALLIS: Splendid. They say Virginia horses are the finest in the world. Come, let's have a look at them. (*He rises.*)

TARLETON: Oh, but the waffles, my lord?

CORNWALLIS: Horses before waffles, my dear Tarleton. (*They exit down right, and* FIFER *re-enters left.*)

JOUETTE (*Sitting up, pounding table with his fist*): No! No! No! They must not do this. I will not let them.

FIFER: Easy, Captain. There's naught you can do. It is forty miles to Charlottesville, and not a horse to be had. (ROBBIE *enters down left.*)

JOUETTE: I must warn Mr. Jefferson, if I have to run those forty miles on foot.

ROBBIE: You'll not run on foot, Captain Jouette. I've a horse all saddled and ready for you.

JOUETTE: What? A horse? How did you work such a miracle, Robbie?

ROBBIE (*Sheepishly*): The Redcoats borrowed all our best horses, so I just returned the favor. I borrowed one of theirs. He's tethered by the woodshed.

JOUETTE: You'll be a general yet, Robbie. Now, friends, wish me well. I'm running a close race with Tarleton. Somehow I shall have to make time to save Mr. Jefferson and the legislature. Farewell. . . . (*He exits.*)

FIFER (*Opening curtains and calling out window*): Keep to the back roads! (*Sound of horse's whinnying is heard from offstage.*)

JOUETTE (*Calling, from offstage*): Away, you British nag! (*Sound of hoofbeats is heard. Hoofbeats continue through dialogue that follows.*)

FIFER: Godspeed! For liberty and for Virginia—ride, Jack Jouette, ride!

MOLLY *and* ROBBIE: Ride, Jack Jouette, ride! (*Curtains close.* CHORUS *enters and stands center, in front of curtain.*   NOTE: *If* CHORUS *is seated in orchestra pit or first row of audience, it stands at this point and faces audience.*)

CHORUS:

> Ride, Jack Jouette, ride.
> Ride, Jack Jouette, ride.

1st Voice: Ride with a rush, over thicket and brush,
Chorus: Ride, Jack Jouette, ride.
2nd Voice:
> Like a bolt from a bow,
> Like a bullet, go.
Chorus: Ride, Jack Jouette, ride.
3rd Voice: Gallop to the rescue of Jefferson,
4th Voice: Gallop 'til the Redcoat race is done,
5th Voice: Gallop for the sake of the world to be won,
Chorus: Ride, Jack Jouette, ride.
6th Voice: Under the moon is a mad steeplechase,
Chorus: On, Jack Jouette, on.
1st Voice: Marathon riders who gallop apace,
Chorus: On, Jack Jouette, on.
2nd Voice: Riding the night down, with no resting place,
Chorus: On, Jack Jouette, on.
3rd Voice: Thirty miles swallowed, and ten more to go,
Chorus: Ride, Jack Jouette, ride.
4th Voice: Minutes ahead of the scurrying foe,
Chorus: Ride, Jack Jouette, ride.
5th Voice: To the east comes the dawn and the sunrise
> glow.
Chorus: Ride, Jack Jouette, ride.
6th Voice:
> Only five more miles down dale and rill,
> Five more miles to Charlottesville,
> Why do you stop at Castle Hill?
Chorus:
> Ride, Jack Jouette, ride.
> Why do you stop at Castle Hill?
> Ride, Jack Jouette, ride.

* * *

SCENE 2

SETTING: *Dining room in the Walker house at Castle Hill. Set is same as Scene 1, but decor has been altered. Draperies replace curtains at windows, and windows are flung open. A sideboard stands in front of window at right. Pots and skillets have been taken down from mantel; candles now stand on mantel. Landscape painting hangs over fireplace, replacing tavern sign. One table and bench have been removed. Remaining table stands at right, covered with a white tablecloth. Candelabra stand on table. There are three ladder-back chairs at table.*

AT RISE: MRS. WALKER *stands at window right, listening.* LIZZIE, *the maid, folds napkins at table.*

MRS. WALKER: Listen. I thought I heard hoofbeats, Lizzie.

LIZZIE: But who would be coming to Castle Hill so early in the morning, mum? (*Hoofbeats are heard from offstage.*)

MRS. WALKER: There. Somebody *is* coming.

JOUETTE (*Offstage*): Whoa . . . (*Sound of knocking on door is heard.*) Let me come in, I pray you. It is urgent. I'm a Continental officer.

MRS. WALKER: Open the door, Lizzie. He's one of our officers. (LIZZIE *opens door right and* JOUETTE, *exhausted, staggers in, and falls into chair.*) Get some water, Lizzie. He's exhausted. (LIZZIE *runs off left, returning quickly with mug, from which* JOUETTE *drinks.*) You must rest, sir.

JOUETTE: There's no time. Madam, you must help me. (*Rousing himself*) The British are following close behind me. They mean to capture Mr. Jefferson and arrest the legislature. I must ride to warn them. (*Drumbeats are heard.*)

MRS. WALKER: Drums. The Redcoats must be here! But what can I do, sir? I'm alone except for Lizzie.

JOUETTE: Detain them. Give me a little time to ride to

Charlottesville. When all is safe I will send up a rocket. Watch for it. (*Loud drum roll is heard.*)

LIZZIE: They're here!

JOUETTE (*Crossing to exit, left*): Remember, ma'am. If you value your country and Mr. Jefferson's life—hold the British! (*He exits, as loud knocking is heard on outside door, right.*)

1ST AIDE (*Offstage*): Open in the name of the King! (LIZZIE *runs to door right and opens it, admitting* COLONEL TARLETON *and* TWO AIDES.)

TARLETON (*Bowing*): My compliments, madam.

2ND AIDE: You have the very great honor of being hostess to Colonel Tarleton of His Majesty's forces. (MRS. WALKER *and* LIZZIE *curtsy.*)

1ST AIDE: Pray bring us one of your fine Virginia breakfasts.

2ND AIDE: And bring it speedily.

MRS. WALKER: Bring a tray of breakfasts, Lizzie. (LIZZIE *exits left.*) How very good of you to offer me your company for breakfast, gentlemen. But wouldn't you like a stroll in the garden before you eat? (LIZZIE *returns, carrying tray with food, places it on sideboard and begins to fan it vigorously.* MRS. WALKER *joins her in this action.*)

TARLETON: Hurry, madam. We have important business hereabouts.

1ST AIDE: If that is our tray, bring it hither.

MRS. WALKER: Ah, but it is too hot. (*She continues to fan food.*)

TARLETON: But that is how a breakfast should be. Come, madam.

MRS. WALKER: Oh, what a shame. Now it is too cold. No British gentlemen shall have cold food in my home. (*She holds out tray to* LIZZIE.) Throw this to the pigs, Lizzie.

LIZZIE (*Grinning broadly*): Yes, mum. (*She picks up tray and exits.*)

TARLETON (*Impatiently*): Bring another breakfast. Immediately!

MRS. WALKER (*Calling*): Lizzie, prepare another tray. (*Emphasizing her words*) Hurry—but mind you do not drop anything! (*Sound of crash of dishes is heard from offstage. LIZZIE runs in, pretending to sob loudly.*)

LIZZIE: Oh, mum, you said to hurry and so I hurried as fast as ever I could, but when I hurried so fast, my hands slipped and I dropped the dishes. Oh! (*Sobs*)

TARLETON: Enough of this bumbling. Can't you Yankee Doodles do anything right? Come, gentlemen. (*He rises. MRS. WALKER crosses to him.*)

MRS. WALKER (*Soothingly*): Dear, dear Colonel, pray do not leave. I myself will prepare you a tasty breakfast of piping hot ham slices swimming in gravy, spoon bread with melted butter, and crisp waffles with sweet sorghum syrup.

TARLETON (*Sitting*): Waffles, eh? I've heard a great deal about your famous waffles. But hark ye, madam. A few minutes, then we must leave. (MRS. WALKER *exits left. LIZZIE crosses to window, peering out anxiously.*)

1ST AIDE: Here, girl. What are you looking for?

2ND AIDE: She's looking for her Continental soldier, I warrant.

1ST AIDE: Look no more, girl. Your army took to their heels at the sound of our military drums. (MRS. WALKER *returns carrying tray. She crosses to* LIZZIE.)

MRS. WALKER (*Whispering*): Any sign of the rocket?

LIZZIE: Not yet. But I saw two hungry British soldiers snooping about outside this very window.

MRS. WALKER: Two hungry soldiers. Now wouldn't it be a shame if they stole this lovely breakfast? (LIZZIE *grins and nods.* MRS. WALKER *sets tray on sideboard and crosses center to distract officers.*) Now, gentlemen, before you breakfast I must tell you an amusing tale about the candelabra you see before you on the table. (TWO SOLDIERS *appear at window. They sniff food.* LIZZIE *pretends not to notice.*)

TARLETON: Three minutes, madam.

MRS. WALKER: But it is such a droll tale, Colonel. It seems there was a silversmith named Jimpson—or was it Simpson?—who practiced his trade in London. (SOLDIERS *reach in through window, remove plates from tray and disappear.*) Now, Jimpson or Simpson as the case may be and often is, had occasion to visit Bond Street, or was it Bank Street?

LIZZIE (*In piercing scream*): Stop! Stop, thief! (*Officers rise, alarmed.*) Your soldiers. They've stolen the breakfast!

TARLETON: This is the last straw! Aides, after those brigands! I'll make them pay for their breakfast, that I will! (AIDES *run offstage right.* TARLETON *bows to* MRS. WALKER.) I regret, madam, that I will not be able to enjoy your waffles this morning. Egad! (*He turns on his heel, and exits indignantly.* MRS. WALKER *and* LIZZIE *cross to window, laughing.*)

LIZZIE: What a sight they are!

MRS. WALKER: Look at them run. Ah, it does my heart good to see the British lion chasing his tail like a silly kitten.

LIZZIE (*Pointing upward*): Oh, look, mum. There it is. The rocket—like a new star bursting.

MRS. WALKER: They're safe. Thanks be! Mr. Jefferson and the legislature have escaped. (*Drums dying away in distance are heard.*)

LIZZIE: Listen, mum. The drums. They're going away.

MRS. WALKER: Yes, Lizzie. The British are going away. Going away from Virginia empty-handed. Somehow, it appears to me, that is a good omen. Somehow, I believe that very soon they'll be going away from our shores forever . . . back to where they came from . . . empty-handed. (*Curtain*)

THE END

Honorable Cat's Decision

Characters

SCRIBE	WISE ONE, *a scholar*
EMPEROR	IVORY CARVER
HONORABLE CAT	WOOD CARVER
LORD HIGH TALE TELLER	STONE CARVER
LORD HIGH BIRD SPOTTER	SHOJI, *the rat catcher*
LORD HIGH DOG CATCHER	OKUSAN, *his wife*
LADY OF THE CREAM BOWL	SHUBO, *his son*
LADY OF THE SILK SKEIN	TWO PROPERTY BOYS
LADY OF THE DOWN PILLOW	

TIME: *Long ago.*

SETTING: *Ancient Japan. Throne room of Emperor is represented by dais up center, consisting of four tiered steps. Down right is Shoji's home, represented by a screen. In front of screen is a low table set with rice bowl and three small bowls and chopsticks. Next to table is a small hibachi with teapot on it.*

AT RISE: EMPEROR *kneels alone on top tier. There is a gong at his side. On second tier his scholar,* WISE ONE, *is kneeling to the left of* EMPEROR. *On the third tier kneel* LORD HIGH TALE TELLER, LORD HIGH BIRD SPOTTER, *and* LORD HIGH DOG CATCHER. *On the bottom tier kneel* LADY OF THE CREAM BOWL, *holding bowl;* LADY OF THE SILK SKEIN, *holding skein of thread; and* LADY OF THE DOWN PILLOW, *holding pillow.* SHOJI, OKUSAN, *and* SHUBO *kneel on pillows at table. Next to* SHOJI *is a butterfly net.* SCRIBE, *unrolling a scroll, enters, crosses downstage and bows to audience.*

SCRIBE: Please to have the attention of your worthy ears. This humble scribe has a story to tell you. This is the story of the first cat who ever came to Japan, and all the trouble he caused. Long ago in the days of the Emperor Mei Tei, there lived a happy rat catcher named Shoji (SHOJI *bows.*), his wife Okusan (OKUSAN *bows.*), and his son, Shubo. (SHUBO *bows.*) You may ask why a rat catcher should be so happy. He was happy because there were plenty of rats for him to catch. Every day, Shoji took his net to the Imperial Palace. (SHOJI, *holding net, crosses to dais and bows to* EMPEROR.)

SHOJI: Permission to capture the royal rats, Your Most Imperial Highness.

EMPEROR: Permission granted. You may begin.

LADIES (*Screaming in high voices; ad lib*): Oh! Oh! Oh! There, Shoji, there. (*Etc. They each point in a different direction.* SHOJI *zig-zags across stage, then brings net down on imaginary rat.*)

SHOJI: It is done. Sayonara, rat! (*He shakes net fiercely.*)

EMPEROR: Well done, rat catcher. (*Takes gold piece from money bag on his belt and passes it to* WISE ONE, *who in turn passes it to* LORD HIGH TALE TELLER, *who gives it to* LADY OF THE CREAM BOWL. *She presents gold piece to* SHOJI.)

SHOJI: A thousand grateful thanks, Your Excellency. (*He bows and crosses to his home and kneels.*)

SCRIBE: Now, Shoji knew that there would always be hundreds of rats for him to catch, so he never bothered to save his daily gold piece. . . . (SHOJI *claps his hands.* 1ST PROPERTY BOY *brings in large bowl of flowers and sets it down on table.* SHOJI *gives him gold piece with a flourish. He exits.* SHOJI *presents flowers to* OKUSAN *and* SHUBO, *who bow.*) However, this was not wise, for one day a visitor from far away, seeking his fortune, came to the imperial palace. (HONORABLE CAT, *with hobo's bundle over shoulder, enters, crosses center and bows to* EMPEROR.)

ALL: Oh-h, look at that.

LORDS: What a fine, fierce set of whiskers.

LADIES: What a nice, soft coat of fur.

ALL: But what is it?

EMPEROR: Rise, strange creature. Tell me who or what you are. Speak, I command you.

HONORABLE CAT: Meeow!

LORD HIGH TALE TELLER: A foreigner, to be sure.

LADY OF THE CREAM BOWL: He does not speak Japanese, that is sure.

EMPEROR: Wise One, what kind of being is this? What language does he speak?

WISE ONE: I will consult the long scroll, Your Highness. Everything that is known about anything is written upon the long scroll. (*He claps his hands.* TWO PROPERTY BOYS *bring on long scroll, unroll it across stage, and stand holding either end.* WISE ONE *puts on his spectacles and peers intently at scroll. When he reaches end, he points at scroll triumphantly.*) Ah, here it is. Strange creature. Short fur. Long whiskers. Long tail. That, Your Highness, is a cat. He comes from the western side of the world.

ALL: Ah-h-h. A cat!

EMPEROR (*To* WISE ONE): Speak to him. Ask him what his business is.

WISE ONE: I regret very much that I cannot speak to him, Your Highness. He speaks Meowese. I have no dictionary for Meowese. (PROPERTY BOYS *roll up scroll and stand upstage of dais.* WISE ONE *returns to his place on tier.*)

EMPEROR: Well, no matter. He shall be made welcome here. A cat, eh? (*He rings gong.* 1ST PROPERTY BOY *brings a ribbon with a large medal and takes* CAT'S *bundle.*) I hereby name you Honorable Cat, chief ambassador of all cats who come to Japan. (EMPEROR *puts ribbon and medal around* CAT'S *neck.* CAT *bows.* 1ST PROPERTY BOY *returns upstage.*)

LADIES (*Screaming and pointing again at floor; ad lib*): Oh! Oh! Oh! There . . . there . . . there . . . (CAT *meows, extends paws and stalks imaginary rat. He chases it offstage, then returns, holding rat by tail.*)

ALL: Ah-h-h. Clever. Clever. (2ND PROPERTY BOY *takes rat away.*)

EMPEROR: Remarkable. Amazing. The cat is useful as well as ornamental. Come here, Honorable Cat. You shall sit beside me in the place of honor. (LORDS *and* LADIES *bow low as* CAT *kneels in place of honor on second tier, next to* WISE ONE.)

SCRIBE: And that is how the first cat to come to Japan became the immediate favorite of the Emperor and his court. But because of this cat, the Emperor no longer called upon Shoji to catch the rats. Day after day, Shoji waited, but no summons came. Day after day, Shoji grew poorer and poorer . . . (PROPERTY BOYS *remove* SHOJI'S *hibachi, screen, and pillows.*) At last one cold day (SHOJI, OKUSAN *and* SHUBO *shiver and blow on their hands.*) there was nothing left in the rice pot but three grains of rice. . . .

OKUSAN: Oh, what a sad day! We have only three grains of rice left. But I must make the best of things. (*Smiling bravely at* SHOJI) Husband, we are most fortunate today. We have three plump grains of rice. One whole grain for each of us.

SHOJI (*To himself*): Three poor grains of rice. Not enough for a bird. But my poor wife has enough troubles. I will not grumble. (*To* OKUSAN) Ah, how well you have cooked this grain of rice, wife. (*Eats rice*) It is as tender as a lotus bud.

SHUBO (*To himself*): Three grains of rice. I could eat a mountain of rice, I am so hungry. But I must not complain to my honorable parents. (*Eats rice; turns to* SHOJI *and* OKUSAN) Yum, yum, that was a delicious breakfast. I can eat no more.

SHOJI: Things must get better. The Emperor cannot forget me forever . . . can he?

SCRIBE: Now, just when matters seemed most desperate,

something curious occurred in the palace. The Honorable Cat became very lazy. He was so pampered and so spoiled that he did nothing all day but sleep, and no one could keep him entertained.

EMPEROR: What is the matter with Honorable Cat? He mopes and sleeps; sleeps and mopes. My lords—my ladies, make him merry again.

LORD HIGH TALE TELLER (*Rising and bowing to* CAT): Most worthy Cat, please allow this poor teller of tales to tickle your ears with stories of illustrious felines. I have a new tale today. Would you like to hear about Puss-in-Boots? (HONORABLE CAT *yawns and shakes his head. As* LORD HIGH TALE TELLER *sits,* LORD HIGH BIRD SPOTTER *rises and bows.*)

LORD HIGH BIRD SPOTTER: Most distinguished Cat, come with me for a romp in the marshes. I will point out a thousand delicious birds for you to stalk. (CAT *yawns again, shaking his head. As* LORD HIGH BIRD SPOTTER *resumes his place,* LORD HIGH DOG CATCHER *rises and bows.*)

LORD HIGH DOG CATCHER: Most noble Cat, I have caught a great big ugly dog in a cage. Let me free him, so that you may chase him and show him who is master of this palace. (CAT *yawns and shakes his head for the third time.* LADIES *rise and hold out their offerings to him.*)

LADY OF THE CREAM BOWL: Sweet little catkin. Here is a bowl of pure, fresh cream with just a hint of catnip grated over the top. Take one small sip. Just for me. (CAT *puts his paws over his mouth.* LADY OF THE CREAM BOWL *kneels.*)

LADY OF THE SILK SKEIN (*Waving silken threads in front of* CAT): Here, kitty, kitty. Playful puss, come on. Play with the nice silk string. Just for me. (CAT *puts his paws over his eyes.* LADY OF THE SILK SKEIN *kneels.*)

LADY OF THE DOWN PILLOW (*Climbing up tiers, and sitting beside* CAT): There, there. Honorable Cat doesn't want food or play. He wants to sleep, doesn't he? Close your furry eyes and sleep, precious pussycat. Just for me. (*She puts pillow under* CAT's *head, and slips away, kneeling in her place*) Shh-h!

LORDS *and* LADIES (*Putting fingers to lips*): Sh-h-h! (EMPEROR *angrily bangs gong.* CAT *wakes with a startled meow*)

EMPEROR: Enough is enough! What is the use of a cat that sleeps all day? Wise One, amuse the cat immediately. Wake him up or I will get myself a new scholar and a new court.

ALL: Oh!

WISE ONE: Yes, Your Highness. Immediately, Your Highness. (*He claps his hands.* PROPERTY BOYS *unroll scroll. He crosses in double time to center, and points at scroll.*) I have it! A contest. (PROPERTY BOYS *remove scroll.*)

EMPEROR: What kind of contest?

WISE ONE: A contest to see who can carve the most lifelike rat. Honorable Cat will judge, and the winner shall receive a bag of gold.

EMPEROR: Well, Honorable Cat? What do you think?

CAT (*Nodding*): Me-e-ow!

EMPEROR: Lord High Tale Teller—announce the contest to all the people, across my kingdom. Do it quickly, before Honorable Cat falls asleep again. (LORD HIGH TALE TELLER *crosses downstage.* SHOJI *and his family cup their ears, listening intently.*)

LORD HIGH TALE TELLER: Hear ye! Hear ye! Our Most Esteemed Emperor will present a bag of gold to the person who carves the most lifelike rat. Honorable Cat himself will be the judge. Hear ye! Hear ye! (*He goes back to his place.*)

SHOJI: A bag of gold for a carving of a rat? Wife, I will enter that contest.

OKUSAN: But you have never carved so much as a carrot, husband.

SHUBO: All the best carvers in Japan will enter their work, Father.

SHOJI (*Smiling*): Nevertheless, I am going to enter that contest. What is more, I am going to win! (*He takes net, and exits right.*)

SCRIBE: So, Shoji the rat catcher went off by himself to carve a rat. Every day he went to the same place, and when he returned home, his net smelled of seaweed. But he would say nothing of what he had been doing, or where he had been. On the day of the contest, he returned with a wooden box. (SHOJI *enters, carrying box and net.*)

SHOJI: I am ready to display my masterpiece. Do not fear, I will bring home that bag of gold. Then, my dear family, how we will feast! (*He stands to one side.*)

SCRIBE: There was the utmost excitement in the Court upon the day of the contest. Skilled carvers from every corner of Japan appeared to display their works. (EMPEROR *sounds gong.* IVORY CARVER *enters holding ivory rat on pillow.* WOOD CARVER *enters holding wooden rat.* STONE CARVER *enters holding stone rat. They kneel in a line before* EMPEROR. SHOJI *kneels at end of line.* CAT *leaps down from dais and stands in front of* IVORY CARVER.)

EMPEROR: Let the contest begin! (IVORY CARVER *holds out cushion with white rat.*)

IVORY CARVER: Behold. The sacred white rat of Kokura, carved with a single knife stroke from the ivory of the King of Elephants. (CAT *examines white rat, then crosses to* WOOD CARVER.)

WOOD CARVER: Behold. The mighty forest rat of Sapporo carved from the tallest teak tree in Japan. (CAT *paws wooden rat, then crosses to* STONE CARVER.)

STONE CARVER: Behold. The magical water rat of Matsushima, carved from the stone of Mt. Fuji-san itself.

ALL: Ah-h. Most skillful. Most beautiful. (CAT *looks closely at stone rat, then moves to* SHOJI, *who removes cover of wooden box.*)

SHOJI: Behold. A special rat for the Honorable Cat. (*All lean forward, then laugh loudly.*)

ALL: Ha, ha, ha. *That* is a rat?

WISE ONE: Very inferior. (CAT *sniffs box, then sniffs again excitedly and takes shapeless rat out of box by tail.*)

EMPEROR: What is your decision, Honorable Cat? (CAT *holds the rat high so all can see.*) *That* is the winner? (CAT *nods.* CARVERS *exit.*) Honorable Cat has chosen. So be it.

ALL: So be it. (EMPEROR *hands bag of gold down to* SHOJI *as before.* SHOJI *receives it, bowing deeply.*)

SHOJI: I am honored. (CAT *resumes his place next to* EMPEROR.)

EMPEROR (*To* SHOJI): Look up at me. Do I not know you? (SHOJI *looks up.*)

SHOJI: I was once your official rat catcher, Your Highness.

EMPEROR: Yes. Now I remember you. You are a most clever fellow. How did you manage to get Honorable Cat to choose your rat over those of the best carvers in Japan?

SHOJI: Perhaps it was because of what my rat was made of.

EMPEROR: And what was your rat made of?

SHOJI: Fish, Your Highness.

ALL: Fish! Ha, ha, ha.

EMPEROR: What a joke! The catcher of the rat caught a fish to catch a cat. Now that is amusing.

LADIES (*Screaming and pointing to floor*): Oh! Oh! Oh! There . . . there . . . there. . . .

EMPEROR: Honorable Cat, do your duty. (CAT *is asleep.* SHOJI *runs across stage, brings his net down and pretends to catch rat.*)

SHOJI: It is done. Sayonara, rat!

EMPEROR: Well done, rat catcher. How would you like your job back—at twice the pay? (SHOJI *nods.*) The Honorable Cat is all very well as a pet, but as a hunter—well, he is almost as good at hunting as you are at carving. (SHOJI *bows, turns, crosses right and sits at his table.*)

SCRIBE: And so, as they say in the western world, they all lived happily ever after. The Emperor had both his Honorable Cat and his Honorable Rat Catcher. And Shoji gave his family a feast with a mountain of rice. (SHOJI *claps his hands.* 1ST PROPERTY BOY *brings on a tray with many dishes of food, and a mound of rice.* SHOJI *gives him a gold piece.*) But, I am pleased to tell you, Shoji always put one gold piece aside, in the old empty rice bowl, to remind him of those other times. (SHOJI *puts a gold piece into rice bowl.* OKUSAN *and* SHUBO *smile and bow to him. Curtains close.*) And that is the story of the Honorable Cat. It must be true, for it is written (*Points to scroll*) right here by the scribes of the ancient times. Sayonara. . . . (*He bows and exits.*)

THE END

The Tall-Tale Tournament

Characters

OREGON SMITH, *master of ceremonies*
MARY ANNE, *a tourist*
JOHN HENRY
BARBARA FRITCHIE
JOHNNY APPLESEED
MOLLY PITCHER } *jury*
CARL BUCK
POCAHONTAS
STRETCH GARRISON
PAUL BUNYAN
PECOS BILL
MIKE FINK
DAVY CROCKETT
CALAMITY JANE
JUG BAND
CHORUS

TIME: *The present, just before high noon.*
SETTING: *A public square in Bloomington, Indiana. It is decorated with gaily-colored pennants. A banner across the back announces:* WELCOME! NINETY-NINTH ANNUAL TALL-TALE TOURNAMENT. *Podium stands down right, bench for jury at center, and chairs for Chorus and Jug Band are placed in semicircle at rear of stage. Gilded, glitter-covered bench stands down left.*

86

At Rise: Oregon Smith *is chalking large X down right center on stage floor.*

Oregon Smith (*To himself*): There. X marks the spot for the tall-tale champion. (*He draws circle on floor left of center.*) And there's the magic circle for the challenger. (*Tipping hat to audience*) Howdy. Welcome to the Grand and Glorious Tall-Tale Tournament. At high noon today there's going to be a meeting of champions. You'll never again hear tales stretched so tall or fetched so far. (*Chimes begin.*) Listen . . . high noon. (Mary Anne, *holding booklet marked* TOURIST ATTRACTIONS, *enters right. On stroke of twelve, she sits on bench left.*)

Mary Anne (*To herself*): High noon. I have just fifteen minutes to explore the public square before my bus tour leaves town. Now let me see . . . (*She consults booklet.*) How interesting. The town square of Bloomington, Indiana, has a famous liar's bench where people used to sit for hours and swap stories. The famous storyteller, Oregon Smith, used to be a kind of master of ceremonies. (*She looks around.*) The liar's bench . . . I wonder where it is. (*To* Oregon) I'm a stranger in town. Would you direct me to the liar's bench?

Oregon (*In consternation*): Land o' Goshen! The liar's bench? You've plunked yourself down on it. Now you're stuck good and proper.

Mary Anne: Stuck? (*She tries to stand but cannot.*) I can't move. Not an inch.

Oregon Smith: You should never sit on the liar's bench at high noon on the day of the Tall-Tale Tournament. Why, that old bench will just keep you sitting there for days, until you tell a tall tale.

Mary Anne: Me? Tell a tall tale? But I'm only a tourist. I can't stay for your tournament. (*She tries to move.*)

Oregon Smith: Now, now. You'll think of something, miss.

MARY ANNE: You mean this bench really won't let me go until I think of a story to tell?

OREGON: That's about the size of it. But I won't call on you until the tag-end of the tournament. That'll give you time to think of something.

MARY ANNE: Oh, what a pickle! I've never told a story in my entire life. I don't even know how to begin.

OREGON: Begin small and build big, Mary Anne. (*Offstage,* JUG BAND *begins to play "She'll Be Comin' 'Round the Mountain."* OREGON *takes place at rostrum, rapping gavel.*) Come on, folks. Welcome one and all to the Ninety-Ninth Grand and Glorious Tall-Tale Tournament! (*Cheers offstage.* JUG BAND *enters and stands in front of chairs.* CHORUS, *singing refrain, enters right and stands beside chairs.*) Ladies and gents, be seated. (JUG BAND *plays chord. All sit.*) Let the members of the jury take their places. (*Raps gavel once for each jury member*) Big John Henry, from the state of West Virginia. (JOHN HENRY *enters, swinging hammer.*)

CHORUS (*Speaking lines*):
> Here he comes, with his hammer in his hand, Lawd, Lawd.
> Here he comes, with his hammer in his hand.

OREGON: Barbara Fritchie, from the state of Maryland. . . .

CHORUS:
> "Shoot, if you must, this old gray head,
> But spare your country's flag," she said.

(BARBARA FRITCHIE *enters, carrying flag.*)

OREGON: Johnny Appleseed, from the state of Ohio. . . .

CHORUS:
> Oh, Johnny came to visit us.
> How do I know? Come, see.
> Johnny left his calling card:
> A blooming apple tree.

(JOHNNY APPLESEED *enters, scattering seeds from knapsack.*)

OREGON: Molly Pitcher and Stretch Garrison from the state of New Jersey. . . .

CHORUS:

> Come, Molly. Bring us some water.
> Bring your cool pitcher this way.
> For Monmouth is dry as a desert,
> And we're fighting for freedom today!

(MOLLY *enters, pretending to pour water into hands of* CHORUS.)

> Old Stretch Garrison had a farm,
> Oh my, oh my, oh.
> He grew string beans as long as your arm!
> Oh my, oh my, oh.

(STRETCH GARRISON *enters, hoeing.*)

OREGON: Pocahontas, Indian maid, from the state of Virginia. (JUG BAND *plays Indian drumbeat as* POCAHONTAS *dances across stage.*) And last, but far from least, from the sovereign state of Idaho, the sharp-shooting gent—Carl Buck. (CARL BUCK *enters, with rifle.*)

CHORUS:

> There's a man with a rifle in the Rockies,
> Do not trifle with that feller in the Rockies,
> For he can shoot a bee's knees,
> Fifty paces through the trees,
> And there's not a sharper shooter in the Rockies.

OREGON: And now, ladies and gentlemen of the jury, let the proceedings begin. (*Jury sits on bench at center.*)

JURY: Let the proceedings begin.

OREGON: There will be three separate and distinct categories of fiction today. Each category will have a champion and a challenger. I now call upon the champion of the Mighty Deeds and Doings category to appear and defend his title. (PAUL BUNYAN *strides on right, shouldering ax.*)

PAUL BUNYAN: Here I am. Champion Paul Bunyan, giant of the North and lord of the lumberjacks! You ask me to tell you some mighty deeds. Well, mighty deeds are just commonplace and everyday happenings with me. For instance, I raised some sawmills up north one time. I needed some ponds to float the logs around in, so I shoveled a few basins here and there. And do you know what they call those ponds today? They call those ponds the Great Lakes.

CHORUS: Amen. The Great Lakes. (PECOS BILL, *twirling lariat, enters left. He steps into challenger's circle, bowing.*)

PECOS BILL: I'll challenge that. I'm Pecos Bill, friend of the coyotes, rider of lightning-streaks and roper of railroad trains. Listen to me. I had this long, long cattle drive. 'Twas from Australia to the North Pole. And I needed a little old water trough. Just a simple little trough to water about a million and a half head of cattle. So I scraped my fingernail along the south of Texas, and I made a watering trough. And do you know what they call that watering trough today? They call it the river Rio Grande!

CHORUS: Hallelujah. The river Rio Grande. (PAUL BUNYAN *and* PECOS BILL *bow to each other.*)

OREGON: Enough. Shake hands with each other, gents, and sit down on the liar's bench yonder. (*They shake hands, raise their hats to* MARY ANNE, *and sit next to her.*) Now we will hear from the champion of the second category, Boasters and Braggers. (MIKE FINK, *pole in hand, vaults onstage from right, with wild yell.*)

MIKE FINK: That's me. A boaster and a bragger. I'm Mike Fink, king of the Ohio River. Why, the Ohio River doesn't flow in the morning until it asks my permission. I'm a land-screamer. I'm a water dog. I'm a snapping turtle, and when I snap my jaws, you'd better snap to it. I can outrun, outdance, outjump, outdive, and outfight anything in the shape of a human for two thousand miles of the big Mississip'. (*He thumps chest.* DAVY CROCKETT *swaggers on left.*)

DAVY CROCKETT: Is that so? Well, you've never made the

acquaintance of your challenger. Allow me to introduce my shining self, Davy Crockett, coonskin Congressman, from the Tennessee canebrake. I was cradled in a sap trough, weaned on a pine cone and I rode an alligator up the Niagara Falls when I was two. I have the roughest horse, the prettiest sister, the surest rifle and the ugliest dog in the entire district.

MIKE FINK: Bet you can't jump like me, Davy. Why, I can jump clear across the Mississip' without hardly bending my knees, and if I want to, I can change my mind in the middle of the air and jump right back to where I was before.

DAVY CROCKETT: Any mangy rabbit can jump. Now, me—I can saddle the sun and ride around the world and get off where I please.

MIKE FINK: Aw, you're nothing but a backwoods ignoramus with a raccoon's tail tickling your nose.

DAVY CROCKETT: That's better'n being a bogwater bushwhacker with mud in his ears.

OREGON: Break it up, fellers. Now shake hands like good sports, and go cool your heels yonder on the liar's bench. (*They shake hands warily, then sit next to others, tipping hats to* MARY ANNE. CALAMITY JANE *enters right.*)

CALAMITY JANE: Yahoo!

OREGON: Well, here she is, Calamity Jane, right on time for the next category: Whoppers.

CALAMITY JANE: Whoppers, you say? Why, I'll take on the whole kit and caboodle of you. I'm the fastest Pony Express rider there ever was. I can ride over mountains so steep my pony gallops upside down.

JOHN HENRY (*Slapping knee*): You call that steep? Why, I come from West Virginia where the mountains are so steep they have to tie down the pumpkins so they won't roll away. (JUG BAND *and* CHORUS *cheer after each whopper.*)

CARL BUCK (*Slapping knee*): You call that steep? Why, over

in the Rockies the cornfields are planted on mountains so steep that a farmer has to climb up the hill on the opposite side and shoot the seed into the ground with his shotgun.

STRETCH GARRISON (*Slapping knee*): You call that steep? Why, the Ramapo Mountains in New Jersey are so steep that I used to look up a chimney to see if the cows were coming home.

OREGON: Now, just a minute here. You have to have a proper challenger, Calamity Jane. You can't just go around pot-shooting and bird-seeding in six directions at once.

CALAMITY JANE: A proper challenger? Well, I don't see one.

OREGON (*Pointing to* MARY ANNE): There she is. She's small but mighty. Whip out a whopper, Miss Mary Anne. (MARY ANNE *shakes her head.*)

BARBARA FRITCHIE: Don't be afraid, child. Tell us where you're from.

MARY ANNE: New York City. I'm afraid that's not as exciting as the Mississippi, or the Rio Grande.

JOHNNY APPLESEED: New York City. A quiet little village. I planted some nice Baldwins there once.

MARY ANNE: Oh, New York isn't a nice quiet little village. It's a big city. More than thirteen million people live there. The buildings are so tall they reach to the clouds. We call them "skyscrapers."

ALL: Skyscrapers! (*They nudge each other and wink.*) Oh, sure, sure.

MARY ANNE: It's true. Honest. (*She stands.*) Why, I'm free. I can move away from the bench.

OREGON: Of course. You just told your first tall tale.

MARY ANNE (*Crossing to circle*): But it's the truth. I came from New York City on a big bus.

MOLLY: And what, prithee, is a big bus?

MARY ANNE: It's a vehicle. People sit inside it, and it takes them where they want to go.

POCAHONTAS: Ugh. Little squaw tell good whoppers. How many horses pull this big bus?

MARY ANNE: Horses don't pull the bus. It runs by itself, with an engine that uses gasoline and oil.

ALL: Ha, ha, ha. That's a real knee-slapper. (*They all slap knees.*)

CALAMITY JANE: Shucks, I can tell one as good as that. I know a feller who trained a swarm of mosquitoes to hunt for him. Every time he wanted a juicy jackrabbit, he'd send out a mosquito to spear it with his stinger. Can you top that, gal?

MARY ANNE: I don't think so. I don't know anything about mosquitoes. Where I come from we just have things like rockets.

CARL BUCK: Fourth of July rockets?

MARY ANNE: Much bigger rockets than that. Last month a rocket over thirty stories high went to the moon. I watched it on television.

MOLLY: And prithee, what is television?

MARY ANNE: That's kind of hard to explain. Television is a moving picture of something that happens. Everybody can watch the pictures on a little box. (*Members of jury whisper excitedly.*)

CHORUS (*Slapping knees and clapping*): Yahoo!

CARL BUCK: That's not only a knee-slapper, that's a bona fide hand-clapper!

OREGON: Ladies and gents of the jury, have you come to a decision? (*Members of jury talk together.*)

JOHN HENRY: We have. As foreman of this jury, I am pleased as punch to announce our unanimous decision. For the mightiest deed, the biggest boast and the wildest whopper, we elect Miss Mary Anne. (*All cheer.* JUG BAND *plays, and* CHORUS *sings to tune of "She'll Be Comin' 'Round the Mountain.")*

CHORUS:

She's the grand and glorious champion of all, yes she is.
She's the grand and glorious champion of all, yes she is.
She is quick and she is able,
To confabulate a fable,
She's the grand and glorious champion of all. Yes she is.

OREGON: Well, I do declare. A dark horse has won the derby. Yes, siree. I reckon we ought to celebrate the event. Let's all have a picnic on Pike's Peak. Last one up the mountain is a knock-kneed nannygoat. (*He waves his hat and exits right. Others shake* MARY ANNE*'s hand as* JUG BAND *continues to play. Members of* CHORUS, *in twos, join hands and dance off right, followed by jury.* JUG BAND *exits left.*)

CALAMITY JANE: Come on, gal. You won—fair and square. (*As she runs off right*) Last one up the mountain is a knock-kneed nannygoat! (*She exits and others follow.*)

MARY ANNE (*Trying unsuccessfully to move her feet*): But my bus tour doesn't go as far as Pike's Peak. And my feet seem to be stuck. (*Horn sounds offstage.*) The bus. It didn't leave without me, after all. (*She raises her feet.*) There. I can move my feet again. (*She crosses down center, addressing audience, a little puzzled.*) Now, did it all really happen? Or did I imagine it all? There's only one way to find out. I'll come back for the One-Hundredth Tall-Tale Tournament. I can't wait to tell them all about things like elevators and submarines. Won't their eyes pop? Why—isn't it funny? The whole twentieth century is one big unbelievable whopper! (*Horn sounds again.*) I'm coming. (*As she runs off*) Last one on the bus is a knock-kneed nannygoat! (*Curtain*)

THE END

How Mothers Came to Be

Characters

MANITOU, *the Great Spirit*	DEER
KIWA, *the boy*	TURTLE
KIWI, *the girl*	SQUIRREL
AIR	BEAVER
FIRE	BEE
WATER	SPIDER
THE MOTHER	THREE MUSICIANS
OWL	CHORUS

SETTING: *The Earth. There is a backdrop at rear with stylized Indian paintings of sun, trees, running water, and other symbols on it. At center, there is a small riser or wooden box.*

AT RISE: MANITOU *is standing on riser at center. In front of him,* KIWA *and* KIWI *kneel, facing each other, with arms folded and heads bowed.* MUSICIANS *are sitting on blanket down right, holding Indian tom-tom, rattle, and bells.* CHORUS *kneels down left, or sits down in orchestra pit.* 1ST MUSICIAN *plays four beats on tom-tom.* 2ND *and* 3RD MUSICIANS *join in as* 1ST MUSICIAN *repeats beat, and* CHORUS *chants in time to tom-tom.*

CHORUS (*Chanting*): *Lis*-ten to us. *Lis*-ten to us. *Lis*-ten to us.
1ST SOLO:
    Many, many moons ago,
    The world was not the same as it is now.
    (MANITOU *indicates symbols on backdrop as* SOLOS *speak.*)

2ND SOLO: There were rustling trees. (2ND MUSICIAN *shakes rattle.*)

3RD SOLO: There were singing brooks. (3RD MUSICIAN *rings bells.*)

4TH SOLO: Many, many animals walked proudly upon the earth. (1ST MUSICIAN *plays quick drumbeats.*)

5TH SOLO: Proudest of all were two creatures who walked upon their hind legs and looked with interest upon the stars.

6TH SOLO: They were a boy creature and a girl creature. (KIWA *and* KIWI *rise and face audience.*)

1ST SOLO: They were called Kiwa and Kiwi. (1ST MUSICIAN *plays three tom-tom beats as* KIWA *and* KIWI *slowly bow with arms folded.*)

But, nowhere,
Nowhere in the high hills or the low valleys,
Nowhere beside the quiet lakes or on the purple plains,
Was there a Mother.

6TH SOLO: There was no Mother at all!

2ND SOLO: Then it was that Great Spirit Manitou went to his hunting lodge beyond the moon. There was no one to watch over Kiwa and Kiwi.

CHORUS: Oh, look! Look! Look! (1ST MUSICIAN *plays four quick tom-tom beats*) *Troub*le coming! *Troub*le coming! *Troub*le coming!

3RD SOLO: Where is little Kiwa? (KIWA *shades his eyes, looking right and left. Then he traces lines down his cheeks with his fingers to indicate falling tears.*)

CHORUS: He is lost. He is lost. He is lost.

4TH SOLO: What is the matter with little Kiwi? (KIWI *pats her stomach, then traces lines down her cheeks with her fingers, as if in tears.*)

5TH SOLO: She is hungry, hungry, hungry.

6TH SOLO: She does not know how to find food.

7TH SOLO: Look—snow is falling. (2ND MUSICIAN *shakes rattle*) KIWA *and* KIWI *pantomime shaking with cold. They fold their arms and stand close to each other.*)

CHORUS: Poor Kiwa. Poor Kiwi. They are cold, cold, cold. Hear how they cry to Great Spirit Manitou.

KIWA *and* KIWI (*Together*): Help us! Help us, Great Spirit Manitou!

8TH SOLO: Do you think such small voices will ever reach Great Spirit Manitou?

9TH SOLO: Oh, yes. In his lodge beyond the moon, Great Spirit Manitou heard their cries.

10TH SOLO: He looked down upon Kiwa and Kiwi. He said:

MANITOU: Poor little creatures. They are lost and cold and hungry. They do not know how to care for themselves. I cannot leave my lodge to help them. What shall I do? I know. I will make a Mother. (MUSICIANS *play instruments.*)

CHORUS (*Chanting*): A Mother! A Mother! Great Spirit Manitou will make a Mother.

KIWA *and* KIWI (*Arms folded, dancing about*): A Mother, a Mother. We shall have a Mother!

MANITOU: How shall I make a Mother? She must have thoughts as clear as air. She must have a heart as warm as fire. She must have feet as swift as running water.

7TH SOLO: Then Great Spirit Manitou summoned three beings.

8TH SOLO: First, he summoned Air. (2ND MUSICIAN *shakes rattle.*)

9TH SOLO: Then, he summoned Fire. (3RD MUSICIAN *shakes bells.*)

10TH SOLO: Finally he summoned Water. (1ST MUSICIAN *beats drum-roll on tom-tom. Together,* AIR, FIRE *and* WATER *dance onstage and stand center.*)

AIR: Here I stand, Great Spirit Manitou. I am the clear Air. I see all, but no one sees me.

FIRE: Here I stand, Great Spirit Manitou. I am Fire. Carry me where darkness falls. I am Fire. Carry me where coldness hides.

WATER: Here I stand, Great Spirit Manitou. I am Water. I move swiftly. Before you have seen my beginning I have run to my end.

AIR, FIRE, *and* WATER (*Together*): Ask of us what you will, Great Spirit Manitou.

MANITOU: Make for me a Mother! (AIR, FIRE *and* WATER *dance in a circle, Indian-style, as* MUSICIANS *keep a steady beat.* THE MOTHER *enters up right, crosses to circle and enters. She kneels.* AIR, FIRE *and* WATER *stop dancing and point to* THE MOTHER.)

AIR, FIRE, *and* WATER: Behold! A Mother! (*They dance away and exit.*)

MANITOU (*Holding up hand*): It is well. But The Mother is not finished. Who will teach her the ways of the Earth? (OWL, DEER, TURTLE, SQUIRREL, BEAVER, BEE, *and* SPIDER *enter from up left and right, and stand across rear of stage. Each carries gift.*)

OWL: We will teach her the ways of the Earth. We are the animals who walk proudly upon the earth. We know all that happens under the sun and the moon. Hear us, Mother of Kiwa and Kiwi. (OWL *flies downstage to* THE MOTHER. CHORUS *chants as he goes.*)

CHORUS: Whoo. Whoo. Whoo.

OWL: Whoo am I? Wisest of the wise, that is whoo I am. Take wisdom from me. Ask me whoo and why and where and how. Take wisdom from me, Mother of Kiwa and Kiwi. (OWL *puts headband on* THE MOTHER, *then flies upstage, as* CHORUS *chants.*)

CHORUS: Whoo. Whoo. Whoo. (DEER *trots downstage.*) Trip-trop. Trip-trop. Trip-trop.

DEER: I am a doe, Mother of Kiwa and Kiwi. I am as gentle as a falling leaf. Take my gentleness for your hands.

You will need my gentleness to comfort Kiwa and Kiwi. (DEER *places small blanket in front of* THE MOTHER.)

CHORUS (*As* DEER *returns to position*): Trip-trop. Trip-trop. Trip-trop. (TURTLE *crosses to* THE MOTHER.) Galumph-ga-lumph. Galumph-galumph. Galumph-galumph.

TURTLE: Patience. I bring you patience, Mother of Kiwa and Kiwi. Let a turtle teach you how to wait for good things. Have patience. (*He gives her a small shell.*)

CHORUS (*As* TURTLE *returns to place*): Galumph-galumph. Galumph-galumph. Galumph-galumph. (SQUIRREL *crosses to* THE MOTHER.) Chip-chip. Chip-chip. Chip-chip.

SQUIRREL: Do you know what you need, Mother of Kiwa and Kiwi? You need a squirrel. You need a squirrel to help you to gather food and store it for the winter. Let me show you how to save and store and hide and hoard. (*He puts a necklace of acorns around her neck.*)

CHORUS (*As* SQUIRREL *returns to place*): Chip-chip. Chip-chip. Chip-chip. (BEAVER *crosses to* THE MOTHER.) Paddle-pad-dle-paddle. Paddle-paddle-paddle. Paddle-paddle-pad-dle. Dive!

BEAVER: If only you had a fine, flat tail like mine, Mother of Kiwa and Kiwi. Then you would be a beaver. But I can teach you to build many things. I can teach you to build teepees and tents to keep the cold away. (*He gives her a small bundle of twigs, then returns to place.*)

CHORUS: Paddle-paddle-paddle. Paddle-paddle-paddle. Paddle-paddle-paddle. Dive! (BEE *circles downstage.*) Zzz. Zzz. Zzz.

BEE: Who will be busier than the bee? The Mother of Kiwa and Kiwi. She will be busier than the bee. Let me whisper the secrets of the flowers. I will tell you what foods are good foods. Hear the secrets of the melons, the corn, and the sweet berries. Listen! (*She puts a flower into* THE MOTHER'*s hand, then whispers in her ear.*) Zzz!

CHORUS (*As* BEE *returns to place*): Zzz! Zzz! Zzz! (SPIDER *creeps downstage.*) Spin, spin, spin. Spin, spin, spin. Spin, spin, spin.

SPIDER: I, the spider, have a silken skill. I, the spider, will show you how to spin, Mother of Kiwa and Kiwi. You shall make clothes for your children. My skill will be your skill. (*She puts a web in front of* THE MOTHER, *then returns to place.*)

CHORUS: Spin, spin, spin. Spin, spin, spin. Spin, spin, spin. (THE MOTHER *stands, extending her arms.*)

ANIMALS: Behold. Here is a Mother!

CHORUS: Behold. Here is a Mother!

MANITOU: Behold. Here is a Mother! Go to your Mother, Kiwa and Kiwi. (KIWA *and* KIWI *go to stand beside* THE MOTHER, *who puts her arms around their shoulders.*)

MOTHER:
>You will never be lost again.
>
>You will never be hungry again.
>
>You will never be cold again.
>
>When Great Manitou goes to his hunting lodge,
>
>I will be there beside you.
>
>When you speak, I will listen.
>
>What you do not know, I will teach you.

CHORUS (*Chanting*): She is greater than all the animals. She is greater than Air, and Fire, and Water. She is Mother.

MANITOU: It is so. I have spoken. She is Mother! (1ST MUSICIAN *plays four beats on tom-tom.* CHORUS *joins* MUSICIANS.)

CHORUS (*Chanting*): *So* it happened. *So* it happened. *So* it happened.

1ST SOLO:
>Many, many moons ago. So it happened.
>
>But they say that The Mother was so great,
>
>The Mother was so good and so kind and so wise,
>
>That Great Spirit Manitou made many, many Mothers

For many, many Kiwas and Kiwis.
They say, that even to this day
Every Kiwa and every Kiwi has a Mother
To keep him healthy, and happy and wise . . .
CHORUS: So . . . they . . . say. (MUSICIANS *play on their instruments. Curtain*)

THE END

Destination: Christmas!

Characters

SCENE 1

BEFORE RISE: CAROLERS *and* CHEERLEADERS *march down right and left aisles of auditorium, mount stage from both sides and form two groups.* CHEERLEADERS *carry red and green pompons.*

CAROLERS *and* CHEERLEADERS (*Singing to tune of "Jingle Bells"*):
Dashing through the sky,
Flashing jet planes fly,
O'er the world they go—
On journeys to and fro.
Carillons begin—

A Merry Christmas chime,
What fun it is to chase the clouds
At Merry Christmas time!
Oh—Jingle jets, Jingle jets,
Jingle through the air,
Oh, what fun to race the sun
To Christmas everywhere.

(*Sleigh bells are heard from offstage.*)

TICKET AGENT (*Entering through curtain, center*): Passengers, have your boarding passes ready, please. Northern Airlines is happy to announce that you may now board Flight 2425, journeying around the world to Christmas in far places. All fares have been reduced, and you may buy your tickets for a song. (CAROLERS *sing "There's a Song in the Air," or some appropriate carol.* TICKET AGENT *walks by them, checking tickets which each* CAROLER *shows him.*) Very good, Carolers. Your tickets are in order. You may board the aircraft. (CAROLERS *file through curtain, center.* TICKET AGENT *turns to* CHEERLEADERS.) But what about you people? Who are you, and what did you bring for Christmas?

1ST CHEERLEADER: Who are we? We're cheerleaders. You can't have a Merry Christmas without good cheer, and what's better than some good-cheerleaders to lead the good cheer? Ready, everybody?

CHEERLEADERS (*Shouting*): Ready! Ready! Ready! Rah! Rah! Rah!

1ST CHEERLEADER: Let's hear it for Christmas. (CHEERLEADERS *go into positions for a cheer.*)

CHEERLEADERS (*Shouting and shaking pompons*): With an H, and an A, and a double P - Y. With an H-O-L-I-D-A-Y. Hip-Hip-Holiday! Hep-Hep-Holiday! Happy-Happy-Holiday! Rah! Rah! Rah! (*They pose with pompons.*)

TICKET AGENT: That was what you'd call a cheer-ful earful. Welcome aboard, Cheerleaders. (*To audience*) Welcome aboard, one and all. (*Curtains open.*)

* * *

TIME: *The Christmas season.*

SETTING: *The interior of a jet plane. Double rows of seats are arranged up left and right, with wide aisle center.*

AT RISE: CAROLERS *are seated up left.* CHEERLEADERS *file upstage to seats up right.* TICKET AGENT *exits downstage as* PILOT *enters, at center, crossing downstage to address audience.*

PILOT: Merry Christmas! I am your pilot, Captain Kris Kringle. Our aircraft is a Donder-and-Blitzen original, manufactured by the elves at the North Pole. We will be flying at an altitude of high, wide and handsome, and we will have stopovers in Denmark, Italy, Ethiopia and Mexico. Please adjust your watches from daylight saving time to Christmas time, and remember—the only sound this aircraft will make in flight is a slight ringing sound—like silver bells. (*Sleigh bells are heard.*) Did you hear that? That's my co-pilot, Dasher, warming up the engines. It's time to be on our way now. Fasten your safety belts, please, and prepare to head northward. Bon voyage and *Bon Noel!* (*He exits up center, as* CUSTOMS AGENT *enters down right, crosses to center. Sleigh bells are heard.*)

CUSTOMS AGENT: Before you take off, you must go through Customs. Have you anything to declare?

CHEERLEADERS (*Together*):
> We solemnly declare, we solemnly declare,
> We will observe the customs of Christmas everywhere.

CUSTOMS AGENT: That's the spirit! What baggage are you carrying, please?

CHEERLEADERS (*Together*):
> One long American stocking—full.
> One Dutch wooden shoe—full.
> One French sabot—full.
> One Italian pocket—full.
> One Mexican piñata—full.

CUSTOMS AGENT: You must declare all this. Declare it!

CHEERLEADERS (*Together*):

>We declare . . . We declare . . .
>Christmas gifts are everywhere,
>In stockings full of knick-a-knacks,
>In pockets full of gimmycracks,
>In wooden shoes with bric-a-bracs.
>We declare . . . We declare . . .
>Christmas gifts from everywhere.

CUSTOMS AGENT: Excellent. Christmas gifts are a wonderful custom. Your baggage has passed the inspection. (*He hangs a large sign on backdrop:* THIS VEHICLE CLEARED FOR A MERRY CHRISTMAS!) You are hereby certified, ratified, notarized and validated for a Christmas visit to whatever country you may choose, select or otherwise designate! (*He exits downstage. Sleigh bells are heard, followed by opening bars of "Now It Is Christmastime," traditional Swedish song.* SCANDINAVIAN STEWARDESS *enters up center, crossing down center to address audience. She carries tray with coffee cups and coffeepot.*)

SCANDINAVIAN STEWARDESS: *God Jul!* That means "glad Christmas" in Swedish. I am your stewardess for the Scandinavian portion of your journey. You may call me Lucia Dagen, for my costume represents St. Lucia. (*Holding out tray*) Will you have coffee, hot chocolate, or cider? They are traditional on December 13, for that is the day St. Lucia comes to waken all the sleeping households. That is the day when Christmas festivities begin. (*Sleigh bells ring.*) Do you hear that? Our aircraft has landed. We are now in Denmark, our first Christmas stopover. I want you to meet someone. But be very quiet while some Danish friends of mine coax him down from the attic where he lives most of the year. Who is he? Someone you never have met. But someone, oh, someone you'll never forget! (STEWARDESS *steps to side of stage. Opening bars of "Now It Is*

Christmastime" are played, as DANISH DANCERS *enter. Two* DANCERS *bring on small Christmas tree, which they leave at center. All carry small bowls. They form a circle around tree and dance a simple round dance, as* CAROLERS *sing "Now It Is Christmastime." At conclusion, all leave bowls in circle around tree, and tiptoe off left. As they exit, they turn to audience and put their fingers to their lips.*)

CHEERLEADERS:

Sh-h-h-h-h! Steal away quietly.

Close the door.

Leave the rice pudding

There on the floor.

1ST CHEERLEADER: Why are you waiting?

2ND CHEERLEADER: What are you wishing for?

3RD CHEERLEADER: What are you baiting?

4TH CHEERLEADER: Who are you fishing for?

ALL FOUR: Cats? Rats? A mouse in the house?

CHEERLEADERS:

Someone as quick as a purry old cat.

Someone as smart as a furry old rat.

Someone as small as a whiskery mouse.

A whispery someone who lives in this house!

1ST CHEERLEADER: In this very same house? Do tell us—where?

CHEERLEADERS: High in the attic. Under the stair.

2ND CHEERLEADER: As small as a mouse? Do tell us—who?

CHEERLEADERS:

Sh-h-h! Somebody's eyeing, spying on—you!

Red cap. Gray beard. A magic gnome.

He pops out at twelve o'clock,

When nobody's home.

(*Triangle is struck twelve times. On last chime,* JULENISSE, *the Danish Christmas elf, jumps out from right, crosses center, then stands with hands on hips, grinning.*)

3RD CHEERLEADER: A goblin! How wonderful. Please, is he tame?

4TH CHEERLEADER: A gnome. How remarkable! What is his name?

CHEERLEADERS:

Julenisse. Julenisse. The jolly Yule elf.

It's roguish and rompish Julenisse himself.

(JULENISSE *takes off cap and makes low bow, which turns into somersault. He capers over to bowls, goes down on hands and knees and sniffs, then nods.*)

Julenisse! Julenisse! We've brought you a treat.

Creamy rice pudding all spicy and sweet.

Julenisse! Julenisse! We beg you to eat.

(JULENISSE *samples rice pudding with his finger.*)

1ST CHEERLEADER: Does it please him?

2ND CHEERLEADER: Is it tasty? (JULENISSE *stacks up dishes and runs off left*)

3RD CHEERLEADER: Oh—he's leaving.

4TH CHEERLEADER: Don't be hasty!

CHEERLEADERS:

Julenisse! Julenisse! Oh, bring us good things.

Trinkets and trumpets and small silver rings,

Bubbles and baubles and bats and balls,

Puppets and poppets and paper dolls!

(JULENISSE *returns, pushing a large sack full of gifts and carrying a switch.*)

JULENISSE (*To audience*):

Have you been good?

Now, search your heart well.

Have you been good?

Julenisse can tell!

(JULENISSE *nods wisely and points to his head.*)

CHEERLEADERS:

Julenisse can tell,

In case you forgot—

Which children are good,

Which children are not.

(JULENISSE *goes down into audience and points to several children,* smiling. *He then frowns, beckons to one, and switches him lightly on the hand. He returns to stage.*)

But if you've been helpful and truthful and sweet,
Well-mannered, well-spoken, respectful and neat—

4TH CHEERLEADER: Neat? Must you be neat? Completely neat? Always and ever, eternally neat?

CHEERLEADERS: Well . . . *almost* always neat.

1ST CHEERLEADER: What then?

CHEERLEADERS:

Then, Julenisse, the generous, gentleman gnome,
Will graciously garnish with good gifts, your home.

(JULENISSE *crosses to sack of gifts and holds up wrapped package.*)

2ND CHEERLEADER: What then?

CHEERLEADERS:

Then, off like a puff of smoke,
Off, like a bee,
Up to the attic stair,
Up, flies he. . . .

(JULENISSE *bows, spins around and runs on tiptoe, pantomiming climbing stairs, as he exits right.* PROPERTY BOYS *enter and take sack off.*)

1ST CHEERLEADER: Now, a word of advice—

2ND CHEERLEADER: A word of cheer—

3RD CHEERLEADER: If you were *not* nice—

4TH CHEERLEADER: There's always next year.

CHEERLEADERS:

A whole long year to be helpful and sweet,
Well-mannered, well-spoken, respectful and—

4TH CHEERLEADER: Neat?

CHEERLEADERS:

On the whole, neat.
There's a whole long year,
To consider and choose,
How you will mind

Your p's and your q's.

1ST CHEERLEADER: And remember—

CHEERLEADERS:

High in the attic, under the stair,

Someone is pondering all that you do.

Red cap. Gray beard. Someone is watching.

Watching—

4TH CHEERLEADER (*Pointing to audience*): *You!*

CHEERLEADERS: Julenisse! (JULENISSE *jumps onstage, bows and jumps off.*)

SCANDINAVIAN STEWARDESS: And that is the story of Denmark's favorite scamp, Julenisse. Now, it is time for me to wish you Merry Christmas in Norwegian—*Gledelig Jul.* Your airplane is now in flight again, headed for sunny Italy. Have a glad, good time. (*She curtsies.*) Your next stewardess will greet you any minute now. (*She exits. Sleigh bells are heard.* ITALIAN STEWARDESS *enters center.*)

ITALIAN STEWARDESS: *Buon Natale!* That's Merry Christmas in Italian, as if you didn't know. Every country has a legend about a jolly person who comes to bring gifts to children at Christmastime. But have you ever heard the strange and wonderful tale from Italy about an old woman who visits the children on Twelfth Night? Listen! (*She crosses upstage to sit with* CAROLERS. *Sound of tambourine is heard.* OLD BEFANA *enters right, sweeping her way to center. She stands center, pantomiming dusting, scrubbing, scouring, and sweeping with her broom.*)

1ST CHEERLEADER: Long, long ago, in the days before your father's father's father . . . there was an old woman— Old Befana.

OLD BEFANA (*In crone's voice*): A busy old woman, Old Befana.

2ND CHEERLEADER:

A stubborn old woman, Old Befana.

She never would leave her house,

From sunrise to sunset,
From Sunday to Sunday,
From summer sun to winter snow.
She was—

OLD BEFANA (*Indignantly*): Too busy!

3RD CHEERLEADER: Too busy scrubbing and scouring, dusting and sweeping. (*Sound of tambourine is heard.*)

OLD BEFANA (*Holding broom like a club*): Who is there? Who dares disturb me at my tasks?

GIRL (*From offstage*): Old Befana—come out. Come out and see the star that shines in the East!

OLD BEFANA: Star? I'm too busy for stars. Some other time. (*She returns to sweeping. Tambourine is heard again.*) Now, who is there? Another interruption! (*She waves broom angrily.*)

BOY (*From offstage*): Old Befana, come out. Come out and hear the angel music that fills the skies.

OLD BEFANA: Music? I'm too busy for music. Some other time. (*She returns to sweeping.*)

2ND BOY CHEERLEADER: And then, in slow procession, hard by the house of Old Befana, came the Three Wise Men— The Magi. . . .

1ST BOY CHEERLEADER: Caspar . . .

2ND BOY CHEERLEADER: Melchior . . .

3RD BOY CHEERLEADER: And Balthazar . . . (THREE WISE MEN *enter single file, right. They cross stage majestically. Tambourine is shaken, as* WISE MEN *proceed across stage.* WISE MEN *stop at center.*)

1ST BOY CHEERLEADER: Old Befana, come out. Come and join us.

2ND BOY CHEERLEADER: Come and follow the star with us.

3RD BOY CHEERLEADER: Come, bring gifts to the Child of Bethlehem.

OLD BEFANA: What? More interruptions? Have you not heard? I am too busy. Too busy by far to follow a star!

THREE BOY CHEERLEADERS: Once more. We ask you once more. Come, come, come with us to Bethlehem.

OLD BEFANA (*Shaking her fist*): And I tell you once more! I cannot go, go, go—until I have finished sweeping, sweeping, sweeping! (*She sweeps again.*)

THREE BOY CHEERLEADERS (*As* WISE MEN *proceed left, slowly, after each line of dialogue*):
So be it. So be it.
You have shaken your head.
You have given your answer.
You have closed your door.
So be it. So be it.
(*They turn to* OLD BEFANA *and shake their heads.*) Amen! (*Tambourine is shaken, as* WISE MEN *exit left.*)

OLD BEFANA: There. Now. Now I have finished scrubbing and scouring, dusting and sweeping. I will go with you now. Wait!

THREE BOY CHEERLEADERS (*Softly, as from distance*): Too late. (OLD BEFANA, *distressed, puts broom over her shoulder and runs left.*)

OLD BEFANA: But I must find the Christ Child too. Only wait. Only wait! (*She exits.*)

THREE BOY CHEERLEADERS (*Very softly*): Too late!

1ST GIRL CHEERLEADER: And it was too late. Old Befana ran after the Wise Men as fast as her stubborn old legs would carry her. The star had gone. The music had gone. The Wise Men had gone. All, all had gone. (OLD BEFANA *enters, crossing to center, dragging broom behind her, and wiping eyes on apron.*)

OLD BEFANA: Oh, woe. Woe is me. I am a stubborn old donkey. (*To audience*) Let this be a lesson to you. When beautiful, extraordinary things happen outside your window—put down your broom and go! Oh, woe is me. Now I shall never see the Christ Child. (*She drops to her knees and flings broom away, hiding her head in apron. Tambourine is shaken.* ANGEL *enters, holding bag of gifts.* OLD BEFANA *stares at* ANGEL *in wonder.*)

ANGEL: Rise, Old Befana! (OLD BEFANA *rises.*) Your prayers have been heard, Old Befana. You shall wander until the end of time, with your broom in your hand. But you shall find the Christ Child. In each good child of Italy you shall find a little of the Christ Child himself. Busy, you wished to be. Busy, you shall be! You shall give each good child in Italy the gift of his dreams. But you shall give each bad child a lump of coal—as dark and as hard as his heart. Now go, Old Befana—on your way, Old Befana. (ANGEL *hands her bag of gifts. Tambourine is shaken.* ANGEL *exits right.* ITALIAN DANCERS *enter, two of them bringing Yule log. They form circle around log, tapping it in time to* CAROLERS' *song, "The Carol of the Bagpipers," traditional Sicilian carol, and do simple circle dance. At end of song,* OLD BEFANA *hands gifts to* DANCERS, *who dance off.* OLD BEFANA *exits.*)

ITALIAN STEWARDESS: And that is the legend of Old Befana, a legend believed by every child in Italy. But I will tell you a secret. Old Befana almost never leaves a lump of coal for anybody. (*Bongo drumbeat is heard.*) Listen! Do you hear a drumbeat? Look below you. Do you see jungles and lazy gray-green rivers? You are about to touch down in Africa, and I must return to my native Italy. *Buon giorno!* (*She exits up center. Drumbeat gets louder, as* AFRICAN STEWARDESS *enters.*)

AFRICAN STEWARDESS: Ladies and gentlemen, please remove your topcoats, earmuffs, galoshes and mittens. You have now arrived in equatorial Africa where palm trees are Christmas trees, and snowflakes are something children only dream about. But you don't need North winds and icicles to have a Merry Christmas—and here are some Ethiopian children to prove it. They are going to show you a very strange, very old game played only around

Christmastime. They call it "Ko-lee." Watch! (*She sits upstage with* CAROLERS.)

1ST CHEERLEADER (*Chanting to drumbeat*):
     Ko-lee, oh Ko-lee,
     Ko-lee, oh Ko-lee.
     Everybody's playing
     The Ko-lee game.

CHEERLEADERS (*Chanting to drum*):
     Ko-lee, oh Ko-lee,
     Ko-lee, oh Ko-lee,
     Everybody's playing
     The Ko-lee game.

(*Drum continues rhythm, as* TWO ETHIOPIAN BOYS *run onstage from left and right. They meet center in front of an imaginary tree.*)

1ST CHEERLEADER: Now, in a certain country—Ethiopia by name . . .

CHEERLEADERS: Oh, yes! Oh, yes!

1ST CHEERLEADER: The boys get together, to play a certain game . . .

CHEERLEADERS: Oh, yes, indeed!

1ST CHEERLEADER: Now, they gather in November to find a certain tree . . .

CHEERLEADERS: Oh, yes! Oh, yes!

1ST CHEERLEADER: And they take a certain branch that's as knobby as can be . . .

CHEERLEADERS: Oh, yes, indeed! (BOYS *pretend to saw off branches on opposite sides of tree.*)

1ST CHEERLEADER: Now, they make themselves a club, and they make themselves a ball . . .

CHEERLEADERS: Oh, yes! Oh, yes! (PROPERTY BOYS *hand clubs and balls to* ETHIOPIAN BOYS.)

1ST CHEERLEADER: And they scrape them and they file them, and you know—that isn't all. (ETHIOPIAN BOYS *scrape and file clubs in pantomime.*)

CHEERLEADERS: Oh, yes, indeed!

1ST CHEERLEADER: For they wax them 'til they shine, then they polish them the same. . . . (BOYS *pantomime waxing clubs.*)

CHEERLEADERS: Oh, yes! Oh, yes!

1ST CHEERLEADER: Then they find themselves a field and they play the Ko-lee game. . . .

CHEERLEADERS: Oh, yes, indeed! (*Using one ball,* ETHIOPIAN BOYS *stand facing each other and shove ball between their sticks, as in hockey. They cross stage left, playing, and exit.*)

1ST CHEERLEADER (*Chanting*):

Ko-lee, oh Ko-lee,
Ko-lee, oh Ko-lee,
Everybody plays the Ko-lee game.
Ko-lee, oh Ko-lee,
Ko-lee, oh Ko-lee,
Everybody plays the Ko-lee game.

Now, I have told you where they play the Ko-lee game, and I have told you when they play the Ko-lee game, and I have even told you how they play the Ko-lee game. But—I have not told you *why!*

CHEERLEADERS: Oh, yes! Oh, yes!

1ST CHEERLEADER: Long, long ago in Bethlehem in Judea there were shepherds in the fields . . . (ETHIOPIAN BOYS *re-enter left in shepherds' robes, playing Ko-lee with their shepherds' crooks.*) And as they watched their sheep, to pass away the time, they played the Ko-lee game . . .

CHEERLEADERS:

Ko-lee, oh Ko-lee!
Ko-lee, oh Ko-lee!
Shepherds were a-playing
The Ko-lee game.

1ST CHEERLEADER: And in the middle of that Ko-lee game, something glorious and wonderful happened . . .

CHEERLEADERS: Oh, yes! Oh, yes!

1ST CHEERLEADER: An angel, yes an angel, white as a cloud and bright as a sun, came right out of that big old empty sky. (ANGEL *enters right.* BOYS *drop to their knees.* ANGEL *points left.*) And that angel told those shepherds about a little bitty baby, who was born in Bethlehem town to be their savior and king.

CHEERLEADERS: Oh, yes! Oh, yes! Oh, yes, indeed! (ANGEL *exits.* BOYS *rise, and exit left.*)

1ST CHEERLEADER: And the shepherds went away, down to Bethlehem town to see that little bitty baby king. And they never, never finished that Ko-lee game . . .

CHEERLEADERS: Oh, no! Oh, no! Oh, no, indeed!

1ST CHEERLEADER: But every year in Ethiopia, in November, all the boys get together and they finish that Ko-lee game the shepherds began so long ago. And that is the way they remember the shepherds . . .

CHEERLEADERS: Oh, yes. Oh, yes.

1ST CHEERLEADER: And the angel from the skies . . .

CHEERLEADERS: Oh, yes. Oh, yes.

1ST CHEERLEADER: And the little bitty baby king!

CHEERLEADERS: Oh, yes, indeed! (BOYS *re-enter in Ethiopian costume and play Ko-lee game, as* CAROLERS *sing, "Rise Up, Shepherd, and Follow." At end of song,* BOYS *raise their sticks, holding pose. Drums begin steady beat;* BOYS *exit.* AFRICAN STEWARDESS *crosses to center.*)

AFRICAN STEWARDESS: In Africa, everybody helps tell the stories and sing the songs. I hope you have enjoyed your stopover here. Now, I wish you—*"Buronya 'du oo, afe oto yen bio."* (*She claps her cupped hands in greeting.*) And that is how you say "It is Christmas—a New Year has come" in Ghana. Now your Jingle Jet has turned westward and I hear the sound of castanets. I must leave you, but your stewardess from Mexico is coming to take good care of you. Walk in peace! (*She exits center. Sleigh bells and castanets are heard.* MEXICAN STEWARDESS *enters center.*)

MEXICAN STEWARDESS: *Feliz Navidad!* Welcome to Mexico. Ah—si! We have fun and fiesta in store for you. Have you ever heard of the custom of "posadas"? Posadas means "lodgings," so in December, boys and girls go from house to house in their villages pretending to be the Holy Family searching for lodgings in Bethlehem. (*Sound of castanets is heard.* JOSEPH *and* MARY, *in Mexican costume, enter from right.* INNKEEPER *enters left, carrying cardboard door.* JOSEPH *crosses with* MARY *and pretends to knock at door. Tambourine is heard, and music begins.* CAROLERS *sing "Las Posadas." In pantomime,* JOSEPH *asks* INNKEEPER *for lodging.* INNKEEPER *shakes his head and motions* JOSEPH *to leave.* JOSEPH *again entreats* INNKEEPER. *At last,* INNKEEPER *flings open door and* MARY *and* JOSEPH *step behind door, as* INNKEEPER *welcomes them. They hold pose till song stops.*) There! The doors of the inn fly open to welcome the Holy Family. And when that happens, then all the village boys and girls flock inside to enjoy the piñata! (*Castanets are heard.* MEXICAN DANCERS *skip on by twos left.* BOY DANCERS *are blindfolded.* NOTE: *Blindfolds are for effect only; the boys are able to see through them. They carry sticks.* DANCERS *are led by* PIÑATA BOY *bearing a piñata on a pole.* MARY, JOSEPH *and* INNKEEPER *join* DANCERS.)

ALL (*Laughing and clapping*): Piñata! *Bienvenido!* Piñata!

CHEERLEADERS:

How we welcome the precious piñata,
As it hangs in the air, tantalizing—
For under the skin of piñata,
Are sweetmeats and tidbits surprising.

(GIRL DANCERS *turn* BOY DANCERS *around three times.*)

GIRL CHEERLEADERS:

Turn around, turn around, oh, amigos,

Till you hum like gay tops set a-spinning,
For that tempting and teasing piñata,
Is your promising prize—for the winning.
(BOY DANCERS *strike at piñata with their sticks, but* BOY *holding
piñata jerks it away, out of their reach.*)
Once again. Once again, caballeros.
Lift your sticks ever higher to reach it,
Swing again. Swing again, caballeros.
One more thrust. Now you must surely breach it!
(BOY *holds piñata steady and* BOY DANCERS *break it with their
sticks. Paper flowers fall out and* GIRL DANCERS *gather them.*
BOY DANCERS *remove their blindfolds.*)

ALL: Olé! (*They cheer and clap. Castanets play.* DANCERS, *led by*
PIÑATA BOY, *exit in twos, followed by* JOSEPH, MARY *and*
INNKEEPER. *Sleigh bells ring.* PILOT *enters center, and crosses
downstage.*)

PILOT: Ladies and gentlemen, directly below you at this
time is New York City. Prepare for your final landing,
please. We all hope you have enjoyed your journey
around the world at Christmastime. Come fly with us
next year. (*Sleigh bells ring. All* DANCERS *and* JOSEPH,
MARY, INNKEEPER, ETHIOPIAN BOYS, THREE WISE MEN,
OLD BEFANA, ANGEL, *and* JULENISSE *enter.*)

ALL (*Singing, to tune of "Jingle Bells"*):
Dashing through the sky.
Flashing jet planes fly.
O'er the world they go,
On journeys to and fro.
Carillons begin—
A Merry Christmas chime,
What fun it is to chase the clouds
At Merry Christmas time!
Oh, jingle jets! Jingle jets!
Jingle through the air.

Oh, what fun to race the sun,
To Christmas everywhere!
(*Curtain.*)
THE END

One Hundred Words

HELGA	UGLY DUCKLING
HANS CHRISTIAN ANDERSEN	SOLDIER
GIRL WITH THE RED SHOES	BALLERINA
MOTHER DUCK	SPIRIT OF THE STREET LAMP
TWO DUCKLINGS	

TIME: *A spring day long ago.*

SETTING: *A park in Copenhagen, Denmark.*

AT RISE: HELGA, *a little girl, is seated on park bench, writing on slate. She writes, then rubs out what she has written, sobbing. HANS, a young boy, enters right, a bundle tied to a stick slung over his shoulder. He saunters across stage, whistling; sees HELGA. He stops whistling and watches her, curiously.*

HANS: Look at that. A lady in distress.

HELGA (*Sobbing again*): I can't. I simply cannot do it!

HANS (*Crossing to HELGA*): Here now, little miss. You'll flood the park and drown the ducks. What's the matter?

HELGA: Oh, it's too, too dreadful.

HANS: Let me guess. You have been kidnapped by pirates and abandoned in the park!

HELGA (*More cheerfully*): Oh, goodness, no! Worse than that.

HANS: Worse than pirates? Hm-m. You are the crown princess of Denmark, under a spell.

119

HELGA (*Smiling and smoothing her hair*): Do I really look like a princess? I'm not, actually.

HANS: Ah, I made you smile. Now things can't be too dreadful, can they?

HELGA (*Frowning again*): Oh, yes, they are. I have to write a composition.

HANS: A composition—is that all?

HELGA (*Wailing*): But it has to be *one hundred words!*

HANS: Please don't cry again. You're making a waterfall, see? (HELGA *giggles.*) Really, one hundred words aren't many. How many have you written so far?

HELGA: None.

HANS: None. Well, then, you haven't made any mistakes in spelling or grammar, have you?

HELGA (*Smiling*): No, that's true.

HANS: See? You should always look on the bright side of things. By the way, what's your name, your ladyship?

HELGA: I'm not a ladyship. I'm only Helga.

HANS: And I'm only Hans. Now about these hundred words. What are you supposed to be writing about?

HELGA: The schoolmaster said we must write about the most interesting person we have ever met.

HANS (*Fanning himself in mock relief*): Whew! That's a relief. Interesting persons are much easier to write about than the exports of Peru.

HELGA (*Chuckling*): Oh, much. Do you think you can help me?

HANS: I think so. When I was a little boy, I used to help my mother wind wool in the spinning room. There were all kinds of old grannies who used to come and spin wool. You should have heard the gossip they spun, too. I heard many a fine old tale from those grannies. Now, Helga, tell me about the most interesting person you have ever met.

HELGA: I've never met one.

HANS: Not one?

HELGA: Not anyone interesting. Not like a king or a queen.

HANS: Hold on. I said "interesting," not "royal." Take it from me, some of the dullest people on earth are kings and queens.

HELGA: Then whom should I write about? And how should I write about him?

HANS (*Pointing to her eyes*): What are those?

HELGA: My eyes, of course.

HANS (*Pointing to her ears*): And those?

HELGA: My ears, of course.

HANS (*Tapping top of her head*): And this—is this a pumpkin?

HELGA: No, silly. It's my head.

HANS: Of course! You are going to use your eyes, your ears, and your head. That's *how* you'll write the story. As for whom you'll write it about, just wait—and watch. (*He sits down beside her.*)

HELGA: You're the most puzzling boy! What are we waiting for?

HANS: For someone to pass by. (GIRL WITH THE RED SHOES *enters.*) And here she is.

HELGA: But I've never met her. I don't know anything about her.

HANS: Watch. Listen. Wonder about her. Don't you hear her telling you a story about herself?

GIRL (*Dancing down center*): My red shoes! My red shoes! They are like two twinkling coals. How they shine and gleam! Aren't they rich and elegant? To tell you the truth, I was supposed to buy plain, black shoes for Sunday. But then, I saw these red shoes in the cobbler's window. I knew I must have them for my very own. How strange they make me feel! People stare at my red shoes wherever I go, and wherever I go, I must dance. (*She begins to dance off left.*) The red shoes make me dance on . . . and on . . . (*She exits dancing.*) And on!

HELGA (*Rising to follow* GIRL): Oh, stop! Tell me more about the red shoes. Why, I really did hear her telling me a story, Hans.

HANS: Of course. Didn't I say you would? Now, sit down. Here come some more interesting characters. (MOTHER DUCK, *followed by her* TWO DUCKLINGS, *waddles on, quacking. Behind them trails* UGLY DUCKLING. *They cross to center.*)

HELGA: But those are only ducks.

HANS: So they are. I dare say ducks know a few things, too. Listen.

MOTHER DUCK: Come along. Come along, little ducklings.

1ST DUCKLING (*To* UGLY DUCKLING, *who sits exhausted at the side*): Come along. Come along, you lazy thing.

UGLY DUCKLING: I'm coming. I'm coming. (*He waddles awkwardly for a few steps, then stops.*)

MOTHER DUCK: Why have you stopped? We must hurry to the marshes.

2ND DUCKLING (*Pointing to* UGLY DUCKLING): It's his fault, Mama.

1ST DUCKLING: He won't even try to keep up with us.

UGLY DUCKLING: I do try, I do. But you keep running away from me.

2ND DUCKLING: I wish we could run away from you—forever!

1ST DUCKLING: I wish the cat would get you, you great, ugly buzzard!

MOTHER DUCK: Children! Children! Stop quarreling. Who started it?

2ND DUCKLING (*Pointing to* UGLY DUCKLING): He did.

MOTHER DUCK (*To* UGLY DUCKLING, *angrily*): It's always you—starting trouble, picking fights, hanging back.

1ST DUCKLING: Bad, bad duckling!

MOTHER DUCK: We must be on our way. But I warn you, if you cannot keep up with us, stay behind!

2ND DUCKLING: There! Stay behind. (MOTHER DUCK *and* TWO DUCKLINGS *exit.* UGLY DUCKLING *follows.*)

UGLY DUCKLING: Wait for me. Oh, please. Wait for me. (*Exits.*)

HELGA: The poor little Ugly Duckling! He doesn't even look like the others. What will happen to him, Hans?

HANS: Sh-h-h. More interesting people are coming. There's a dancer on her way home from the Royal Danish Ballet. And over there—there's a soldier, coming the other way. (BALLERINA *enters right,* SOLDIER *enters left. They stroll toward each other.*)

HELGA: All I see are two people passing each other. Thousands of people pass each other in this park every single day. Nothing worth mentioning ever happens. (BALLERINA *and* SOLDIER *collide, center.*)

SOLDIER: Please excuse me, miss. It was my fault entirely.

BALLERINA: Not at all. I wasn't looking where I was going.

SOLDIER (*To audience*): What a lovely creature! But she is as far above me as the stars. She must live in a palace. As for me, I'm only a poor corporal who lives in rough barracks. Yet—I must see her again. I must! (*He bows to* BALLERINA.) Pleased to have met you, ma'am.

BALLERINA (*To audience*): What a handsome fellow! He must be at least a general in the Army. He's too good for me, that's certain. I'm only a poor dancer in the chorus of the ballet. Yet, I must see him again. I must! (*She curtsies to* SOLDIER.) Charmed to have met you, sir. (BALLERINA *exits left,* SOLDIER, *right.*)

HELGA: Oh . . . they began a wonderful story. Will they meet again, Hans? Don't keep me in suspense.

HANS: Perhaps they will, and perhaps they won't.

HELGA: Oh, Hans! You are about as helpful as that old street lamp there. (*She points to street lamp.*)

HANS: Sh-h-h. Lower your voice, Helga. The street lamp

will hear you. (HELGA *rises, then crosses to street lamp and puts her hand on it.*)

HELGA: You're not going to tell me that street lamps have feelings!

HANS: No, Helga. I am not going to tell you. The street lamp will tell you. Listen. (HELGA *puts her head close to street lamp.* SPIRIT OF THE STREET LAMP, *an old man with a cane, enters down left.*)

STREET LAMP SPIRIT: I'm an old, old lamp, I am. But I've been a faithful lamp these last forty years. I've shone over this very bench through rain and snow. I've frightened away robbers, and I've given light to the weary. Now, it's all over. Tonight is my last night to give light to the park. Tomorrow they'll take me down and send me away to be melted down in a foundry. Melted down! Like an old wax candle. Oh, it's a sad thing. My last night as a street lamp. My very last night! (*He shuffles off left.*)

HELGA: How sad to think this is the street lamp's last night after all the years he's stood here!

HANS: There. You see what miracles happen when you use your eyes, and your ears, and your imagination? Try writing your composition now. Surely, from all those characters, one will strike your fancy.

HELGA (*Taking slate and chalk and sitting down*): Oh, yes. Someone has struck my fancy, that's true. (*She begins to write very fast.* HANS *begins to saunter off, his bundle over his shoulder.* HELGA *calls him back.*) Oh, please, don't go, Hans. Look! I've written ninety-eight words already. (HANS *crosses back and sits next to* HELGA)

HANS: I knew you could do it. Will you read your composition to me?

HELGA (*Reading slowly*): "Today I met the most interesting person in the whole world. He was not a king or prince. He was just a cheerful, kind boy who stopped to help me with a composition. He showed me how to look and listen. He showed me the stories that people tell as they walk through the park. Now I know that there are stories everywhere. Even ducks and street lamps can tell tales. I do not know where this boy came from, or where he is going, but he will become someone great. I will always remember my friend, Hans."

HANS (*Smiling proudly*): Thank you, Helga. Imagine—I never suspected that I was an interesting person.

HELGA: Oh, but you are. Why, you ought to be a storyteller yourself.

HANS (*Teasing*): What? And have to write thousands and thousands of words? (*Sobbing mockingly*) I can't! I simply cannot do it!

HELGA: Stop teasing me, Hans. It's really not hard at all. Once you get the idea, the words come all by themselves. Well, almost all of them. I still need two words.

HANS (*Studying slate*): Let me see. Very simple. Put the rest of my name right there.

HELGA (*Reading*): "I will always remember my friend, Hans." (*Looking up*) Hans, what?

HANS (*Tipping his hat, as he rises*): Hans Christian Andersen. (*He bows, slings bundle over shoulder and exits left, whistling.*)

HELGA: Why, that's one hundred words exactly! (*She repeats sentence slowly and with feeling.*) "I will always remember my friend, *Hans Christian Andersen!*" (*Curtain*)

THE END

Number One Apple Tree Lane

Characters

MOTHER ROBIN   BLUE JAY
FATHER ROBIN   SQUIRREL
EARLY-ONE ⎫   CAT
ME TOO   ⎬ *baby robins*   BOY
CHEEPER   ⎭   CHORUS

SETTING: *A nest in an apple tree.*

AT RISE: MOTHER ROBIN *and* FATHER ROBIN *are perched left and right on nest, watching eggs inside. Members of* CHORUS *enter, binoculars to their eyes. They sit on apron of stage.*

CHORUS:
>   Good morning. Good morning.
>   It's a very good morning
>   For visiting friends in a tree.
>   For dropping in on neighbors
>   In a nest.
>   For chatting with Robins,
>   Hobnobbin' with Robins,
>   At Number One Apple Tree Lane.
>   Bring your eyes and your ears
>   And come along with us.
>   Come along with us,
>   To Number One Apple Tree Lane.

1ST SOLO (*Putting finger to lips*):

Sh-h-h! Can you be quiet?
So quiet that even the grass
Does not hear your footsteps?

2ND SOLO (*Holding up hand*):
Wait! Can you be patient?
So patient that the Morning Glory
Winds around your ankle?

3RD SOLO (*Cupping hand to ear*):
Listen! Can you listen?
Can you listen so intently
That you can hear the breathing
Of a bee?

4TH SOLO (*Shading eyes*):
Look! Can you look?
Can you see so keenly,
That you can see three blue eggs,
In the hidden nest,
On the topmost branch
Of the blossoming tree?

CHORUS: At Number One Apple Tree Lane. (*They all turn, and sit cross-legged, backs to audience, watching birds through binoculars.*)

MOTHER *and* FATHER ROBIN: Chirrup! Chirrup!

FATHER: Where are they? Where are they, Mother Robin? Half-past dawn and where are our new robins? Still in their eggs. All right, all you robins in your shells. Out. Everybody out of your shells!

MOTHER: Now, now, Father Robin. Give them time. Oh. Oh, look. There's a crack in one of the eggs. It's getting wider. Oh, here he comes. Here he comes! (EARLY-ONE *pops his head up over edge of nest. He looks around.*)

EARLY-ONE: Who am I? Where am I? What am I?

FATHER: Answer to Question One: You are the Early-One. Answer to Question Two: You are in our nest. Answer to

Question Three: You are a Robin, you lucky, lucky creature.

MOTHER: Oh, here comes another one. (ME TOO *peeps over nest, with mouth open.*)

EARLY-ONE (*Opening and closing mouth greedily*): Feed me! Feed me! Feed me!

ME TOO (*Mimicking* EARLY-ONE): Me too! Me too! Me too!

MOTHER (*Counting bills*): Early-One. Me Too. Only one more Robin not accounted for. Come on, little slowpoke. Open up.

EARLY-ONE *and* ME TOO: Open up! Open up! (CHEEPER *reluctantly puts his head over nest*)

CHEEPER: Cheep-cheep-cheep-cheep.

MOTHER: What a talky little Robin. I shall name you Cheeper.

BABY ROBINS: Feed me! Feed me! Feed me!

FATHER: All right. One at a time. Quiet down. I'll go find a fat juicy worm. (*He flies off up left as* BLUE JAY *flies in from right, circling nest. He has raucous voice*)

BLUE JAY (*Haughtily*): A-ak. If it isn't Mrs. Robin. So—your eggs *finally* hatched. Our little jays hatched two weeks ago.

MOTHER (*Ruffling her feathers*): Well! First is not always best, Blue Jay.

BLUE JAY (*Pecking at baby Robins*): What have we here? Toadstools? Oh, pardon me. I see you are fledgling Robins. How odd little Robins look, all puffy and furry. Just like toadstools.

MOTHER (*Putting her wings over baby robins*): Toadstools, indeed! We think they are beautiful. Much more beautiful than some birds I could name. Some baby birds look just like pink, wrinkled prunes. Isn't that so, Blue Jay?

BLUE JAY: A-ak. All right. All right, so my fledglings are born without feathers. Even so, they are smarter than robins. One of my jays flew around the nest yesterday. I don't see any of those—those feathered toadstools flying around your nest.

MOTHER: They'll fly soon enough, Blue Jay, soon enough. (FATHER *flies in and flaps around* BLUE JAY.)

FATHER (*Irritated*): Are you annoying Mrs. Robin again, you nest-robber? Buzz off! This is Robin territory! (*He chases* BLUE JAY *right.*)

BLUE JAY: A-ak. Robins! May the great, black cat get you, Robins! (*Exits right*)

FATHER (*Perching next to* MOTHER): I came back when I saw that big blue bully bothering you.

MOTHER: Thank you! You must be tired. This time, I'll go find the food. You teach the babies to fly. (*She flies off down left.*)

FATHER: Attention, fledglings. Time for flight drill.

EARLY-ONE: What is flight?

FATHER (*Demonstrating by doing aerobatics around nest*): This is flight.

EARLY-ONE: I can do it! I can do it! (*He perches on edge of nest and flaps his wings awkwardly.*)

ME TOO: Me too! Me too! (*He imitates* EARLY-ONE. *Both fall into nest*)

FATHER: It takes practice, fledglings. Hours and hours of practice. Now, perch for flight. Three toes forward, one toe backward. (*They all lean forward expectantly.*) Practice your wing strokes. Up stroke. (*He lifts his wing.*) Open your feathers, let the air rush through. Now down stroke. (*He brings his wings down sharply.*) Close your feathers tightly. Push, push, push the air. Now, rest. Ready? Follow me. (*Baby robins imitate him.*) Up. Down. Rest. Up. Down. Rest. (*He watches them.*) Pull those feathers open, Early-One. Harder, harder, Me Too. (CHEEPER *stops, hanging his head.*) What's the matter, Cheeper?

CHEEPER: I can't.

EARLY-ONE *and* ME TOO: You can. You can. If we can do it,

you can do it. (SQUIRREL *scampers onstage, stands left of nest, an ear of corn in his paws.*)

FATHER: Never say, "I can't." I never knew a robin who couldn't fly. Remember that.

SQUIRREL: Chip-chip. Good morning, robin. Teaching the babies to fly?

FATHER: Good morning, Squirrel. What's that in your paws?

SQUIRREL: Corn. I've been storing it in the hollow tree. Lots of corn. Chip-chip. Come and see. It's not far. Come with me. Chip-chip.

FATHER: Attention, fledglings. This is important. I must find food for all of us. You must take care of yourselves for a few minutes. Do not let anyone into the nest, unless he has feathers. If anyone comes to the nest, you must say, "Let me see your feathers." Now, what did I just say?

EARLY-ONE: If anyone comes to the nest we must say, "Let me see your feathers."

FATHER: Now put your heads down. (*They retire into nest*)

SQUIRREL: Chip-chip. This way, Robin. Follow me. Chip-chip. (*He scampers off,* FATHER *flying behind him. They exit up left as* CAT *creeps on right. She sneaks up to nest and crouches.*)

CAT (*Plaintively*): Meow.

EARLY-ONE (*Popping up*): Who's there?

ME TOO: Stay down. (*Pulls him down*)

CAT: Meow. I'm a poor old cat-bird. Let me in.

EARLY-ONE (*Popping up*): It says it is a bird.

ME TOO (*Popping up*): Are you a bird?

CHEEPER (*Slowly lifting head above nest*): Show us your feathers.

CAT: Gladly, but my feathers are very small. I must come closer . . . and closer. (*She puts her paws up on side of nest.*)

EARLY-ONE: I don't see any feathers.

ME TOO: Me too. I don't see any feathers.

CAT: I must come still closer. (*She leaps into nest.*)

BABY ROBINS (*Frightened*): We don't see any feathers!

CAT: But I see feathers. Delicious, delectable feathers. (*She licks her lips and springs. Robins squawk and beat their wings.*) Meow!

BABY ROBINS: Help! Mother! Father! (MOTHER *flies in left. She beats* CAT *with her wings furiously.* CAT *falls out of nest, rolls over and goes right.* MOTHER *goes back to nest screaming at* CAT)

MOTHER: Assassin! Murderer! (CHORUS *turns, calling* CAT)

CHORUS: Pssst. Here, kitty, kitty. (CAT *crosses to* 1ST SOLO, *who grabs her by scruff of neck.* CHORUS *lectures* CAT.)

> Do you know what we'll do
> With a cat like you?
> With an awful, claw-full,
> Bird-in-the-jaw-ful,
> Prowler unlawful,
> Skinful of sinful
> Cat like you?
> We'll tell you—
> We'll bell you!

(1ST SOLO *fastens collar with bells around* CAT's *neck.* CAT *slinks off right, ashamed, as* CHORUS *recites.*)

> Now wherever you slink it'll
> Jingle and tinkle,
> So, buzz off.
> Buzz off. Buzz off!
> This is Robin territory.

MOTHER (*Scolding babies*): Silly Robins. Never play with a cat. I see you will not be safe until you learn how to fly. Who'd like to give it a try?

EARLY-ONE: Me first! Me first! Here goes. (*He gets out of nest, flying awkwardly.*)

ME TOO: Me too. Me too. Up, and over. Happy landing. (*He flutters behind* EARLY-ONE.)

EARLY-ONE *and* ME TOO: We can fly.

MOTHER: That is what you were born to do. Now you are citizens of the sky. You are free, lucky, lucky robins. All right, Cheeper, up, and over you go.

CHEEPER: I can't. I can't.

EARLY-ONE *and* ME TOO: If we can, you can.

CHEEPER: I'm afraid.

MOTHER (*Nudging him out of nest*): Up, and over you go, little slowpoke.

CHEEPER (*Fluttering*): My wings won't hold me up. I know it.

MOTHER: But look at yourself. You are flying. You are really flying.

CHEEPER: I am? I am. (FATHER *flies in right, joining* MOTHER. *Baby Robins fly around excitedly.*)

ROBINS: Look, Father, look. We can fly. (BOY *with toy rifle enters, pointing his gun at birds*)

FATHER: Danger! Danger! Come back to the nest. (EARLY-ONE *and* ME TOO *fly into nest, but* CHEEPER *keeps flying.* FATHER *enters nest.*)

CHEEPER: I can soar. I can dip. Did you see how cleverly I banked? Watch me hover, Mother. Watch me fly into the sun, Father. Up. Up. Up. (BOY *takes aim.*)

MOTHER: Cheeper! Come back! (*Climbs into nest.*)

BOY: Ready . . . aim . . .

1ST SOLO (*Standing indignantly, holding up his hand*): Stop!

CHORUS (*Rising*): Stop the action. (BOY *holds his pose,* CHEEPER *stops, with wings raised.*)

2ND SOLO: Do you think for one minute we will let such a thing happen?

CHORUS (*Facing audience*):
Not for one minute.
Not ever. No never,
At Number One Apple Tree Lane.

3RD SOLO (*Advancing to* BOY): Hey, you, was that big fierce Robin bothering you?

BOY (*Putting down rifle*): What's it to you?

4TH SOLO: There must be some reason you're shooting a robin.

BOY: I want to shoot something.

CHORUS (*Moving toward* BOY, *a step at a time*): Shoot something? A robin is not *something*. A robin is *somebody*. A cheeky, talky, breezy somebody.

5TH SOLO: Somebody with bright, black eyes and a red coat.

6TH SOLO: A hopper and a chirper and a digger and a doer.

4TH SOLO: Somebody with a right to live.

CHORUS: A robin has a right to live. (BOY *puts rifle behind his back.*)

5TH SOLO: You want to shoot something? Shoot targets.

6TH SOLO: Shoot tin cans.

7TH SOLO: Shoot marbles.

CHORUS:
Shoot pictures, shoot cue balls, shoot the chutes.
But don't shoot robins.
Now buzz off.

8TH SOLO: Buzz off.

CHORUS: This is robin territory. (BOY *slowly exits left.* CHEEPER *flies into nest.* CHORUS *sits in semicircle around nest.*)

MOTHER: Oh, Cheeper, are you all right?

CHEEPER: Cheer-up. I'm perfectly fine. Cheer-up, I'm perfectly fine. Listen! (*He whistles trill. Other robins join him.*)

CHORUS:
Listen! The robins are singing,
At Number One Apple Tree Lane.

1ST SOLO: The world is sweet again for Robins. (MOTHER *spreads wings over baby robins.* FATHER *puts head under his wing.*)

CHORUS:
Sh-h-h! Darkness is spreading his midnight wings.
Can you be silent?
Can you be so still
That you can hear—

1ST SOLO:
>The whispering of stars?

2ND SOLO:
>The drifting sound
>Of apple petals wafting down?

3RD SOLO:
>Can you hear
>The rustle of robins, nestling?

4TH SOLO:
>Can you hear
>The flutter of dreaming wings?

(Curtains begin to close.)

CHORUS:
>Oh, rock-a-bye, rock-a-bye
>Rock-a-bye robins,
>Swayed in your cradle,
>Swung in your cradle,
>Hush-a-by, hush-a-by,
>Hush-a-by robins,
>Rocked in your cradle of straw,
>High in the star-peppered sky,
>High in the star-blossomed tree,

1ST SOLO: At Number One Apple Tree Lane.

CHORUS: At Number One Apple Tree Lane. *(Curtain)*

THE END

The Little Red Hen

Characters

BOY NARRATOR	GRAHAM QUACKER, *the duck*
GIRL NARRATOR	PERCIVAL, *the pig*
THE LITTLE RED HEN	FARMER
CHIP-CHIP	SCARECROW
PECK-A-BIT } *her chicks*	MILLER
CLUCKET	CHORUS
TABITHA, *the cat*	

BEFORE RISE: *Down right in front of curtain stands* BOY NARRATOR. *Seated about him informally are several members of* CHORUS, *wearing farm clothes. Down left is* GIRL NARRATOR, *with several other* CHORUS *members grouped about her.*

BOY NARRATOR: Something has happened down on the farm.

CHORUS: Down on the farm in the fall of the year.

GIRL NARRATOR: Something has happened that you should hear. (*She points to audience.*)

CHORUS: That you should hear. (*They point to audience.*) So you will know. (*They point to their heads.*) So you can help.

BOY: Oh, you must help. We need your help.

GIRL: We need your ears. (*She points to her ears.*) So listen, please.

CHORUS: Do listen, please. We need your ears.

135

Boy: Listen and judge. Oyez, oyez! (*He pretends to rap gavel.*) The case of the Little Red Hen versus her friends.

Chorus: The story begins in the spring of the year. (*Curtains open.*)

* * *

Setting: *A farmyard. A pile of hoes and scythes is at one side. Backdrop shows fields and a red barn.*

At Rise: *Stage is empty.*

Girl: The story begins in the farmyard of Old MacDonald.

Boy: The story begins with a little red hen.

Chorus: Enter, Little Red Hen. (Little Red Hen *enters from right, flapping her wings.*)

Little Red Hen (*Looking off right and calling*): Here, chick. Here, chick, chick, chick. (Chip-Chip, Peck-a-Bit *and* Clucket *enter from left with tiny, quick steps.* Red Hen *calls them by name.*) Chip-Chip?

Chip-Chip: Here, Mama. (*She scratches ground.*)

Red Hen: Peck-a-Bit?

Peck-a-Bit: Here, Mama. (*She pecks at ground.*)

Red Hen: Clucket?

Clucket: Present, Mama. Cluck-cluck-cluck.

Red Hen: Be quiet, my chicks. I am about to present the world with an Idea.

Chicks: Oh! An Idea! (*They shush each other.*) Sh-h-h-h!

Chorus: Sh-h. Your respectful attention, please. The Little Red Hen is about to have an Idea.

Red Hen (*Running about in circles*): Cluck-cluck-cadacket! Cluck-cluck-cadacket! (*She stops center, flaps her wings and announces*) I have it! I have an Idea. We shall make some bread!

Chicks (*Imitating their mother*): Yes. We shall. We shall make some bread!

Chorus: What a glorious idea! Bread, bread. Make some

bread. Bread full of cream. Bread full of grain. Bread full of butter. Bread full of *bread.*

BOY: Everyone likes bread.

CHORUS: Everyone.

GIRL: Especially the three *so-called* friends of the Little Red Hen.

CHORUS: The three *uninvited* friends of the Little Red Hen. (RED HEN *stands center, with chicks clustered right of her.* TABITHA, *the cat, slinks on, down left. She extends an elegant paw to* RED HEN, *then stands left of her.*)

TABITHA: Meow. Good mousing, dear Little Red Hen. Did I hear you mention bread? I adore bread. It's so full of creamy cream. (*She licks her whiskers.* GRAHAM QUACKER *waddles on down left, and nods to* RED HEN. *He stands left of* TABITHA.)

GRAHAM QUACKER: Quack, quack. My best friend, the Little Red Hen. Did I hear you say bread? I'm very fond of bread. It's so full of rich, ripe grain. (*To* TABITHA) What are you doing here, you sly old cat?

TABITHA: Meow. I have as much right to be here as you have, you damp old duck. (PERCIVAL, *the pig, trots on left. He bows to* RED HEN *and stands left of* QUACKER.)

PERCIVAL: Oink, oink. Am I too late? I ran as soon as I heard the good news. (*Bowing to* RED HEN *again.*) Ah, here she is—the beautiful queen of the barnyard. My favorite animal, the Little Red Hen. So we're going to have bread. Ah, I love bread. It's so full of soft, golden butter. (*He eyes* QUACKER *and* TABITHA *with disdain.*) Depart, duck. Shoo, cat. I am the official bread taster.

TABITHA *and* QUACKER: Not on your curly tail. If you stay, we stay.

RED HEN: Now, first things first. First we must plant the wheat to make the bread. First we must work.

TABITHA: Work? Me?

QUACKER: Plant? Me?

PERCIVAL: Work and plant? Me?

RED HEN: Don't fret. There's enough work for everybody. Many hands make light work. Now, who will plant the wheat?

TABITHA: Well, I *would,* but I might spoil my lovely, long nails. (*She curls up down left and watches others.*) No, not I.

QUACKER: Well, I *would,* but I might ruffle my fine feathers. (*He sits down next to* TABITHA.) No, not I.

PERCIVAL: I would, too. I really *would.* But you know how pigs hate to grub about in the mud. No, not I. (PERCIVAL *sits down beside* QUACKER *and watches proceedings.*)

RED HEN: Oh, dear. Then who will plant the wheat? (FARMER *enters, doffs his hat.*)

FARMER: Allow me, Little Red Hen. A farmer's a fellow who works with a will. I'll put my shoulder to the wheel, my hands to the hoe, my nose to the grindstone, and my feet to the plow. Here, chicks. (*He hands a hoe to each and to* RED HEN.) It's time for a hoedown. (*They raise hoes and pose.*)

TABITHA: Who's that farmer creature? Is he on the Little Red Hen's official list of friends? He bears watching.

QUACKER: Never mind. Let's sit here and keep them company. I love to watch workers work. It's so healthy.

PERCIVAL: Why don't we sing for the Little Red Hen? It makes the work go faster. (RED HEN, FARMER, *and chicks hoe in rhythm, as others clap and sing.*)

CHORUS, TABITHA, QUACKER, *and* PERCIVAL (*Singing to tune of "Old MacDonald Had a Farm"*):

The Little Red Hen, she planted grain,
See them, see them hoe.
The sun came down—
(*All wipe their brows.*)
And so did the rain—
(*All turn up collars.*)
See those wheat stalks grow.

CHIP-CHIP: Look, Mama. The wheat is knee high. (*Points to knee*)

ALL (*Singing*):
With a little weed here, and a big weed there—
(*They pull weeds.*)
Here a weed, there a weed, everywhere a weed-weed.
Little Red Hen, she planted grain.
See those wheat stalks grow.

PECK-A-BIT: Look, Mama. The wheat is wing-high. (*She raises wing.*)

BOY: And the days went by . . . (*They lean on hoes.*)

GIRL: And the weeks went by . . . (FARMER, *shouldering hoe, exits waving. All wave.*)

CHORUS: And the summer went by. And then . . .

CLUCKET: Oh, Mama, look. (*All look up.*) The wheat is high, high, high over my head. (*She puts wing above her head.* SCARECROW *enters from right and stands with hands out-stretched.*)

RED HEN: To be sure. It's time to cut the wheat and bring it to the mill. Many hands make light work. Now, who will cut the wheat?

TABITHA (*Coughing delicately*): Oh! I have such a *dreadful* cough. I'm so sorry. Not this time. Not I.

QUACKER: Oh! (*He sneezes loudly.*) I have an allergy to wheat. What a shame! So sorry. Not I.

PERCIVAL (*Rising*): I'll try. (*He groans and feels his back.*) Oh! My aching back. I have a terrible crick in my back. No, Little Red Hen. Not I.

RED HEN: Oh, dear. Then, who will cut the wheat?

SCARECROW (*Doffing hat*): Allow me, Little Red Hen. I'm only an old scarecrow, but there's not much about wheat fields that I don't know. Why, I've seen half a hundred wheat crops come and go. Here, chicks, here are the scythes. (*He hands out scythes to chicks and* RED HEN)

TABITHA: Hm-m-m. A mere scarecrow. I suppose we should do something.

PERCIVAL: We could lend our voices again. (SCARECROW, RED HEN *and chicks line up across stage and swing scythes, slowly advancing downstage, as if cutting wheat, as others sing*)

CHORUS, TABITHA, QUACKER *and* PERCIVAL (*Singing to tune of "Little Brown Jug"*):

The Little Red Hen, she cut the grain

With a chip and a chop

And a might and a main.

She bundled the sheaves,

(*Workers pantomime gathering sheaves*)

The sheaves were bound,

And stacked up neatly

On the ground.

(RED HEN *and* SCARECROW *skip around, as chicks join together and cirlce around them.*)

Circle round with a one-two-three—

The wheat's all in

And so are we!

(*Chicks collapse at left, as* SCARECROW *exits right, waving.*)

CHIP-CHIP: That's what I call work! Are we ready to bake the bread now, Mama?

CHICKS: Now, Mama?

RED HEN: Oh, dear me, no. Now we grind the flour. Oh my, I almost hate to ask. Ahem. Would someone—somebody, anyone—*anybody* volunteer to grind the flour?

TABITHA: Why, I've never ground flour. I wouldn't know where to begin. Not I—but perhaps the duck will.

QUACKER: What do you mean—"the duck will"? I'd only be in the way, Little Red Hen. Not I. But Percival is a likely fellow.

PERCIVAL: Percival is an *un*likely fellow. Don't believe him, Little Red Hen. I have two left knuckles at that sort of thing. Not I. (MILLER, *carrying grindstone and sacks, enters.*)

RED HEN: Then who will grind the flour?

MILLER (*Doffing cap*): Allow me, Little Red Hen. Dusty Miller is my name. Anything you grow is grist for my mill. I've ground sweet rye, sour rye, buckwheat, spring wheat, winter wheat and graham wheat. Groat meal, oatmeal, branmeal, and corn. Corn for pone, corn for johnny cake, corn for spoonbread. How shall I grind it for you, Little Red Hen? Coarse for fodder, medium for mash, or fine for bread?

RED HEN: Fine for bread, if you please.

MILLER (*Holding out sacks*): Hold the sacks, chicks. (RED HEN *and chicks hold sacks, as* MILLER *turns grindstone.*)

CHORUS, TABITHA, QUACKER, *and* PERCIVAL (*Singing to tune of "Go Round and Round the Village"*):

> Go round and round the millstones,
> Go round and round the millstones,
> Go round and round the millstones,
> And grind the grain to flour.

(*At conclusion,* MILLER *exits, waving*)

PECK-A-BIT (*Putting sack over her wing*): Whew. That's heavy, hard, hot work. Now, is it time to bake the bread, Mama?

RED HEN: Now!

TABITHA, QUACKER, *and* PERCIVAL: Now! At last!

TABITHA: We really *should* do something.

QUACKER: Yes, we should. Some little something.

PERCIVAL: Have you some small tasks, some odd jobs for us, Little Red Hen?

RED HEN: Small tasks? Odd jobs? Oh, yes. How thoughtful! (*She recites tasks, going faster and faster, until she runs out of breath*) First we must sift the flour for half an hour. Borrow or beg a large round egg. Skim the milk through cloth of silk, and far from least, we must find yeast. Then carry from the dairy a lump of butter. . . .

TABITHA: Stop! I almost forgot. I have an urgent appointment with a mouse. Let me know when the bread is baked, my dear. (*She exits left.*)

QUACKER: Stop! A goldfish is waiting for me at the bottom of the pond. Do give me a call when the bread is finished. (*He exits left.*)

PERCIVAL: Wait for me, Graham Quacker. I suddenly remembered—this is my day to dig for mushrooms. But I'll have plenty of time after that to enjoy the bread. Do save me a large slice. (*He exits left.*)

RED HEN: Oh, dear. Who will help me bake the bread?

CHICKS: We will, Mama. (CHIP-CHIP *and* PECK-A-BIT *exit and bring on table with bread pans, bowl, spoons, egg, milk bottle. They put flour sacks on table as* CLUCKET *exits and re-enters carrying oven. She pantomimes lighting oven.* RED HEN *and chicks sing to tune of "Here We Go 'Round the Mulberry Bush."*)

RED HEN (*Singing*):
This is the way we make the bread,

CHIP-CHIP (*Singing*):
Egg for the bread,
(*Pantomimes breaking egg*)

PECK-A-BIT (*Singing*):
Milk for the bread,
(*Pantomimes pouring milk*)

RED HEN *and* CHICKS (*Singing*):
This is the way we make the bread,
We knead and knead and knead it.
(*They pantomime kneading bread dough.* RED HEN *puts dough into pans.*)

RED HEN (*Singing*):
This is the way we bake the bread,

CHIP-CHIP (*Singing*):
Batter up!
(*Holds bread pans up over head*)

PECK-A-BIT (*Singing*):
Batter in!

(*Takes bread pans and pops them into oven*)

RED HEN *and* CHICKS (*Singing*):

This is the way we bake the bread,

We wait and wait and wait for it.

(RED HEN *stands at oven, while chicks remove bread-baking utensils, and bring in seven chairs and a pile of plates. They set table and put chairs around it. Bell rings offstage. All cheer and run to oven.* CHIP-CHIP *and* PECK-A-BIT *open oven door, and* CLUCKET *tests bread with long straw, which she hands to* RED HEN. *She examines it carefully.*)

CHIP-CHIP: Is the bread moist and spongy and springy on the inside?

PECK-A-BIT: Is it crisp and crusty and toasty on the outside?

CLUCKET: In other words—is it done?

RED HEN: It is done. (*She puts pans of bread on table.*)

CHICKS: Done, done, done!

RED HEN: Now. There is one small matter. Who will help us eat the bread? (TABITHA, QUACKER, *and* PERCIVAL *rush in from left with napkins tied around their necks. They carry knives and forks which they bang together.*)

TABITHA, QUACKER, *and* PERCIVAL: Eat? Eat? Did someone say eat?

TABITHA: I heard your call, and I came immediately. I will eat the bread.

QUACKER: At your service, Little Red Hen. I will eat the bread.

PERCIVAL: Out of my way. Let a pig do the honors. My most favorite friend, *I* will eat the bread.

TABITHA, QUACKER *and* PERCIVAL: We will eat the bread. We are your friends.

CHICKS (*Shaking their heads*): No, no, no. You are not our friends. Friends help. Friends work beside you.

CHORUS: Friends help. Friends work beside you. (FARMER, SCARECROW *and* MILLER *enter and stand upstage.*)

CHICKS: Who sowed the wheat? Who cut the wheat? Who ground the wheat? (*Pointing upstage*) The Farmer. The Scarecrow. The Miller.

RED HEN (*Running about in circles*): But I only have room for three guests. Only three. Three only. (*She stops at center, addresses audience*) But which three? Which three are truly the friends of the Little Red Hen?

TABITHA, QUACKER, *and* PERCIVAL: We are, of course.

CHICKS (*Pointing to* FARMER, SCARECROW, *and* MILLER): They are, of course.

RED HEN: We are. They are. (*She shakes her head dizzily.*) We. They. We. They. Cluck-cluck-cadacket!

CHORUS: Do you see?

BOY: Do you see what has happened down on the farm?

GIRL (*To audience*): You can help. You must vote for the true friends of the Little Red Hen. Clap for the true friends of the Little Red Hen.

CHORUS: Clap for the true friends of the Little Red Hen. (TABITHA *and* FARMER *go to first chair at table and stand beside it.*)

BOY: Tabitha?

GIRL: Or the Farmer? (*When audience claps for* FARMER, *he sits, and* TABITHA *slinks down left.* SCARECROW *and* QUACKER *stand beside second chair.*) Graham Quacker?

BOY: Or the Scarecrow? (SCARECROW *sits when audience applauds for him, and* QUACKER *joins* TABITHA. MILLER *and* PERCIVAL *stand at third chair.*)

GIRL: Percival?

BOY: Or the Miller? (MILLER *sits as audience applauds, and* PERCIVAL *joins others.*)

CHICKS (*Applauding*): Our true friends. We know our true friends. (*They sit at table, with* RED HEN *at the head.*)

RED HEN: And now, good friends, we shall cut the bread. (*She poses, with bread knife ready to cut.*)

CHORUS: Bread. Bread. Glorious bread. Bread full of

cream. Bread full of grain. Bread full of butter. Bread full of bread. Glorious bread!

TABITHA (*Going off, nose in the air*): Meow! True friends, indeed. Freeloaders! That's what I call them. Goodbye!

QUACKER (*Exciting*): You see how some folks treat their real friends? After all the kind advice I gave. After all the work I watched. That's gratitude for you. Goodbye!

PERCIVAL: Humph. Bread. Who likes bread, anyhow? No doubt it's stale. No doubt it's dry. I never cared for bread. (*Sadly*) Especially bread with rich golden butter. Goodbye! (*Exits*)

ALL (*Singing to tune of "Old MacDonald Had a Farm"*):
> The Little Red Hen, she had three friends,
> Helpers, helpers, all.
> They sowed beside her in the fields,
> Till the wheat grew tall.
> With a hoe-hoe here,
> And a cut-cut there,
> Mind the wheat, bind the wheat,
> Everybody grind the wheat.
> The Little Red Hen, she had three friends.
> (*All join hands around the table*)
> The very best friends of all!

(Curtain)

THE END

May Basket Fantasia

BOY NARRATOR
GIRL NARRATOR
OLD-FASHIONED GIRL
TWO MODERN GIRLS
SIX MAYBASKETEERS, *three boys and three girls*
SECRET AGENT
PHANTOM
JOHN ALDEN
CHILD
FLORIDA GIRL
ESKIMO
COWBOY
MANY-ARMED GODDESS, *three girls*
MARTIAN
WALKING MAY BASKET
WESTERN UNION MESSENGER

BEFORE RISE: BOY NARRATOR *and* GIRL NARRATOR *enter in front of curtain and stand down left.*

BOY NARRATOR: Something happens on a doorstep on the first day of May.
GIRL NARRATOR: On the first day of May, something happens on a doorstep that is not quite a valentine . . .
BOY NARRATOR: Not quite an Easter basket.

146

GIRL NARRATOR: Something sweet and pretty.

BOY NARRATOR: Something rather friendly.

GIRL NARRATOR: Something that wasn't there the day before.

BOY NARRATOR: Something that won't be there the day after.

GIRL NARRATOR: On the first day of May, something happens to coax the door open.

BOY NARRATOR: Open in the name of May!

GIRL NARRATOR: Sh-h-h. I said "coax." Now, see if you can answer this riddle: What holds flowers, but is not a flowerpot?

BOY NARRATOR: Hm-m-m. A flour sifter?

GIRL NARRATOR: Guess again. What has a handle you can handle?

BOY NARRATOR: Handlebars?

GIRL NARRATOR: Guess again. What is pink and blue and yellow and green and sits on a doorstep?

BOY NARRATOR: A pink and blue and yellow and green doorstep-sitter?

GIRL NARRATOR: No, silly. (Two MODERN GIRLS *tiptoe on from right, put May baskets in front of* BOY NARRATOR, *and tiptoe off left.*)

BOY NARRATOR (*Loudly*): Oh. Why didn't you say so? May baskets!

GIRL NARRATOR: Sh-h-h! May baskets are quiet things.

BOY NARRATOR (*Whispering*): May baskets. Is that better? (*She nods.* BOY NARRATOR *and* GIRL NARRATOR *step to one side as curtains open.*)

* * *

SETTING: *Three flowered archways representing doors are at center.*

AT RISE: OLD-FASHIONED GIRL *sits in first archway.* TWO MODERN GIRLS *sit in other archways.*

GIRL NARRATOR: Ahem. (*Formally*) The May basket. The May basket is a very old tradition.

BOY NARRATOR: Even older than I am.

GIRL NARRATOR: Much older than you are. Some people believe the custom originated when the Romans presented gifts to Maia, the Goddess of Spring.

BOY NARRATOR: I wouldn't be a bit surprised.

GIRL NARRATOR: Today, this delightful tradition is observed in only a few places. If you live in one of these localities, May morning is a time of great anticipation.

BOY NARRATOR: The rest of you folks don't get any May baskets. Sorry about that.

GIRL NARRATOR: Sh-h-h! Let me demonstrate some of the fine points of constructing, delivering and accepting the May basket. Maybasketeer—if you please! (GIRL NARRATOR *claps her hands.* 1ST MAYBASKETEER, *a girl in crinolines, skips across stage from right, carrying straw May basket.*) First, the classical May basket.

1ST MAYBASKETEER (*Curtsying*): Your servant, ma'am. The classical May basket is constructed of woven straw. If you would so kindly observe—the classical contents of the classical basket are as follows: The first blue violets plucked at dawn; five wild hepaticas fresh with dew; a large bunch of assorted cowslips newly opened; and of course, above all, Mayflowers, twining about the handle.

GIRL NARRATOR: Your grandmother probably received a basket like this on her doorstep. Now, watch. Here is the proper manner of presenting a May basket. (*"Spring Song" is played during pantomime.* 1ST MAYBASKETEER *tiptoes to first archway, holding up May basket. She makes elaborate pirouette, then sets basket down. She knocks three times at imaginary door. Three knocks are heard. She pirouettes, then skips off left.* OLD-FASHIONED GIRL *pantomimes opening of door. She looks left, right, up, and finally down. She discovers May basket and picks it up, with delight.*) Now, pay close attention. For there is an

equally proper manner of accepting a basket. First, exclaim upon its size and shape, in case the giver is hiding
in the bushes.

OLD-FASHIONED GIRL: Oh, joy! Oh, rapture! A May basket.
How remarkably large it is. How very well made it is.
Ah! It is full of my most favorite flowers. (*She declaims in
Victorian fashion, using extravagant gestures.*)

Now fancy this!
Now fancy that!
A fancy basket of May.
With drops of snow,
And bits of blue,
To signal this sweet
Spring day.

But tell me, do,
But tell me, do,
Who sent it?
It doth not say.
For, the giver hath gone.
But, blessings upon—
This anonymous basket of May.

(*She smiles, and, with her finger under her chin, curtsies, then sits
down and holds May basket in her lap.*)

BOY NARRATOR: Oh, no. That's not for me. I'd just drop the
basket and run. But on to more modern May baskets.
Don't be surprised if someone puts a basket on your doorknob filled with fresh wild strawberries, or cherries—if
they're ripe. But the best kind of May basket is the candy
May basket.

GIRL NARRATOR: You can really let your imagination go
with a May basket. You can fill a basket with gumdrops,
or fudge, or cookies or mints.

BOY NARRATOR: Japanese folding paper birds . . .

GIRL NARRATOR: Hair ribbons . . .

BOY NARRATOR: Horoscopes . . .

GIRL NARRATOR: A hundred brand-new pennies . . .

BOY NARRATOR: A hundred brand-new marbles . . .

GIRL NARRATOR: One fluffy kitten!

BOY NARRATOR: But the most important thing is this—don't get caught. If you want to be sure you are not discovered, try the old secret agent disguise trick. (*Mysterious music is heard, as* SECRET AGENT, *wearing trench coat, false beard and big spectacles, sneaks in from right, putting May basket on the doorstep of* 1ST MODERN GIRL. *As he starts to sneak off left, she taps him on shoulder.*)

1ST GIRL: Thank you, Arnold. Happy May Day. (SECRET AGENT *hides his head in his collar and dashes off left.*)

BOY NARRATOR: There is always a chance that the old secret agent disguise trick won't work. In that case, try the old Phantom-of-the-Opera trick. (*Spooky music is heard.* PHANTOM *enters, wearing sheet. As he puts his basket down on the doorstep of* 2ND MODERN GIRL, *she reaches out and pulls off sheet.*)

2ND GIRL: Thank you, Robert. Happy May Day. (*He runs off left.*)

BOY NARRATOR: Just in case the old Phantom-of-the-Opera trick doesn't work, there is one sure-fire way of avoiding detection while leaving a May basket—the old John Alden switcheroo. (*"Beautiful Dreamer" is played during pantomime, as* JOHN ALDEN, *carrying May basket, enters, followed by* CHILD *on tricycle.* JOHN *gives* CHILD *basket and points to* 2ND MODERN GIRL. CHILD *nods vigorously, pedals to archway, sets down basket.* 2ND MODERN GIRL *steps out, pats* CHILD's *head, then motions for him to wait. She gets huge, candy-filled basket and gives it to* CHILD, *who pedals off with it.* JOHN *runs across the stage to center, waving to* CHILD *to stop.*)

JOHN: Stop! Thief! Stop! (*To audience*) Oh, why didn't I speak for myself! (*He runs off left in pursuit.*)

BOY NARRATOR: See? I told you it was sure-fire.

GIRL NARRATOR: Of course, there are fashions in May baskets. Here comes the very latest in May baskets. (2ND MAYBASKETEER, *in a modern dress, enters right with basket full of balloons. She dances across stage, exiting left, accompanied by popular music.*)

BOY NARRATOR: What was that? What kind of a May basket is a basket full of balloons?

GIRL NARRATOR: I just told you. It's the latest thing. *Pop* art.

BOY NARRATOR: Well, it just goes to show you. Almost anything that's fun to do, or eat, or look at can go into a May basket.

GIRL NARRATOR: Naturally, you lucky people who receive dozens of baskets are very happy about the whole thing. It makes you feel so wanted, somehow. (1ST MAYBASKETEER *brings in large tray full of May baskets, which she places on doorstep of* OLD-FASHIONED GIRL, *who smiles happily.* 1ST MAYBASKETEER *exits.*)

BOY NARRATOR: But should you receive only one May basket, don't be disappointed. Good things come in small packages sometimes. (3RD MAYBASKETEER, *a girl, brings in one large May basket and puts it at door of* 2ND MODERN GIRL, *who pantomimes disappointment at first. She picks it up, takes out several smaller baskets, then happily, a tiny basket holding forget-me-nots. "Spring Song" is heard being played during action.*)

GIRL NARRATOR: May baskets! Everybody should get a May basket. May baskets should sprout from doorknob and doorstep everywhere. In sunny Florida . . . (FLORIDA GIRL, *dressed in sunclothes, and carrying beach bag, enters right.* 1ST MAYBASKETEER *crosses to her, puts May basket into her beach bag. They stand together.*)

BOY NARRATOR: In frosty Alaska . . . (ESKIMO *enters right, on snowshoes with ski poles.* 2ND MAYBASKETEER *enters and puts May basket on ski pole. They join* FLORIDA GIRL *down right.*)

GIRL NARRATOR: In the Far West . . . (COWBOY *enters right, twirling lasso. He throws rope across stage.* 3RD MAYBASKETEER *enters and fastens May basket to rope.* COWBOY *pulls May basket to him, stands with* 3RD MAYBASKETEER *and others at center.*)

BOY NARRATOR: In the Far East . . . (MANY-ARMED GODDESS *enters.* NOTE: *To get proper effect, one girl holds her arms out sideways, as two others, their bodies hidden under her robe, stretch their arms sideways at different levels.* 4TH *and* 5TH MAYBASKETEERS *enter, each carrying three May baskets. They hang one May basket on each hand of* MANY-ARMED GODDESS. *They join others in line across stage.*) Yes, in every town and country across the globe, May ought to come with a bang and a basket.

GIRL NARRATOR: And even out of this world . . . (MARTIAN *with antennas enters.*)

MARTIAN: Take me to your May basket! (6TH MAY-BASKETEER *enters and hangs a basket from* MARTIAN's *antenna. Fanfare is heard.*)

MAYBASKETEERS: Surprise! Surprise! (*Others discover their May baskets and hold them out.*)

ALL:
   Surprise! Surprise!
   Out of the blue came a basket.
   A bonnie bedecked bit of basket.
   A well-created, decorated
   Beautiful, bountiful basket!

FLORIDA GIRL: Did we bargain at all for a basket?

ESKIMO: No, I hadn't a notion to ask it.

COWBOY: Who could have suspected?

GODDESS: Who would have expected?

ALL: A bolt-from-the-blue, blooming basket!

MARTIAN: Take me to your May basket! (WESTERN UNION MESSENGER *runs in, blowing whistle.*)

MESSENGER: Western Union. Western Union May basket. Sign here, please. (MARTIAN *signs pad. All step back, as* WALKING MAY BASKET *enters and stands center.*)

MARTIAN (*Kneeling and holding up his arms*): All hail the May
  basket. May baskets have taken over the Earth.

ALL:

> Surprise! Surprise!
>
> Out of the blue came a basket.
>
> A flowering bower of a basket,
>
> A basket romantic,
>
> A basket gigantic,
>
> The basket to end all May baskets.

WALKING MAY BASKET (*Bursting out*): Surprise! Surprise!
  (*She throws paper flowers*) Happy May Day. (*Curtain*)

GIRL NARRATOR (*Coming to front of stage with* BOY NARRATOR):
  By now, you have undoubtedly received our message—

BOY NARRATOR: Be it ever so humble, there's no basket like
  a May basket. Or—

GIRL NARRATOR: One good May basket deserves another.

BOY NARRATOR: But, what if your town doesn't celebrate
  May Day in this way?

GIRL NARRATOR: Then you can be a committee of one to
  change things. Leave a May basket at the home of a
  friend.

BOY NARRATOR: And who knows? By next May, you may
  have started a whole new thing.

GIRL NARRATOR: A May basket thing. May baskets are con-
  tagious. May baskets have a way of spreading. Now it's
  time for everybody to go out and find a doorstep for a de-
  serving May basket.

BOY NARRATOR: There's no better way to coax a winter
  door open. So long . . . (*He turns to go,* GIRL NARRATOR
  reaches behind curtain, brings out basket which she hands to BOY,
  then runs off left. BOY *steps forward, smiling.*) Just wait till she
  gets home! I left her a May basket with a hundred marbles—all aggies! (*He bows and exits right.*)

THE END

The Wild Rabbit Chase

Characters

SAM JONES
TAG-ALONG JONES, *his younger brother*
THREE BOYS
MOTHER RABBIT
BUNNY TWINS
JACK RABBIT
CANE-CUTTER RABBIT
ARCTIC HARE
WHITE RABBIT
MARCH HARE
POOKA
PETER RABBIT
FLOPSY
MOPSY
COTTONTAIL
MAGICIAN'S RABBIT
EASTER RABBIT
PROPERTY BOYS

BEFORE RISE: SAM JONES, *accompanied by* THREE BOYS, *enters right, in front of the curtain. They wear baseball uniforms, and carry bat, ball, gloves.*

SAM (*Looking back over his shoulder*): Hurry up. My little

brother is on my trail again. He's harder to shake than a bloodhound.

1st Boy: Tag-Along again? We don't want that little squirt butting in.

Tag-Along (*Calling from offstage*): Sam? Where are you, Sam?

Sam: Sh-h-h. Pretend you didn't hear him. (Tag-Along *enters right, catching up with* Sam, *and pulling his arm.*)

Tag-Along: So this is where you are! You're harder to find than a bank robber at the policemen's ball. Well—can I play ball today? Can I? Can I? Can I?

Sam: Quit nagging. Some other time, Tag-Along.

1st Boy: Yeah, like the next time the moon is blue.

2nd Boy: I know—come back on June 31st.

3rd Boy: Better still—don't call us. We'll call you.

Tag-Along: Today, Sam. Today. You promised today.

1st Boy: You didn't promise him, did you, Sam?

Sam (*Sheepishly*): Yes. I promised him. A sacred promise.

2nd Boy: A sacred promise. The worst kind.

3rd Boy: Yeah. A sacred promise is absolutely airtight and unbreakable.

Sam: I know. He brought me breakfast in bed. Then he cleaned my room, and shined my shoes. I had to do something for him.

Tag-Along: Oh, great! Then I can play with you? Can I play first base? Can I catch? Can I be first at bat? Can I? Can I? Can I?

3rd Boy: Oh, no. If he plays, I quit.

1st *and* 2nd Boys: Me, too. (*They start to cross left.* Sam *calls them back.*)

Sam: Wait, you guys. (*To* Tag-Along) See what you did? If you play, we'll lose the game for sure. I told you before— you're too small, too slow, and too dumb. (*He pulls visor on* Tag-Along's *hat over his eyes.*)

Tag-Along (*Pulling his cap up*): But you made a sacred

promise. If you break it, lightning could strike you. I don't want lightning to strike you, Sam.

SAM: I know. Hey—I have an idea. Come here, you guys. (SAM *and* BOYS *go into a huddle*) I know how to keep Tag-Along very busy until dinner time and yet not break my promise. Have you heard of a wild goose chase?

BOYS: Sure.

SAM: Well, this is a wild *rabbit* chase. Get this. (*To* TAG-ALONG) Tag-Along, old sport, I'll let you play ball with us on one condition.

TAG-ALONG (*Eagerly*): What, Sam?

SAM: You know how baseball players have to train with special diets? Well, we can't win this season without lots of eggs.

TAG-ALONG: I'll get you eggs, Sam.

SAM: Wait. We need special eggs, with all kinds of vitamins and minerals and stuff. You have to get us one dozen Gobi Desert Rainbow Eggs before sundown.

TAG-ALONG: Gobi Desert Rainbow Eggs?

SAM: Gobi Desert Rainbow Eggs. Right, you guys?

BOYS: Right, Sam.

SAM: And do you know the only place in the world you can get those eggs?

TAG-ALONG: Where, Sam?

SAM: From the Easter Rabbit. (*To* BOYS) Let's get to the field before somebody else does. (SAM *and* BOYS *start off left*)

TAG-ALONG: But, Sam—where will I find the Easter Rabbit?

SAM (*Looking back*): Look in the bushes—in the tall grass.

TAG-ALONG: But, Sam—how do I catch the Easter Rabbit?

SAM (*Laughing*): Put salt on his tail. (BOYS *laugh and punch* SAM *gleefully as they exit.* TAG-ALONG *stands center, deep in thought.*)

TAG-ALONG: Salt? Salt on his tail? (*He crosses left and calls off.*) Hey, Sam, what kind of salt—plain, or iodized? (*He runs off right, as curtains open.*)

* * *

SETTING: *A forest. A large tree is left; rocky hill with cave, center; blue sky backdrop, bushes at right, and border of tall grass center, across stage.*

AT RISE: TAG-ALONG *crawls in on his hands and knees. A small butterfly net is stuck in his belt, and a saltshaker is in his back pocket.*

TAG-ALONG (*Crawling to center*): Here, bunny, bunny, bunny. Here, bunny. Here's some tall grass. Now, how do I get the Easter Rabbit to come out? (*He stands up, takes out butterfly net and saltshaker, and whistles, then pokes through tall grass with net.* MOTHER RABBIT *hops out furiously and leaps at* TAG-ALONG, *who backs away.* BUNNY TWINS *hop out and watch.*)

MOTHER RABBIT: How dare you! If I've told you owls once, I've told you a hundred times, leave us alone!

TAG-ALONG: Please don't hit me. I'm not an owl. I'm a boy. I was looking for the Easter Rabbit. Are you the Easter Rabbit?

MOTHER RABBIT: A boy? Oh, so you are. The way you swooped, I thought you must be an owl. You thought I was the Easter Rabbit? How flattering. Isn't that flattering, my dears?

TWINS (*Giggling*): We're merely cottontails. Common cottontails.

MOTHER RABBIT: Those are my offspring—the last two to leave the nest. I'm sorry I hopped on you, but you were destroying my nest, and I've just finished lining it with my winter fur.

TAG-ALONG: I'm sorry. Maybe I can help you fix it up. Where is it?

MOTHER RABBIT: Right in front of your nose, in the tall grass. It's our home. Never mind, boy, you really didn't disturb the nest too much. I'll just line it with cool leaves

—that's much better for spring anyway. It isn't as fine as the Easter Rabbit's warren, but we call it home.

TAG-ALONG: Do you know the Easter Rabbit personally? Please help me find him. It's urgent.

MOTHER RABBIT: Why, of course. We'll send him a rabbit-gram. Ready, children?

TWINS: Ready, Mother. (*With their feet, they thump in rhythm, pause briefly to listen, then thump again.*)

MOTHER RABBIT: This is how rabbits communicate. You'd be surprised how far the sound travels. Ah, somebody's coming. (JACK RABBIT *bounds in, from left.* TAG-ALONG *extends his hand.*)

TAG-ALONG: Easter Rabbit? Am I glad to meet you!

1ST TWIN: That's not the Easter Rabbit.

2ND TWIN: That's only Jack Rabbit. A common jack rabbit.

JACK RABBIT: That's true, son. I'm not the Easter Rabbit, but I can help you find him. My ears are tingling right now. Somebunny's sending a message from down South. The Easter Rabbit is down there, looking over the sugar cane for candy eggs. Look before you leap, now, son. We're on our way. (*Curtains close as* JACK RABBIT, *followed by* TAG-ALONG, *runs off left. Down right,* PROPERTY BOYS *put hollow log and sign,* MARSHCANE SWAMP. JACK RABBIT *bounds in left, followed by* TAG-ALONG, *panting and staggering.*)

JACK RABBIT: Hurry up! You're slower than a turtle in a molasses vat.

TAG-ALONG: I can't help it. I can't leap as fast as you can.

JACK RABBIT: Why, there's nothing whatever to it. Just coil yourself in a ball, and then uncoil—like a rattlesnake on a cactus burr. See? (*He demonstrates.*) I can cover twenty feet at a bound.

TAG-ALONG: Please, can't we rest?

JACK RABBIT: That's the trouble with you humans. You rest too much. Never mind, son. We're here—Marshcane

Swamp. (*He thumps his foot.*) Hey, down there. Swim up and thump howdy. (CANE-CUTTER RABBIT *pokes his head up over hollow log. He wears diving mask and snorkel.*)

TAG-ALONG: The Easter Rabbit! I didn't know you could swim.

CANE-CUTTER: Sure 'nough, I can swim. Doesn't every-bunny? (*He sits on log, and holds out waterlily pad.*) Would y'all care to join me in a nibble of waterlily pad?

TAG-ALONG: No thanks, Mr. Easter Rabbit.

CANE-CUTTER: Easter Rabbit? Why, upon my ears, I'm not the Easter Rabbit. I'm just little old Cane-Cutter, the swamp rabbit. The Easter Rabbit came through here fifteen minutes ago, heading north. Can you swim, boy?

TAG-ALONG: Well, yes, but—

CANE-CUTTER: No buts. You haven't any time for buts. All aboard, boy. We'll head for the North Pole, up the Mis-sissippi and swamp-to-swamp until we come to Hudson Bay.

TAG-ALONG: You rabbits don't waste any time, do you?

JACK RABBIT: That's because it's leap year, son. Goodbye— I'm off for the prairies to race the antelope. (*He hops off right.* CANE-CUTTER *and* TAG-ALONG *pantomime swimming across stage apron, left, as* PROPERTY BOYS *remove log and sign and slide on an igloo, with striped pole and banner reading,* NORTH POLE.)

CANE-CUTTER: Br-r-r-r. Here we are. Just thump on the igloo yonder. Br-r-r. I'd like to stay and chew the fat with the Easter Rabbit, but it's too cold for a swamp rabbit. Y'all come down and visit me in the marsh sometime, you hear?

TAG-ALONG (*Waving as* CANE-CUTTER *swims right and exits*): I will, Cane-Cutter. Thanks a lot. (*He stamps his foot and then listens. He stamps again.*) Hello. Anybody in there? Hello. (ARCTIC HARE *cautiously pokes his head out of igloo, then starts to pull back, but not before* TAG-ALONG *spies him and grabs hold of his ears.*) Got you! Come out, please, Mr. Easter Rabbit.

ARCTIC HARE (*Furiously*): Let go. Let go, I say!

TAG-ALONG: But I'm only holding you by the ears. I thought that was the proper way to hold a rabbit. (*He lets go, and* ARCTIC HARE *promptly pulls* TAG-ALONG's *ears.*) Ow! Let go!

ARCTIC HARE: Do you like it, Short Ears? Hurts, doesn't it? Think how much it hurts me when you dangle me by my ears.

TAG-ALONG (*Rubbing his ears*): I never thought of it that way before.

ARCTIC HARE: You will the next time you pick up a rabbit. If you must hold a rabbit, hold him by the scruff of the neck. Better still, don't hold us at all. It offends our dignity. Now then, Short Ears, let's not bandy words. He isn't here.

TAG-ALONG: You mean, you are not the Easter Rabbit?

ARCTIC HARE: I never was and never will be. He left here five minutes ago. News travels fast among rabbits.

TAG-ALONG: Missed him again. Where in the world is he?

ARCTIC HARE: That's the point. He's not in the world now. He's out of this world now.

TAG-ALONG: Then where will I find him? It's getting dark already.

ARCTIC HARE: It's time for the midnight sun to set. Time for me to go back into my snow burrow. I'm sorry I can't help you, Short Ears. Find an unreal rabbit. That's it. An unreal rabbit. (*He wiggles back into igloo, waving to* TAG-ALONG *as he disappears.*) Ta-ta. (*Lights dim,* TAG-ALONG *sits disconsolately.* PROPERTY BOYS *enter and remove igloo.*)

TAG-ALONG: I'll never find the Easter Rabbit. And how am I going to get home from the North Pole in time for dinner? I wonder if there's a bus stop at the North Pole. What a topsy-turvy day! Find an unreal rabbit. I don't know any unreal rabbits. This is almost as bad as Alice in Wonderland.

WHITE RABBIT (*Offstage*): Oh, my ears and whiskers!

TAG-ALONG: Now I'm hearing things. All I said was "Alice in Wonderland." (WHITE RABBIT, *carrying fan, enters left, pauses to fan himself, then looks* TAG-ALONG *over.*)

WHITE RABBIT: Oh, there you are, my dear. Come along, Alice. We shall be late. (*He takes* TAG-ALONG *by hand and pulls him through curtain. Curtain opens, disclosing same forest, but set pieces have been turned around, so that tree, border and bushes are painted pink, blue and yellow. Cave is silver, with glitter, and has door marked,* E. RABBIT, BY APPOINTMENT ONLY. *There is a rainbow on backdrop.*)

TAG-ALONG: Hey, just a minute. I am not Alice.

WHITE RABBIT (*Peering at* TAG-ALONG): Ah, just so. I see that now. I'm very nearsighted, you know. Which character are you, then?

TAG-ALONG: I'm not a character. I'm a real person. At least I was a few minutes ago. Where on earth are we?

WHITE RABBIT: Nowhere on earth at all. We are in the realm of the imagination—another part of the forest. It's the place where rabbits out of fables and stories and hats meet and mingle. (*He calls out.*) Come out and see this. A real person has come to call. (MARCH HARE, POOKA, PETER RABBIT *and* MAGICIAN'S RABBIT *hop out from behind tree and bushes.*)

MARCH HARE (*Poking* TAG-ALONG): Real, is he? He seems solid enough. Here, person. Riddle me this—Hare today, gone tomorrow. Mad as a hatter, who am I?

TAG-ALONG: The March Hare—right?

PETER (*Coming forward*): We shouldn't be standing here, out in the open like this. He might be Mr. McGregor. He might have a big, long rake.

TAG-ALONG: Hello, Peter Rabbit. I'm not Mr. McGregor, and I don't have a rake.

PETER: Good. In that case (*Turning to bushes*), you can come out now, girls. (FLOPSY, MOPSY *and* COTTONTAIL *scamper down right.*)

FLOPSY, MOPSY *and* COTTONTAIL (*Wiggling their noses*): Pleased to meet you, person.

POOKA: Top of the day to ye, me bucko. I happen to be a Pooka from Kildare. I change me shape at the drop of a hat. Would ye like to see my imitation of a lion? It frightened all the kings of Ireland once. (*He drops to all fours and roars feebly.*) How was that? Did I sound like a lion?

TAG-ALONG (*Laughing*): No. You sounded like a rabbit growling.

MAGICIAN'S RABBIT: Ha! See that, Pooka? I keep telling him to drop his act and be my assistant—but those Pookas have a one-trick mind. Look here. How would you like me to pull a magician out of the hat?

TAG-ALONG: Some other time, honestly. Right now, I have to find the Easter Rabbit before sundown.

WHITE RABBIT: The Easter Rabbit? Why didn't you say so?

MARCH HARE: He's dyeing eggs in his cave. Knock twice and state your business.

MAGICIAN'S RABBIT: But when he comes out, shake salt on his tail quickly. He's faster than the wind. He never stays in the same place once. (TAG-ALONG *crosses to cave timidly.*)

PETER: Go ahead. He won't bite.

FLOPSY, MOPSY, *and* COTTONTAIL: Knock twice. Once and once. That's twice. (TAG-ALONG *knocks twice timidly.* EASTER RABBIT *pops head out.*)

EASTER RABBIT: E. Rabbit speaking. State your business.

TAG-ALONG (*Startled*): Um. Well. It's about baseball.

EASTER RABBIT: I never use baseballs. I only dye eggs. Goodbye. (*He pops back in again.*)

TAG-ALONG: Oh, please, please, Easter Rabbit—(EASTER RABBIT *leaps out and runs down left.* TAG-ALONG *chases him, shaking saltshaker.*)

EASTER RABBIT: Who put salt on my tail? Who dares to stop the Easter Rabbit on his swift appointed rounds?

TAG-ALONG: I did. Please, Mr. Easter Rabbit. I must have your help. You see, I want to play baseball more than anything in the world, but my brother won't let me play with him. He says I'm too short, too slow and too dumb.

MARCH HARE: Hm-m-m. That reminds me of what I used to tell a certain tortoise . . .

EASTER RABBIT: But what does baseball have to do with me?

TAG-ALONG: My brother said I could play baseball with him if I brought him a dozen Gobi Desert Rainbow Eggs from the Easter Rabbit before sundown. Please, sir, may I have a dozen Gobi Desert Rainbow Eggs?

EASTER RABBIT: Gobi Desert Rainbow Eggs?

ALL: Gobi Desert Rainbow Eggs!

EASTER RABBIT: I'd be more than happy to give you *two* dozen Gobi Desert Rainbow Eggs—

TAG-ALONG: Oh, thank you.

EASTER RABBIT: Except for one small fact. I've never heard of them.

TAG-ALONG: Oh, no!

EASTER RABBIT: And neither has anyone else. Somebody is pulling your ear—or in your case, your leg. Somebody has sent you on a wild rabbit chase.

ALL (*Ad lib*): Tsk, tsk. Oh, no! A wild rabbit chase! (*Etc.*)

TAG-ALONG (*Crossing slowly center, then sadly*): I've been to the four corners of the earth today, and then some. I've swum up rivers, and leaped boulders, and when I finally found the Easter Rabbit, I also found something I knew in my heart all along. I really am too small, too slow, and too dumb. Especially too dumb. (*He buries face in hands.*)

EASTER RABBIT: Nonsense, child. You may be small, but time will take care of that. As for being too slow and too dumb, why, just consider the pluck, daring and cleverness, not to mention the incredible swiftness, it took to find and hold the Easter Rabbit. I'm most impressed. In fact, I am so impressed that I'll tell you what I'm going to do.

ALL: Tell us what you're going to do.

EASTER RABBIT: I'm going to make it possible for you to play baseball. You will have such a remarkable talent that your brother will beg you on bended knee to join his team. I am going to whisper to you the eternal and well-guarded Secret of the Hare.

ALL: Yes, yes. Tell him the Secret of the Hare.

EASTER RABBIT: Listen well. I can repeat it but once. (TAG-ALONG *cups his hand to his ear.* EASTER RABBIT *bends over and whispers. Others put their hands to their mouths and make whispering sounds also.*)

TAG-ALONG (*Suspiciously*): No fooling? (EASTER RABBIT *nods.*) Imagine that! The Secret of the Hare! (*Quick curtain.* SAM JONES *and* THREE BOYS *enter left in front of curtain, then cross right.*)

1ST BOY: So we lost the game, Sam. It's only one game. It's early in the season. We'll make it up.

2ND BOY: Aw, don't be angry.

3RD BOY: Yeah, don't be angry.

SAM (*Loudly*): Angry? I'm not angry. I'm just wondering which team you were playing for—our side or the other team.

1ST BOY: All right. We were a little slow.

SAM: Slow? Slow? I could have gotten better running from Girl Scouts with burlap sacks tied over them. (TAG-ALONG *bounds in, zooms back and forth across stage, and exits.*)

SAM: Wow! Who was that?

1ST BOY: He ran so fast, his face was a blur.

2ND BOY: I think he broke the sound barrier.

3RD BOY: Boy, could a guy like that run bases!

SAM: Could he ever! (TAG-ALONG *zooms back on, pausing briefly as* SAM *calls out to him.*) Hey, Speedy!

TAG-ALONG (*Not turning around*): Were you speaking to me?

SAM (*Crossing to him*): I sure was. I was wondering—are you on anybody's baseball team around here? Because if you aren't, we sure could use a runner like you. Want to join us?

TAG-ALONG (*Still not turning*): Nope. I don't think so. If you knew who I was, you wouldn't want me.

SAM: Of course I would. I don't care what your name is. All I care about is that you're the fastest thing on two legs I ever saw. Please—join up with us.

TAG-ALONG: Ask me on bended knee, old sport.

SAM: On bended knee. Now just a minute—

1ST BOY (*Nudging* SAM): Go on.

2ND BOY: Don't let him get away, Sam.

3RD BOY: Somebody else will snap him up, Sam. (TAG-ALONG *begins to saunter off.*)

BOYS: He's leaving, Sam.

SAM: Aw. This is goofy, but all right. (*He goes down on one knee.*) Will you play on our team?

TAG-ALONG: Say, "Pretty please with sugar on it."

SAM: Aw.

BOYS: Sam!

SAM: Pretty please with sugar on it.

TAG-ALONG: You won't change your mind when I turn around?

SAM: I promise I won't.

TAG-ALONG (*Raising his hand*): Sacred promise?

SAM (*Raising his hand*): Sacred promise.

TAG-ALONG: If I join, will you serve me orange juice and pancakes in bed and clean my room and shine my shoes?

SAM: Anything. Anything, as long as you stay with us, Speedy.

TAG-ALONG: Well, I don't know . . .

ALL: *Please.*

TAG-ALONG: O.K. It's a deal. (*He turns around, grins broadly.*)

ALL: Tag-Along!

TAG-ALONG: There's been a slight change in the lineup. It's "Speedy" now.

SAM: But how—?

TAG-ALONG: Don't ask. Because I won't tell you. Or maybe I will. It was all because of that omelet.

ALL: Omelet?

TAG-ALONG: Sure. The one I scrambled with all those nice, big Gobi Desert Rainbow Eggs. (*He pushes them off, laughing.*) Come on, team. Play ball! (*They exit right.*)

THE END

Pandora's Perilous Predicament

Characters

PANDORA PINKERTON
GRACIE GREENFIELD
GAX ⎫
TIMIX ⎭ *smugglers from outer space*
DETECTOR
CHIEF SKY-WATCHER
PRETZEL BIRD
COPYCAT
SCREAMING MIMI
RAYDOX
HELIX
HELICA
MASTER ROBOT
HOUSEHOLD ROBOT
CITIZENS OF ULTIMA
ANTENNA MUFF SALESMAN
WING WAX SALESMAN

SCENE 1

SETTING: *City park. Two park benches are placed in front of curtain, down right and left. Small sign reads:* CITY PARK: PLEASE KEEP OFF THE GRASS. *This scene is played before the curtain.*

BEFORE CURTAIN: GAX, *in sorcerer's hat and robe, tiptoes onstage through center opening in curtain. He carries silver hoop and glit-*

tery flashlight-shaped device. He beckons offstage and TIMIX *enters through curtain, carrying coins.* GAX *places hoop at center, on ground, while* TIMIX *places coins on ground, in a line leading up to hoop.* GAX *places dollar bill in hoop, then dusts off his hands and beckons to* TIMIX. *They hide behind bench down left. In a moment,* PANDORA *and* GRACIE *enter right.*

PANDORA (*Skipping ahead*): What a wonderful day! I hope something amazing and astonishing and truly fantastic happens to me.

GRACIE: Oh, I don't. I just want a nice, ordinary day. Surprises make me nervous, Pandora.

PANDORA (*Spying penny*): A penny! (*Recites*)
  See a penny and pick it up.
  All the day you'll have good luck.

GRACIE: Pandora, there's another rhyme:
  See a penny. Let it lie.
  Then bad luck will pass you by.

PANDORA (*Following trail of coins*): My goodness. There's a treasure here. (*As she picks up coins*) A nickel. A dime. A quarter!

GRACIE: It's a joke. Nobody's that careless. You know, Pandora, the trouble with you is—you don't look before you leap.

PANDORA: You know, Gracie, the trouble with you is—you always tell me what the trouble is with me. O-ho—somebody left a hoop! (*Going to hoop*) And there's a dollar bill inside the hoop. Finders keepers.

GRACIE: Pandora! Look before you leap. It might be a trap.

PANDORA (*Stepping into hoop*): How can a little old hoop be a trap? (GAX *peers over bench, then points flashlight at hoop. There is sound of loud buzzing. Surprised,* PANDORA *starts to reach out to* GRACIE, *then stops suddenly, as if she has touched an invisible wall.* PANDORA *mouths "help."*)

GRACIE (*Tearfully*): Oh, Pandora! It *is* a trap! (GRACIE *hurries to hoop and moves her hands around air above hoop as if touching invisible dome which walls off* PANDORA.) I can't hear you! It's as if you were in an invisible glass jar. (PANDORA *begins to cry.*) I'll get a policeman. Don't go away. (GRACIE *runs off right. As she exits,* GAX *and* TIMIX *come out from behind bench.* GAX *swaggers over to hoop.*)

GAX (*Boastfully*): I caught one. A real live human being. That makes me the number one smuggler from outer space. Right, Timix?

TIMIX: We shouldn't take a human being, Gax. It's against the galaxy law. The Sky-Watchers will get us.

GAX: Sky-Watchers—bah. I'm quicker, sneakier and crook-eder than all the Sky-Watchers put together. (*He waves at* PANDORA, *who is still crying.*) Greetings, my pet. You're going to make me a rich smuggler.

TIMIX: Where in the universe are we going to set up our pet shop?

GAX: We're going to the last planet, on the last spiral of the farthest arm of the galaxy.

TIMIX: You mean the planet Ultima?

GAX: I mean the planet Ultima, the last stop in the known universe. They'll never find us there. Now, push the hoop into the space buggy. (TIMIX *bends and pushes hoop left.* PANDORA *cowers inside, walking with hoop.*)

TIMIX: Are we going faster than light?

GAX: Too slow. We're going faster than thought. There's nothing faster than that. (*They exit left.* DETECTOR *enters right. He holds out long, silver wand which chimes. He is followed by* CHIEF SKY-WATCHER. *They wear long silver capes, under which are police uniforms. Under their silver hoods are police caps. As* DETECTOR *crosses center, wand begins to chime rapidly. He stops the chiming.*)

DETECTOR: Here . . . here, Chief Sky-Watcher. There was an illegal human hoop-trap right here. (*Points to center*)

SKY-WATCHER: Gax, again. He's broken the strictest law in the galaxy. He's captured an intelligent species.

DETECTOR: That means imprisonment for the rest of his unnatural life.

SKY-WATCHER: When I get my hands on Gax, I'll put him away on a small cold planet somewhere north of nowhere. With pleasure!

DETECTOR (*As wand begins to chime rapidly*): Sir. A human child is approaching.

SKY-WATCHER: Scan her mind. (DETECTOR *points wand toward exit right.*)

DETECTOR: She is looking for a policeman.

SKY-WATCHER: Then we shall appear to her as policemen. (*They remove robes and hoods, revealing police uniforms.* GRACIE *enters and sees* SKY-WATCHER *and* DETECTOR. *She runs over to them.*)

GRACIE: Help! Police! Help!

SKY-WATCHER: May I be of service, miss?

GRACIE (*Pointing center*): A trap . . . why, it's gone. And Pandora's gone, too. It was right there—a girl-eating trap!

DETECTOR: Was the trap a hoop kind-of-a-thing?

GRACIE: That's the kind-of-a-thing it was.

SKY-WATCHER: And did it catch a human being?

GRACIE: Yes, sir. My friend, Pandora. She never looks before she leaps, and now she's gone. (*She begins to sob.*)

SKY-WATCHER: Please don't get upset. We'll find her.

DETECTOR: You just go along home. Before you can say "Declination is equivalent to longitude," we'll have Pandora leaping back to you. Off with you now. (GRACIE, *wiping her eyes, exits right.*)

SKY-WATCHER: This is a tough one to solve, Detector. Now where would I go if I were Gax? I'd go to the last place in the universe anyone would think of.

DETECTOR: The last place in the universe is the planet Ultima, sir.

SKY-WATCHER: The planet Ultima! Of course. Good thinking, Detector. You have lived up to the motto of the Royal Cosmic Mounted Sky-Watchers.

DETECTOR *and* SKY-WATCHER (*Hands on hearts*): We Always Get Our Creature!

SKY-WATCHER: To the planet Ultima. Tally ho-ho-ho. (*They exit left, taking their robes. As benches and sign are removed, curtains open.*)

* * *

SCENE 2

SETTING: *Marketplace of Ultimate City, on the planet Ultima. Backdrop shows a large red sun and a small yellow sun, jagged blue mountains and a city of mushroom-shaped buildings. There is a gaudy awning with sign proclaiming:* ULTIMATE CITY PUBLIC MARKETPLACE. *There are several tables under awning.*

AT RISE: ANTENNA MUFF SALESMAN *and* WING WAX SALESMAN *stand behind two of the tables.* CITIZENS OF ULTIMA, *wearing polka-dot tunics, small butterfly wings and caps with antennas, enter right and left, gathering before tables.*

1ST CITIZEN (*Touching antennas with* 2ND CITIZEN): Happy double sunrise, Citizen.

2ND CITIZEN (*Nodding*): And to you, Citizen. May both of our suns shine on your antennas all the day.

ANTENNA MUFF SALESMAN: Citizens, attention. Are your antennas cold and tingly? (*To* 1ST CITIZEN) How about your antennas, Citizen? I have some hand-knit antenna muffs. (*Shows them*) Nice, eh? Very stylish, Citizen. (1ST CITIZEN *shakes his head and exits left.* ANTENNA MUFF SALESMAN *follows him, holding out handful of muffs*) Wait. You haven't even looked at them. Two shells a pair. Only two shells. (*Exits*)

WING WAX SALESMAN (*To* 2ND CITIZEN): Say, Citizen. You have a fine pair of wings there. (2ND CITIZEN *looks at his wings proudly.*) I'll bet you can do thirty miles an hour in a good stiff breeze. (2ND CITIZEN *nods.*) How'd you like to do fifty miles an hour? I just happen to have here a jar of Winixes Wonderful Wing Wax. One application of Winixes Wonderful Wing Wax and you'll zoom off like a Zinglebird. (2ND CITIZEN *starts to exit right.* WING WAX SALESMAN *follows, holding out jar of wax.*) Wait. I'll give you a free trial. Wait . . . (*They exit.* GAX *enters, bringing with him* PRETZEL BIRD, COPYCAT, SCREAMING MIMI *and* PANDORA, *chained together.* TIMIX *brings up rear, urging them on with feather duster.*)

GAX: Right here, Timix. The Public Market of Ultimate City. (*Calling to* CITIZENS) Step right up, folks. You'll never again see creatures like these. Pets for sale. Pets from here, there and absolutely everywhere. (CITIZENS *gather in front of* GAX. RAYDOX *enters right;* HELIX *and* HELICA *from left.*)

3RD CITIZEN: What kind of animals are those, stranger?

GAX: I'm glad you asked me that, Citizen. You see before you the rare and exotic Pretzel Bird from Pegasus. Go into your act, Pretzel Bird. (TIMIX *tickles* PRETZEL BIRD *with feather duster.* PRETZEL BIRD *does several contortions, then twists its arms and legs together and rolls into a ball.* CITIZENS *laugh and stamp their feet approvingly*)

RAYDOX (*Sourly*): Is that all it can do?

GAX: Isn't that enough? However, if you don't like birds, how about a never-before-seen Copycat from Vega? (*To* HELICA) Here, little girl. Do a dance for the Copycat.

HELICA: A dance? (*To* HELIX) May I, Father?

HELIX: Go ahead, child. You might like the Copycat for a pet. I promised you any pet you wanted. (HELICA *does short dance.* COPYCAT *mimes her dance steps. All applaud and stamp their feet.*)

RAYDOX (*Yawning*): What a bore!

GAX: Drat! (*In a hiss, to* RAYDOX) Go away, boy. You're spoiling my pitch.

RAYDOX (*Loudly*): You call these pets? They're old stuff.

GAX (*Quickly*): Here, folks. Over here is a brand-new animal, brought to you at great expense from the constellation Mensa. You've never heard a sound like this before. (TIMIX *tickles* SCREAMING MIMI. *She makes loud hooting sound.* CITIZENS *cover their ears*) There you are, folks. Screaming Mimi—the living burglar alarm.

RAYDOX: All that old thing does is make noise. I want to see something different.

GAX (*Laughing falsely*): Bless his little antennas. He wants to see something different. (*To* RAYDOX, *with a sneer*) How about a boy-eating Boojum from Bootes? (*He claps his hands.*) Well, Citizens, I have saved the best until the last. (TIMIX *tickles* PANDORA, *so that she steps forward.*) Here she is, folks. A human being from the planet Earth.

4TH CITIZEN: Earth? Never heard of it.

HELICA: Oh, she's sweet. What nice long fur. (*She strokes* PANDORA'*s hair.*) Does she do tricks?

GAX: Does she do tricks! Why, she's almost intelligent. Ah-ha. I said "almost" intelligent.

PANDORA (*Indignantly*): I'm not "almost" intelligent. I'm really, truly intelligent. I want to go home. (CITIZENS *murmur in awe.*)

HELIX: She can speak! What a remarkable animal! How can she speak if she cannot reason?

GAX: That's a very good question, Citizen. How can she speak if she cannot reason, Timix?

TIMIX: Uh—ventriloquism?

GAX: Right. Ventriloquism.

RAYDOX: I want her. Give me the human being. How much?

HELICA: Oh, Father. This is the pet I want most of all. Please, may I have her?

HELIX: Certainly. She appears to be clean and gentle.

GAX: You both want her?

RAYDOX *and* HELIX: Yes!

GAX (*To* TIMIX): This is better than I had hoped. (*To* HELIX) We'll have to auction her off. (*He takes out small gavel.*) Oyez, oyez, the auction of the human being is now open. Do I hear a bid of zog-zog shells?

5TH CITIZEN: Zog-zog shells.

RAYDOX: Zog-zog-og shells.

5TH CITIZEN: That lets me out. (*He exits down right with other* CITIZENS, *leaving behind* RAYDOX, HELIX, *and* HELICA.)

HELIX: Zog-zog-tog shells.

RAYDOX: Zog-zog-throg.

HELIX: Zog-zog-fog.

RAYDOX: Zog-zog-frog shells. (HELIX *pauses.*)

GAX: Zog-zog-frog shells. Do I hear zog-zog-sog?

HELICA: *Please,* Father.

HELIX: That's a lot of shells, Helica.

GAX: Going . . . going . . .

HELIX: Zog-zog-sog shells.

RAYDOX: That's all I have. I can't bid any more.

GAX (*Grinning*): Aw, too bad. (*Quickly*) Going, going, gone to the fine, upstanding Citizen with zog-zog-sog shells. (HELIX *hands him bag.* RAYDOX *crosses down right, watching.* GAX *unchains* PANDORA, *and fastens leash to her wrist. He gives other end to* HELICA) There you are. You'll be the only citizen on the block with your own human being.

HELICA (*Pulling leash gently*): Come on, little human. I think I'll name you Duk-Duk. Come, Duk-Duk.

PANDORA: My name is Pandora. I won't answer to Duk-Duk. (*She stands firmly.*)

HELIX (*Laughing*): Extraordinary! You'd better call her Pandora, my dear. I wonder how she does that ventriloquism?

HELICA: All right then, Pandora. Come along. (*They exit left,* PANDORA *following reluctantly.* RAYDOX *follows them across stage.*)

GAX (*To* RAYDOX): Hey, you. Where do you think you're going?

RAYDOX: None of your business. But if it were your business I'd tell you this: I saw that creature first. Finders keepers. Nobody, but nobody, puts anything over on Raydox. (*He exits left.*)

TIMIX: You ought to go after him, Gax. He's up to no good.

GAX: But he's right, Timix. It is none of my business. My business is to get my business off this planet before some snoopy Sky-Watcher catches me. Come on! (*Curtains close.* MASTER ROBOT *enters stiffly, in front of curtain. He carries sign reading,* THE HOME OF THE HELIX FAMILY. PLEASE WIPE YOUR WINGS BEFORE FLYING IN. MASTER ROBOT *rotates dish antenna on top of his head, as if listening, then sets sign on floor.*)

MASTER ROBOT: Ah. I sense that the child Helica is flying home. (*Calls*) Attention, Household Robot. (*He listens, then calls again, louder.*) Attention, Household Robot. Yoo-hoo, Household Robot! (HOUSEHOLD ROBOT *glides in, dragging broom and reading avidly from computer punch card.*)

HOUSEHOLD ROBOT (*Without lifting eyes from card*): You hollered, Master Robot?

MASTER ROBOT: Take your eye sockets off that Popular Computer Romance card, Household. Prepare the room for the child Helica.

HOUSEHOLD ROBOT: It shall be done. (*She does not move.*)

MASTER ROBOT: It shall be done *now*. Or do you want me to put sand in your bearings again?

HOUSEHOLD ROBOT: Eek. Don't put sand in my bearings. Look—I'm working. (*She pushes blow-up chair onstage, then pushes in low table with exotic-looking plant on it. Then she sweeps in one spot rapidly and inefficiently.*)

MASTER ROBOT (*As he exits right*): I must remind my memory bank to send her in for a thousand-mile checkup. They just don't make robots the way they used to! (HELICA *enters, dragging* PANDORA *by leash.*)

HELICA: You may go now, Household.

HOUSEHOLD ROBOT: I-may-go-now. (*Glides away, dragging broom and reading computer card*) I-may-go-now. (*She exits.* PANDORA *sinks into chair and puts her head in her hands.*)

HELICA (*Jerking leash*): No, no, Pandora. Not on the chair. Pets must not sit in chairs.

PANDORA (*Rising, angrily*): I am not a pet. I am a person. At home I sit on chairs whenever I please.

HELICA: My cosmos, if I didn't know it was ventriloquism, I'd swear you could talk.

PANDORA: I *can* talk. I can also think.

HELICA: Sh-h-h. Don't say that. If you could think, you'd be intelligent. If you were intelligent, I'd have to send you back to your planet. That's the law.

PANDORA: But it's true. Why won't you believe me?

HELICA: Can you actually prove that you can think? Can you prove that you are intelligent?

PANDORA: I don't know. I never had to prove anything at home. How shall I prove that I am intelligent?

HELICA: Well, for instance, can you do zongles with your antennas?

PANDORA: I don't have any antennas. But if I did, I could probably do zongles.

HELICA: You could? Well, try this. Calculate the angle of flight when you must take off in a high wind with only one of your wings in working condition.

PANDORA: I don't have any wings, either.

HELICA: I'll make a bargain with you. I'll count up to zog.

If you haven't proved that you can think by then, I get to keep you forever and ever.

PANDORA: Oh, but that's not fair—

HELICA: Ready? I'm counting. Og, tog, throg, fog, frog, sog, slog, eetog, nog, zog . . .

PANDORA: Wait! Listen! I can prove that I can think. I can think in your language. Og and og are tog. Frog take away og leaves fog. Throg and frog and slog and nog are prime ogs. And listen to this: zog and og together equal zog-og.

HELICA (*Sighing*): My cosmos! You can do arithmetic. You *can* think.

PANDORA: Now, please take me back to my planet. Please.

HELICA: I suppose I have to. It's the law. Oh . . . I like you so much. If I let you off the leash, would you consider being my pet?

PANDORA: I'm sorry, Helica. People will never be pets. But, I'll be your friend.

HELICA: All right. You stay here. My father will find the Sky-Watcher. He'll find a way to return you to your planet. (*She hands leash to* PANDORA *and exits left, as* RAYDOX *sneaks in, center, carrying whip. He crosses to* PANDORA, *grabbing leash from her, and pulls her center.*)

RAYDOX: I have you! You're going to learn some new tricks, my pet! (*He flourishes whip, and pulls her through curtain, center.* HOUSEHOLD ROBOT *enters and removes table and chair. There is a brief interlude of electronic music, then curtains open on marketplace scene.* RAYDOX *and* PANDORA *stand center.* RAYDOX *addresses group of* CITIZENS.) Fellow Citizens. Come and see what I have brought at great expense for your entertainment. I have here a human animal. She's a regular circus. She prances, she dances. She jumps through hoops.

1ST CITIZEN: Here's a shell. Let's see her dance. (*Throws shell onto ground*)

RAYDOX (*Flicking whip; to* PANDORA): Dance! Dance, I say!

PANDORA (*Stubbornly*): I won't. No matter what you do, I won't dance one single step for you.

2ND CITIZEN: Why, the animal can answer back.

PANDORA (*Desperately*): I'm intelligent. Won't you believe me? Og and og are tog. Tog and tog are fog. (RAYDOX *puts his hand over her mouth.* SKY-WATCHER, *in his robe, followed by* HELIX *and* HELICA, *enters from left.*)

RAYDOX (*To* CITIZENS): It's only ventriloquism.

HELIX (*Pointing to* RAYDOX): There he is! (RAYDOX *turns, sees* SKY-WATCHER, *jerks leash and starts to run down right.*) Stop, thief! (CITIZENS *block his way. Two grab* RAYDOX *by antennas.*)

RAYDOX: Ow! Let go. You're hurting me!

SKY-WATCHER: Take him away. Take him away to a small, cold planet, somewhere north of nowhere. (CITIZENS *lead* RAYDOX *off right.*)

HELICA: You've found her. Please, Sky-Watcher, may she stay here?

SKY-WATCHER: No, child. She must return to her own planet. But she may help me capture the smuggler Gax, if she so chooses.

PANDORA: I'll do anything to help you catch him. Just tell me how.

SKY-WATCHER: We will return you to the day-before-yesterday. You see, Sky-Watchers can control time, as well as space. We will return you to the moment that Gax set his trap for you. We must catch him in the act of trapping you. Are you afraid?

PANDORA: A little. What if you don't catch him?

SKY-WATCHER: Then you will go back through all of this again. But we will be most careful, mark my word.

PANDORA: I'll—I'll help you.

SKY-WATCHER: Good. You have courage as well as intelligence. (*He waves his hand, as curtains close*) Back . . . back we go, to the day . . . before . . . yesterday. (*Curtains close.* SKY-WATCHER *and* DETECTOR *enter in front of curtains and place benches and sign as they were in Scene 1.* SKY-WATCHER *and* DETECTOR *hide behind bench, right.* GAX *enters, as before, with hoop and flashlight device. He beckons offstage and* TIMIX *enters, puts coins on floor. Both pace their actions double-time to appear to resemble a speeded-up movie.* GAX *puts dollar bill in hoop, dusts off his hands and beckons* TIMIX *to hide behind bench, left.* PANDORA *and* GRACIE *enter right.* PANDORA *skips ahead, picks up penny.* GRACIE *shakes her head.* PANDORA *picks up trail of coins.* GRACIE *shakes her head harder.* PANDORA *points to dollar bill in hoop.* GRACIE *tries to pull* PANDORA *back, but* PANDORA *enters hoop.* GAX *peers over bench, points his flashlight at hoop, and* PANDORA *tries to escape from invisible dome.* GRACIE *runs up to hoop, turns and runs off right.*)

GAX: I caught one. A real, live human being. (SKY-WATCHER *and* DETECTOR *jump from behind bench.*)

SKY-WATCHER: And we caught two. Two real, live smugglers. Let her go, Gax. (GAX *points flashlight at hoop. There is buzzing sound.* PANDORA *steps out of hoop.*)

PANDORA: Whew! I'm glad that's over.

TIMIX: I told you so, Gax, I told you the Sky-Watchers would get us.

SKY-WATCHER *and* DETECTOR: We Always Get Our Creature.

GAX: Are you taking us away?

SKY-WATCHER: Very far away. To a small, cold planet, somewhere north of nowhere. Up and away you go. Tally ho-ho-ho. (DETECTOR *prods* GAX *and* TIMIX *with wand. They exit left.* GRACIE *runs on right*)

GRACIE (*Crossing to* PANDORA): You're here! What happened, Pandora?

PANDORA: Well, you see, Gracie, it *was* a trap. A smuggler from outer space had me in a trap. He took me to a planet far out in the galaxy and he sold me as a pet. . . .

GRACIE: Pandora, you are too much. I never know when to believe you. Come down to earth.

PANDORA: Gladly, Gracie, gladly. I should have listened to you. I should have looked before I leaped.

GRACIE: It's about time you learned that lesson. By the way, what are you going to do with the money you found?

PANDORA: Oh, that. I hadn't thought about it.

GRACIE: Well, since those smugglers from outer space tried to make a pet of you, why don't you give the money to the S.P.C.A.?

PANDORA (*Seriously*): The Society for the Prevention of Cruelty to Animals. Not a bad idea. Not a bad idea at all! (*They exit right.*)

THE END

Snowflake

Characters

TWO NARRATORS, *a boy and a girl*
SPRING
SUMMER
AUTUMN
FROST KING
OLD MAN
OLD WOMAN
IVAN THE OLDER
BLACKSMITH'S WIFE
IVAN THE YOUNGER ⎫
OLGA   ⎬ *children*
MISCHA
KATYA   ⎭
SNOWFLAKE
VILLAGERS
DANCING SNOWFLAKES, *boys and girls*
TWO PROPERTY BOYS

TIME: *Long, long ago.*
SETTING: *A small clearing near a large forest in old Russia. There is a backdrop of sky, hills, and forest. At rear of stage, there is a row of fir trees, with two large trees center, and a thatched cottage at left.*
AT RISE: VILLAGERS, IVAN THE YOUNGER, OLGA, MISCHA, *and* KATYA *stand in tableau.* TWO NARRATORS, *wearing Rus-*

sian peasant costumes, enter, cross downstage, stand at one side and face audience.

1ST NARRATOR: Long, long ago in old Russia, in a far-off forest, there was a small, happy village.

2ND NARRATOR: At least, the village was happy for three seasons of the year. (SPRING, *dressed in green peasant dress and carrying basket of flowers, enters dancing, as* VILLAGERS *break their tableau formation, and begin to sing.*)

VILLAGERS (*Singing to tune of "Minka"*):
Joyful Spring, you bring us flowers,
Melting snows and rainbow showers,
But how brief are springtime's hours,
Stay, we beg you, stay.

(SPRING *dances off.*)

1ST NARRATOR: Spring vanished almost as soon as she came, and Summer arrived. . . . (SUMMER, *wearing gaily colored dress, and flowers in her hair, dances in, moving quickly around stage, as* VILLAGERS *sing.*)

VILLAGERS (*Singing to tune of "Minka"*):
Blazing summer sun is coming,
Lazy days with warm winds humming,
Dance, while soft guitars are strumming,
Soon the summer's gone.

(SUMMER *dances off.*)

2ND NARRATOR: Then, before the village had a chance to catch its breath, Autumn leaped across the landscape. (AUTUMN, *a boy in Cossack uniform, strides on, squats and does Russian Cossack dance, as* VILLAGERS *begin to clap and sing, first slowly, then faster as they go along.*)

VILLAGERS (*Singing to tune of "Minka"*):
Red and golden come the fall days,
Harvest brings the best of all days,
But alas, what swift and small days,
Autumn dances by, hey!

(AUTUMN *rises, folds arms, and strides offstage.*)

1ST NARRATOR: And then came Winter.

2ND NARRATOR: Winter, the time of the Frost King. (*Sounds of wind howling and of sleigh bells are heard from offstage.* FROST KING, *wearing long white cloak trimmed with silver, a tall hat and boots, enters center, stands majestically, and raises his arms commandingly.*)

1ST NARRATOR: Then the villagers were not happy.

VILLAGERS (*Singing mournfully to tune of "Minka"*):

Seven slow and snowy moontimes,

Frost upon the sun at noontimes,

How we long for happy Junetimes,

Endless winter days.

(VILLAGERS, FROST KING, *and children exit, repeating song as they go off.*)

2ND NARRATOR: Now there were two lonely old people in this village who had no children to keep them company or to comfort them. (OLD MAN *and* OLD WOMAN *enter from cottage.*)

1ST NARRATOR: Somehow, nobody seemed to have time for them. (IVAN THE OLDER *and* IVAN THE YOUNGER *enter, carrying hatchets over their shoulders and whistling.*)

OLD MAN (*To boy*): Good morning, young Ivan. Where are you going in such a hurry? Stop a minute and talk with us. (*Takes wooden whistle from his pocket and holds it toward boy*) See, I've made a wooden whistle for you, little Ivan.

IVAN THE OLDER (*Waving him away*): Some other time, Old Man. Today my son and I must go deep into the forest to cut wood. My son is going to be the best woodcutter in the province, eh, my boy? (*Boy nods proudly.*) Come on, then, son. (*They exit.*)

OLD MAN: Did you hear that, wife? Did you hear how proudly Ivan Ivanovitch called the boy "my son"? Ah, I tell you, wife, if I had a child I'd think I were in heaven. (BLACKSMITH'S WIFE *and* OLGA *enter and hurry across stage.*)

BLACKSMITH'S WIFE (*To* OLGA): Hurry, child. Don't lag behind.

OLD WOMAN: Why, it's the Blacksmith's Wife and little Olga. How are you this morning? How cold little Olga looks. Will you stop and have a nice cup of tea with us?

BLACKSMITH'S WIFE (*Impatiently*): I haven't a moment to spare, Old Woman. Winter is upon us, and this child has no mittens. We must get wool from the carder's this very day.

OLGA: Oh, I wish we could stay. (*She lags behind, then waves to* OLD WOMAN.)

BLACKSMITH'S WIFE (*Pushing* OLGA *toward exit*): Stop dawdling, child, and get along! (*They exit.*)

OLD WOMAN (*Sighing*): She's too busy. But then, if I had a pretty daughter like that, I'd be busy too. Ah, me.

OLD MAN (*Sadly*): Ah, me. (*They exit into cottage.*)

1ST NARRATOR: But the children were not too busy to think of their old friends who had always been so kind to them. The next day, even though it had snowed the whole night and the ground was covered with snow, they gathered in front of the cottage and tried to think of a way to repay the old couple. (OLGA, IVAN, MISCHA, *and* KATYA *enter, hands behind their backs, as if deep in thought, and walk over to cottage door.*)

IVAN (*Pacing back and forth*): What to do, what to do! (*He looks around at snow.*) I know what we shall do for our friends.

CHILDREN (*Ad lib*): What? Tell us! What can we do? (*Etc.*)

IVAN (*Picking up handful of snow*): We can make a snow child!

CHILDREN (*Ad lib*): Wonderful! What a good idea! Let's get started. (*Etc.*)

IVAN: Mischa, you and Katya roll the large ball. Olga, you can roll the small one for the head, and I'll roll the middle-size one for the body. (NOTE: *A reprise of "Minka" may be played in background during following action.*)

MISCHA: Good! Come on, Katya. (MISCHA *and* KATYA *run offstage, left, and return rolling a large ball of snow.* IVAN *goes behind bushes right, and* OLGA *behind trees, left, and soon reappear, rolling balls of snow.*)

IVAN: Wonderful! Now let's put this together. (*They begin to assemble figure, placing snowballs on top of each other. Head has been prepared with eyes, nose and mouth.*)

OLGA: We must make her as lovely as their daughter might have been.

KATYA (*Standing back to look at snow figure*): She is beautiful, but we must dress her up a bit. (*She takes off her shawl and drapes it around figure.*)

OLGA (*Pretending to put eyes, nose, and mouth into head*): There, now, eyes to see, ears to hear, and a mouth to smile with. And she needs just one more thing.

MISCHA: What else? She looks pretty enough.

OLGA (*Taking off her cap and putting it on snow figure*): Just this cap to make her look like a real child.

IVAN (*Turning figure around to face audience*): There! She's almost as good as a real live child. (*Sound of howling wind is heard. Children all shiver.*)

KATYA: Br-r-r. The Frost Demons are singing.

MISCHA: It's time to go home.

IVAN: Well, at least our old friends will have a pleasant surprise when they come out again. (*All cross to exit.*)

OLGA (*Turning to wave to snow figure*): Goodbye, snow child. I wish with all my heart you were a real, live child. (*Children exit.*)

CHILDREN (*In offstage echo*): A real live child . . . a real live child . . . a real live child. . . .

2ND NARRATOR: Then the wind heard the wish that Olga made, and carried it north, until it reached the ears of the Frost King himself. (*Offstage sleigh bells are heard.* FROST KING *enters, center.*)

1ST NARRATOR: And the Frost King took pity on the Old

Man and the Old Woman, for he lived alone at the top of the world, and he knew what it was like to be lonely. (FROST KING *crosses to snow figure.*)

FROST KING (*Singing to tune of "Minka"*):
Little doll of snow forsaken,
Ere dawn night has overtaken,
As a real child you shall waken,
Spellbound till the spring.

(*He removes his cloak, waves it with flourish in front of snow figure, and holds it there, as* DANCING SNOWFLAKES *dance in left and right, each waving a scarf.* FROST KING *repeats his song and* DANCING SNOWFLAKES *dance around him, waving scarves. Meanwhile,* PROPERTY BOYS *move snow figure offstage, and* SNOWFLAKE *enters upstage and stands behind* FROST KING's *cloak in place of snow figure. This action is hidden from audience by* DANCING SNOWFLAKES. *As dance ends,* DANCING SNOWFLAKES *bow low to* FROST KING. *He puts his cloak back on and exits center, followed by* DANCING SNOWFLAKES. *The snow child,* SNOWFLAKE, *remains at center, motionless, as* OLD MAN *and* OLD WOMAN *enter from cottage.*)

OLD WOMAN (*Running center*): Music—I heard music—singing—here, in this very clearing.

OLD MAN: No, no, wife. You heard the wind. Only the Frost Demons were singing. Only the snowflakes were dancing.

OLD WOMAN: I heard what I heard, husband. (*Seeing* SNOWFLAKE *and stepping back in wonder.*) And now I see what I see. (*She points to* SNOWFLAKE) Look at this. The children must have made us a little daughter of snow. How kind of them. (*Sound of rooster crowing is heard from offstage.*)

OLD MAN: It's dawn already. The rooster crowed. (*Crossing to* SNOWFLAKE) Well, wife, say good morning to your daughter.

OLD WOMAN: I would, but alas, she could not answer me.

(*Startled*) Oh. How lifelike they have made her! I thought I saw her blink.

OLD MAN: That was a trick of the light, wife. (*He circles around* SNOWFLAKE, *inspecting her.*) Well, somebody should greet her. Good morning, child.

SNOWFLAKE (*Curtsying*): Good morning, Papa. (*She returns to her motionless position.*)

OLD MAN (*Looking around, in wonder*): Oh, oh! (*He puts his hands to his ears and closes his eyes for a moment.*) What a funny dream I am having, wife. I dreamed the snow child said, "Good morning, Papa."

OLD WOMAN (*Clapping delightedly*): Then I must be having the same dream, because I heard her say it, too. (*Touches* SNOWFLAKE *timidly*) Why, child, you are alive! But what are you doing here, waiting alone in the snow?

SNOWFLAKE (*Taking* OLD MAN *and* OLD WOMAN *by the hand*): I'm waiting for you, Mama—Papa!

OLD MAN (*In great excitement*): She called us Mama and Papa! Did you hear? I'm really awake. It's all true. It's a miracle.

OLD WOMAN: After all these years, we have a daughter.

OLD MAN: But why? How? When?

OLD WOMAN: Don't you understand? We have been given our hearts' desire. Never, never ask how, why, or when. Just be grateful.

OLD MAN (*Excitedly*): The first thing I shall do is tell Ivan Ivanovitch. No, on second thought, the first thing I shall do is arrange a feast. (*Turning to* SNOWFLAKE) On the other hand, perhaps you would like a pair of new boots, my child. (SNOWFLAKE *claps her hands.*) My child! Oh, how proud I'm going to be today. It will be my daughter this —my daughter that. Have you met my daughter, the prettiest girl in the village? Here is my daughter—uh— now, what is my daughter's name?

SNOWFLAKE (*Curtsying*): Snowflake, Papa. My name is

Snowflake. (OLD MAN, OLD WOMAN *and* SNOWFLAKE *cross left to cottage and hold their positions.*)

2ND NARRATOR: And so, Snowflake came to stay with the Old Man and the Old Woman, and they were happy beyond measure.

1ST NARRATOR: And the days of the winter slipped by, white and wonderful, for everyone in the village.

2ND NARRATOR: But one day, something strange and terrible happened. (IVAN, MISCHA, OLGA, *and* KATYA *enter.* OLD MAN *and* OLD WOMAN *go into cottage.*)

IVAN: Snowflake, come and play with us. (SNOWFLAKE *joins children.*) Now close your eyes, everyone. (*All join hands in circle, and close their eyes.*) Now listen carefully. What do you hear? (*Sound of bird call is heard.*)

OLGA (*Excitedly*): A bluebird! The very first bluebird is singing. (SNOWFLAKE *slips out of circle and moves, unnoticed, upstage, forlornly.*)

SNOWFLAKE: A bluebird. (*Shivering in fright*) I am afraid. I cannot stay here.

IVAN: Now, take a deep breath. Lift your faces to the sky. What do you smell? What do you feel?

MISCHA: Oh-h-h! The south wind has come back. I smell apple blossoms.

KATYA (*Taking off her cap and scarf*): I feel the warm sun. It is too warm for caps and scarves. (OLGA, IVAN, *and* MISCHA *also take off their hats and scarves.*)

SNOWFLAKE (*Sadly, to herself*): Too warm. It's too warm for snowflakes. Oh, where shall I go? What shall I do? (*She buries her head in her hands.*) They have forgotten me.

IVAN: Now, this is the best part of the game. Open your eyes. (*He points to center of circle.*) Look. What do you see?

MISCHA: Why—something is blooming in the snow.

OLGA (*Looking down*): It's a crocus—the first crocus of spring! (*Sound of distant sleigh bells is heard from offstage.*

FROST KING *enters up center and approaches* SNOWFLAKE, *who turns to look at him.* FROST KING *beckons to her commandingly, and starts toward exit.* SNOWFLAKE *nods sadly and follows him, turning to wave at children, before she and* FROST KING *exit, unnoticed by children. She drops her cap at center as she goes off.*)

KATYA (*Turning as she calls*): Snowflake, why are you so quiet? Come see the crocus, Snowflake. (*Suddenly*) Why, she's gone! Where could she be? I must go find her. (*Calling as she exits left*) Snowflake! Snowflake!

IVAN (*Calling*): Snowflake, where are you? (*He exits right.*)

MISCHA: Maybe she went into the forest. She should never go into the forest alone. (*He calls.*) Snowflake . . . (*He exits up center.*)

OLGA: You're teasing us, aren't you, Snowflake? (*She listens.*) It's so still. So lonely now. (*She calls.*) Snowflake . . . (OLD MAN *and* OLD WOMAN *enter from cottage.*)

OLD WOMAN: Why, Olga—what is the matter?

OLGA (*Beginning to cry*): She's gone. Snowflake has gone.

OLD MAN (*Patting her shoulder*): Now, now. She's playing hide-and-seek. She'll come back. (OLD WOMAN *crosses center, sees cap, picks it up and holds it close.*)

OLD WOMAN (*Sobbing*): No. She will not come back. Here is her cap. She never goes anywhere without her cap. Oh— something dark and cold whispered to me—gone forever. Gone forever. (*She runs up center, calling urgently.*) Snowflake . . .

OLD MAN (*Going off left, calling*): Snowflake . . .

VOICES (*Echoing from offstage*): Snowflake . . . Snowflake . . . Snowflake. . . .

2ND NARRATOR: But Snowflake could not be found. Not that day, or the next, or the next. (OLD MAN *and* OLD WOMAN *re-enter left, heads down.* OLD WOMAN *wipes her eyes, as* OLD MAN *tries to comfort her.*)

1ST NARRATOR: When the Old Man and the Old Woman found that Snowflake had indeed gone, they could not be consoled.

2ND NARRATOR: The boys and girls came to comfort them, but they no longer smiled. (OLGA, IVAN, MISCHA, *and* KATYA *re-enter, cross left to stand beside* OLD MAN *and* OLD WOMAN.)

1ST NARRATOR: Spring came, dancing green and gold across the countryside. (SPRING *dances in and crosses stage, with musical interlude in background, if desired. She exits.*)

2ND NARRATOR: But it was not the same. (*All shake their heads sadly.*)

1ST NARRATOR: Summer followed Spring, with blazing sun and brilliant blossoms. (SUMMER *enters, dances across stage and exits.*)

2ND NARRATOR: But it was not the same. (*All shake their heads again.*)

1ST NARRATOR: And then, Autumn leaped across the fields and forests, more colorful than ever before. (AUTUMN *enters, does brief Cossack dance, exits.*)

2ND NARRATOR: But it was not the same. (*All shake their heads again.*)

1ST NARRATOR: And then, it was Winter. Still the children watched and waited, keeping a vigil with the Old Man and the Old Woman.

2ND NARRATOR: November stretched on, gray and empty and endless.

1ST NARRATOR: And then the wind began to rise. (*Howling wind is heard from offstage.*)

2ND NARRATOR: And then, soft as kittens' paws, the first snow began to fall. (*Sound of approaching sleigh bells is heard.*)

1ST NARRATOR: And *then*, something strange and wonderful happened! (*Fanfare is heard from offstage.*)

2ND NARRATOR: From the top of the world, on the back of the North Wind, came a glittering white sleigh . . .

(Two Property Boys *enter, pulling sleigh on wheels down center.* Snowflake, *wearing tall, white crown, rides in sleigh.*)

All (*Ad lib*): Snowflake! It's Snowflake! She's back! (*Etc.* Old Man *and* Old Woman *run to sleigh.* Villagers *enter.*)

Old Woman: My dear child. We have waited for you so long. (*She takes* Snowflake's *hand.*)

Old Man: Why, you're a princess! But, then—I always knew you were a princess. (*Happily*) Listen, everybody. Let me introduce my daughter—Princess Snowflake. (*He bows, pointing to* Snowflake. *All clap and cheer.*)

Snowflake: Good people, did you think I would go away and leave you forever? I would never do such a thing. But you must remember, I am a creature of the frost and snow. I cannot live in the days of sun and flowers. And so, every year, I must leave you for a while. But every year, sure as the snow falls, I will return to you. (*She begins to sing to tune of "Minka."*)

When the snow moon shimmers brightly,
And the frost-rime shimmers whitely,
Listen for my bells so spritely, (*Sound of sleigh bells*)
Snowflake's coming home.

Villagers (*Singing to tune of "Minka"*):
Welcome, silvery winter treasure,
Welcome, frosty winter pleasure,
Welcome, beauty, without measure,
Snowflake, welcome home.

(*Everyone holds arms out to* Snowflake, *as* Frost King *enters, center, his arms raised in greeting.* Dancing Snowflakes *enter, followed first by* Spring, *then* Summer, *and* Autumn. *They dance around stage in pairs with* Dancing Snowflakes. 1st Narrator *and* 2nd Narrator *step forward to apron of stage, as curtains close behind them.*)

2nd Narrator: From that day to this, when the first crystals of snow touch the earth, Snowflake returns to the village just as she promised.

1ST NARRATOR: And even though Snowflake must return to the Frost King when the first crocus appears—nobody grumbles or complains.

2ND NARRATOR: For there is an old proverb that everybody in the village knows by heart.

NARRATORS (*Together, slowly*): A snow child is better than no child. (NARRATORS *turn and bow and curtsy to each other, then exit at opposite sides of stage.*)

THE END

Ah See and the Six-Colored Heaven

Characters

Two Narrators
Ding Ling, *emperor*
Ming Ling, *empress*
Sing Ling, *princess*
So Low, *the magician*
Two Handmaidens

Prince Ching
Prince Chong
Prince Chung
Ah See, *the humble servant*
Two Property Boys
Four Musicians

Before Rise: Four Musicians *are seated on cushions, down left, with gong, woodblocks, flute, slide whistle, and tambourine. Woodblocks are struck three times.* Two Narrators *enter and take their places down right, where they remain throughout play.* Narrators *bow.*

1st Narrator: Honorable audience: Please to tune your eyes and your ears most delicately.
2nd Narrator: We are about to paint a scene for you of ancient China.
Both: Listen, we beg you, to the tale of Ah See and the Six-Colored Heaven. (*Gong is struck once. Curtains open.*)

*   *   *

Time: *Long ago.*
Setting: *China.*
At Rise: *The stage is bare.*

1ST NARRATOR: The tale begins in the Middle Kingdom of Cathay. (PROPERTY BOYS *bring on red pagoda. They set it center stage and exit.*)

2ND NARRATOR: In that kingdom there lived a high and mighty Emperor. He was named by the gods, Ding Ling. (DING LING *enters, and stands in front of pagoda, hand upraised. Gong sounds. Gong is struck each time* DING LING *takes a step across stage.*)

1ST NARRATOR: In due time, Ding Ling married a lady of high degree, named by her father, Ming Ling. (*Tambourine is shaken, as* MING LING *enters and minces across stage.* DING LING *extends his arm.* MING LING *puts her hand on his arm, and they stand together.*)

2ND NARRATOR: In due time a royal princess was born. (SING LING *enters.*) She was more beautiful than a young pear tree. She was named by her mother—

MING LING: Sing Ling.

1ST NARRATOR: Ah, but they were happy.

DING LING: I am most humbly happy.

MING LING: Who could not be happy here?

SING LING: The sun shines every day throughout the year. (PROPERTY BOYS *bring on sun, which they fasten to backdrop, and exit.*)

1ST NARRATOR: The princess grew more radiant every year. It must have been all that sunshine! (Two HANDMAIDENS *bring on mirror.* 1ST MAIDEN *holds mirror before* SING LING. 2ND MAIDEN *arranges her hair. They smile and nod at her.*)

2ND NARRATOR: At last, when she was sixteen years young, there was no one in all China who could compare with Princess Sing Ling.

DING LING: Our daughter grows more beautiful than the flowering pear tree.

MING LING: And more radiant than the sunrise.

SING LING: I am most grateful to my honorable parents. (HANDMAIDENS *kneel and bow very low.* DING LING *and* MING

LING *exit.* PROPERTY BOYS *enter and remove pagoda and mirror, then exit.*)

1ST NARRATOR: But—(*Gong is struck once.*)

2ND NARRATOR: There is always a "but" in fairy tales.

1ST NARRATOR: But—one day the princess was alone in the garden with her handmaidens. (PROPERTY BOYS *bring on willow tree, place it at center, and exit.*) As Sing Ling stood by the willow tree, wind began to ripple through the willow leaves, even though it was not the time of the wind. (SO LOW, *wearing demon mask, dances on, carrying two fans. Slide whistle is heard, as he dances behind willow tree.*)

2ND NARRATOR: Did you say the wind? That is no gentle breeze, that is a magician! (SO LOW *crosses to center, removes his mask and bows.*)

1ST *and* 2ND NARRATORS: That is an evil magician—wonder of the underworld, named by the demons, So Low! (SO LOW *sneaks behind* HANDMAIDENS, *makes quick fanning motions, and they sink down, fold hands on their cheeks, and pantomime sleep. Slide whistle makes a wavery sound during this action.*)

2ND NARRATOR: So Low had come to inspect the princess. (SO LOW *slowly circles* SING LING, *who looks left and right, puzzled.*)

SO LOW: Beautiful! Enchanting. Even better than advertised.

1ST NARRATOR: Instantly (*Gong is struck once.*)—if not sooner, So Low fell violently in love. (SO LOW *clutches his heart, dropping mask. He hunches over, tottering a few steps downstage.*)

2ND NARRATOR: It was the only way So Low could fall in love. So Low went down on his knees. (SO LOW *drops to his knees, lifting his folded hands skyward.*)

1ST NARRATOR: He beat his breast. He tore his hair. (*Woodblocks are rapped three times.* SO LOW *thumps his chest in time to woodblocks. He pulls his hair.*)

2ND NARRATOR: Naturally, Princess Sing Ling was startled out of her wits.

SING LING: Oh! I am most humbly astonished.

2ND NARRATOR: So Low was nothing much to look at in the first place.

1ST NARRATOR: In the second place, at that moment he looked like a madman.

2ND NARRATOR: Princess Sing Ling did not even pause. She did what any sensible princess should do. She ran away. (*She runs mincingly offstage. Woodblocks are tapped together quickly.*) The handmaidens woke, and, frightened, they followed the Princess. (HANDMAIDENS *get up, look around fearfully, then run offstage after* SING LING. PROPERTY BOYS *enter, take off willow tree, and bring on red pagoda. They exit.*)

1ST NARRATOR: There was So Low—all by himself, looking very foolish. (So LOW *scratches his head.*)

2ND NARRATOR: Word of warning: Never make a magician look foolish.

1ST NARRATOR: So Low's love turned to anger. (So LOW *frowns.*) So Low beat his breast. He tore his hair. (*Woodblocks are rapped three times, as* So LOW *thumps his chest and pulls his hair.*)

So LOW: Woe unto you, Princess Sing Ling. If I cannot have you, no one shall have you. Behold: a spell! (*Gong is struck once.*) I, the low and loathsome So Low, do hereby cover the sun with clouds. (PROPERTY BOYS *bring on clouds, covering the sun. They turn red pagoda around, revealing the gray side.*) No longer shall the sun shine on this Middle Kingdom. All the six colors of the spectrum shall henceforth and forevermore fade from view. Gray and grisly shall this kingdom be. But (*Gong is struck once.*)—if there is one prince who can show the Princess the Six-Colored Heaven, the spell will vanish and the Princess may be married and live (*He coughs.*)—happily ever after.

2ND NARRATOR: See how he chokes on the words, happily ever after?

SO LOW: So Low has said it; so be it! (*He puts on mask and dances offstage.*)

1ST *and* 2ND NARRATORS: So be it. So was it. (*Tambourine is shaken, as* DING LING, MING LING *and* SING LING *enter, wearing gray robes, their heads bowed.*)

1ST NARRATOR: Then, you may imagine, there was a time of great sorrow. (*All pantomime weeping.*)

2ND NARRATOR: Terrible times followed. Travel fell off. Who wishes to visit a kingdom of gray rivers, gray mountains and gray flowers?

DING LING, MING LING *and* SING LING (*Shaking their heads*): No one.

1ST NARRATOR: Trade dwindled to nothing. Who wishes to buy gray silks, gray pottery, and (heaven forbid) gray tea?

DING LING, MING LING *and* SING LING (*Shaking their heads again*): Absolutely no one. (*They bow their heads.*)

2ND NARRATOR: However—(*Gong is struck once.*) However, there were three haughty Princes who heard of the spell cast on the Middle Kingdom. They decided to try their luck. In the order of their importance they were: Prince Ching, Prince Chong, and Prince Chung. (*Tambourine is shaken, as the* PRINCES, *followed by* AH SEE, *enter, marching single file.*)

PRINCE CHING (*Facing audience*): Without question, Princess Sing Ling will marry me—Prince Ching. (*Pointing to his head*) I have much upstairs. Not so, my brothers.

PRINCE CHONG (*Facing audience*): Without question, Princess Sing Ling will marry me, Prince Chong. I have eyes like a hawk. Not so, my brothers.

PRINCE CHUNG (*Facing audience*): Without question, Princess Sing Ling will marry me, Prince Chung. I am most elegant. Most refined. Not so, my brothers.

1ST NARRATOR: Little did they know that right behind them was someone more clever, more keen-sighted and more refined than all three brothers put together.

2ND NARRATOR: Who was that somebody? (*Flute trills, as* AH SEE *bows to audience.*)

AH SEE: I am Ah See, a humble servant of no importance. I am so insignificant that I hardly ever think about myself. But—being of such unimportance, I have time to enjoy the world. (*He looks left.*) I am a student of different colors. For example: there are five hundred and twenty different shades of green among the leaves of the willow. (*He looks right.*) As for the mountains, there are shades of blue from hazy morning blue to midnight blue. I am also an expert on the sunrise. I know the thousand fires of dawn, and also the thousand glowing coals of sunset. Thank you. (*He bows.*)

1ST NARRATOR: Keep your eye on him. (AH SEE *rises.* PRINCES *march in place, followed by* AH SEE. PROPERTY BOYS *bring on torii gate and place it in front of imperial family.* SO LOW, *in gatekeeper's disguise, is hiding behind gate.*)

2ND NARRATOR: At last they came to the Emperor's gate. And whom do you think they met?

So Low (*Stepping from behind gate*): Halt. Who goes there?

1ST NARRATOR: It is our old friend, So Low, disguised as a gatekeeper. He is keeping an eye on things.

PRINCES: We are important princes, from important places. We have come to break the spell and marry the Princess.

So Low: Have you really? Let me help you.

PRINCES: Ah!

So Low: For a small fee.

PRINCES: Oh. (*They hand him three bags of gold.* So Low *takes gold. He hands lantern to* PRINCE CHING.)

So Low: Here. Take this lantern. It will enlighten your mind. (*He hands* PRINCE CHONG *folded fan.*) There. Take this fan. It will blow your doubts away. (*He hands* PRINCE

CHUNG *pair of spectacles.*) Take these. They are magic spectacles. They will help you to see the truth. Now, you may pass through the gate. (*Tambourines are shaken, as* PRINCES *and* AH SEE *go through gate and kneel before the imperial family.* PROPERTY BOYS *remove gate.*) Ha ha! Try very hard, haughty Princes. But try as you will, you will never break the spell. (So LOW *sneaks downstage, watching from side.*)

DING LING: Who comes to my kingdom of dismay?

PRINCE CHING (*Standing*): Prince Ching, O illustrious Emperor.

PRINCE CHONG (*Standing*): Prince Chong, O honored Emperor.

PRINCE CHUNG (*Standing*): Prince Chung, O mighty Emperor.

PRINCES (*Together*): Important princes from important places. We will break the spell and marry the princess.

DING LING: Go ahead. Try. Thousands have tried before you. Thousands have failed before you. But, go ahead. Show us the Six-Colored Heaven and break the spell.

PRINCE CHING (*Stepping center*): My turn, first. (*He holds up lantern.*) See this lantern? It will show us the way to the Six-Colored Heaven. Enlighten us, lantern. (*Pauses. Woodblocks mark passage of time by rapping slowly three times.*) One more moment, Your Imperial Highness.

DING LING: No more moments, you fraud! You have failed. Be off! (*He points off right. There is quick tapping on woodblocks, as* PRINCE CHING *gives lantern to* AH SEE *and runs offstage.*)

PRINCE CHUNG (*Stepping center*): My turn now. Notice these magic spectacles. With these glasses I will describe for you the wonders of the Six-Colored Heaven. (*He dons spectacles.*) Oh! They are backwards spectacles. Instead of showing the outside world, they show the inside of my mind.

DING LING: And what is inside your mind?

PRINCE CHUNG (*Smugly*): My mind is full of the wonders of me. Shall I describe my wonderful self?

DING LING: Decidedly not. You have failed. Be off! (*Woodblocks tap quickly, as* PRINCE CHUNG *gives spectacles to* AH SEE *and runs offstage.*)

PRINCE CHONG: At last my unworthy brothers have gone. Now I shall break the spell. Here is a fan. I shall blow away all the clouds of doubt from your kingdom. (*He opens fan. It has large hole in middle.*) Oh! I've been cheated. The fan has a hole in it!

DING LING: Be off—before I chop off your head and use it for a bowling ball! (*Woodblocks tap quickly as* PRINCE CHONG, *holding his head, gives fan to* AH SEE, *then runs off.*)

SO LOW (*Swaggering center*): And now (*Gong is struck once.*)—it is *my* turn. You have run out of princes, Emperor Ding Ling. You must consider magicians now, Sing Ling. Marry me!

SING LING: I most humbly beg to answer your request with a small word. No! (AH SEE *puts on spectacles. He rises, and raises his hands in wonder.*)

AH SEE: Ah—marvelous! Oh—wonderful!

ALL (*Ad lib*): What? What is it? What do you see? (*Etc.*)

AH SEE: I see . . . the Six-Colored Heaven. It is here, inside my mind. But, I cannot be so selfish as to keep it inside myself. I will find the Six-Colored Heaven for you, too. (*Holds up lantern, which he lights*) Here is the lantern of enlightenment. Prince Ching forgot to light the candle inside. I will search for the sun. . . . (*Tambourine is shaken, as* AH SEE *runs around stage, holding lantern high, and searching for sun. He points to backdrop.*) The honorable sun! (*Gong is struck once.* PROPERTY BOYS *enter and remove clouds, disclosing sun. They hold clouds high above their heads.*) Now I will show you the Six-Colored Heaven. Turn to the sky, if you please. (*All turn toward backdrop, shading their eyes.*) Watch, if you please, as the sky changes. For when you stand between sun and mist, the Six-Colored Heaven will appear. (AH SEE *begins to fan. He holds his hand over hole in fan. Flute trill is heard.* PROPERTY BOYS *put down clouds, exit and re-enter with large rainbow, which they hang over sun. They place clouds left and right, beyond edge of rainbow.*)

ALL: Ah! The beautiful Six-Colored Heaven! (PROPERTY BOYS *turn pagoda to red side. They remove gray robes from shoulders of imperial family.*)

SO LOW: The upstart! (*All turn to face* SO LOW.) He has broken my unbreakable spell. But—he is a humble servant of no importance. He is not a prince. Therefore, he cannot marry the Princess.

DING LING: Nonsense. He can be a prince with a clap of my imperial hands. (*He claps his hands.* PROPERTY BOYS *bring on Chinese crown, which they place on* AH SEE'S *head.*) Ah See —you are now Prince Ah See. (SO LOW *beats his breast and pulls his hair. Woodblocks are tapped three times.*)

SO LOW: Gr-r-r-r-r! Now I will become a roaring wind. I will blow your kingdom off the face of the earth! (*Slide whistle is heard.* SO LOW *runs back and forth across stage menacingly.* PROPERTY BOYS *make red pagoda sway back and forth.*)

ALL (*Swaying back and forth*): Oh! Oh! (AH SEE *creeps up behind* SO LOW *and begins to fan him with circular motions.* SO LOW *runs around in spiral, finally spinning around, center, then runs offstage, still turning.*)

1ST NARRATOR: Bold little Ah See has turned the evil magician's magic against him.

2ND NARRATOR: Bold little Ah See has curled that mighty wind around and around. So Low has been trapped in his own hot air.

1ST *and* 2ND NARRATORS: Farewell, So Low! (*They wave.*)

ALL (*Waving*): Farewell, So Low.

1ST NARRATOR: However—(*Gong is struck once.* AH SEE *and* SING LING *kneel before* DING LING *and* MING LING, *heads bowed.*)

2ND NARRATOR: However, Prince Ah See and Princess Sing Ling were united that very day in celestial bliss for all eternity and then some. (PROPERTY BOYS *bring on baskets of multicolored paper flowers, which they shower on bridal pair.*)

1ST NARRATOR: Which means that they all lived happily ever after. (MUSICIANS *play fanfare, and imperial family bows to audience as curtains close.*)

THE END

What Ever Happened to Mother Nature?

Characters

MOTHER GOOSE	MARY CONTRARY
FROG	LITTLE MISS MUFFET
MOTHER NATURE	BOY BLUE
BO-PEEP	SPIDER
JACK	MAIDEN
JILL	MAN
STAR CHILD	WATER COMMISSIONER

BEFORE RISE: *There is a large door frame left. On it is sign:* DO NOT DISTURB. FROG *squats beside door.* MOTHER GOOSE *enters right on broomstick fitted out to look like a large goose.*

MOTHER GOOSE: Here I come, just as I said I would. Once a century I visit Mother Nature down on Earth. Here I am. (*She alights from broom and speaks to* FROG.) Ah, here's Mother Nature's page. Will you tell Mother Nature that Mother Goose has come calling, please?

FROG: Go away.

MOTHER GOOSE: What kind of welcome is that, pray tell?

FROG: It's all the welcome you'll get. Mother Nature is not to be disturbed. She's brooding. Go away.

MOTHER GOOSE: Stuff and nonsense. Mother Nature always has time for Mother Goose. Announce my presence this instant.

FROG: Very well, but you'll be sorry. (*He hops off left.*)

MOTHER GOOSE: What a rude frog. Dear Mother Nature! I remember her so well. Such a beautiful lady. So stylish. She never wore the same season twice. (MOTHER NATURE *enters down left, wearing gray smock, construction helmet, earmuffs, goggles, and a surgical mask. She carries a canteen.*)

MOTHER GOOSE: Is that you, Mother Nature?

MOTHER NATURE (*Pulling down mask*): Mother Goose? (*She walks toward* MOTHER GOOSE.) Oh, dear. Is it once-a-century again?

MOTHER GOOSE: What have you done to yourself? You've grown such great fuzzy ears. What is that bucket on your head? Why are you wearing a mask?

MOTHER NATURE: It's a long, sad tale, Mother Goose. I wear these horrid things to protect me. To protect me from—*them.*

MOTHER GOOSE: Them? You mean the frogs? Your frog was very rude to me.

MOTHER NATURE: Don't be too hard on poor froggie. He's having a hard time. You see, they polluted his lily pond, and now he lives from puddle to puddle. It's the dry season here, and he's very cross.

MOTHER GOOSE: Who is doing these dreadful things? Georgie Porgie? Tom, the Piper's son?

MOTHER NATURE: People. Ordinary people. Come with me. I'll take you to my favorite meadow. You won't believe what's been happening since you visited last century. (*Curtain opens*)

*   *   *

SETTING: *A deteriorated landscape. Backdrop shows factories belching smoke into a gray sky. There are crates and old boxes helter-skelter onstage. Down right, there is a dilapidated wishing well with sign:* POLLUTED. NO DRINKING, WASHING OR WISHING. *Down left, there is pile of trash with sign:* DON'T PICK THE FLOWERS.

AT RISE: MOTHER GOOSE *and* MOTHER NATURE *walk up center.*

MOTHER GOOSE (*Dismayed*): What in the wide world is this awful place? Where is your lovely meadow?

MOTHER NATURE: This *is* my meadow.

MOTHER GOOSE: But where are the flowers hiding? Why does the sky frown like that? Who slaughtered the trees? And where are the birds? I don't hear the birds. I don't hear anything.

MOTHER NATURE: You will. (*She adjusts earmuffs. There is loud cacophony of auto horns.* MOTHER GOOSE *holds her ears.*)

MOTHER GOOSE: What a row! It's worse than the Kilkenny cats fighting.

MOTHER NATURE: Now you see why I must wear earmuffs and a mask. It's all very discouraging. Confidentially, if people don't stop using my world for their private wastebasket, I'm going to change my address.

MOTHER GOOSE: Mother Nature, you wouldn't!

MOTHER NATURE: Oh, yes, I would. I'm already looking for another planet.

MOTHER GOOSE: Another planet! Why, Earth would become a ball of mud without you, Mother Nature. We must find a way to stop this. Perhaps my children can help. (*She takes small handbell from pocket and rings it.*) Come one! Come all! From your lane and your little house. Come one! Come all! From Bo-Peep to Tom Tittlemouse. (STAR CHILD, *holding telescope,* JACK, JILL, BO-PEEP, MARY CONTRARY, *and* MISS MUFFET *enter. They form semicircle around* MOTHER GOOSE. MOTHER NATURE *sits on crate down left, observing them.*)

CHILDREN: All present and accounted for, Mother Goose.

MOTHER GOOSE: Look around you, children. What do you see?

STAR CHILD (*Looking at backdrop through telescope*):

Star light, star bright,
Where are the stars I see at night?
I wish I may, I wish I might,
See through the smoke this murky night.

(JACK *and* JILL *join hands, and cross to well, as others sit on boxes and crates.*)

JACK: Jack—
JILL: And Jill,
BOTH:

Went up the hill,
To fetch a pail of water.

(*They take bucket from well, and examine it.*)

JACK: They found a spring . . . (*He holds up coil.*)
JILL: And some slimy string . . . (*She holds up greenish rope.*)
BOTH: But not a drop of water! (*Auto horn sounds loudly.* BOY BLUE *enters on tricycle, beeping bulb-type horn.*)
CHILDREN (*Putting hands on ears*):

Little Boy Blue, don't blow your horn,
You'll wake all the neighbors this quiet morn.

BO-PEEP (*Yawning and rubbing her eyes*):

I'm little Bo-Peep,
I've lost my sleep,
Because of Little Boy Blue.
Please keep the noise down,
When you travel through town,
Or I'll lose my poor head, too!

(*She holds her head.* BOY BLUE *parks tricycle and joins others.* MARY CONTRARY *angrily crosses to dump, pointing at litter.*)

MARY: Shame, shame. Shame on somebody!
CHILDREN:

Mary, Mary, quite contrary;
How does your garden grow?

MARY: You'd be contrary, too, if somebody dumped rubbish on your jonquils and trash on your trillium. How does my garden grow, indeed? (*She holds up each item as she names it.*) With bottle caps, and litter scraps, and rusty cans all in a row. Humph! (*She crosses back to seat, tossing her head.* MISS MUFFET *crosses to her, waving spray can.*)

MISS MUFFET: I have something for your garden, Mary! (*She pretends to spray can around stage.*) Insecticide! (*Pulls up box and sits, still spraying*)

CHILDREN:

Little Miss Muffet,

Sat on a tuffet,

Using a garden spray . . .

(SPIDER *staggers in. He waves white flag of truce, then goes down on his knees.*)

SPIDER: Goodbye, cruel world. Little did Miss Muffet know —I was one of the good bugs. I caught flies and mosquitoes and all kinds of garden pests. Now it's too late. (*He flops down onto floor, feet up. Children stand, hands on hearts.* JACK *and* BOY BLUE *drag* SPIDER *offstage and return.*)

CHILDREN: Who did this to the world? Who?

MOTHER NATURE: People. Ordinary people. This is the world the people made.

CHILDREN:

This is the world the people made.

What a woeful world the people made.

BO-PEEP: Look at the smoke that fouls the air,

CHILDREN: In the woeful world that people made.

JACK: Look at the slime that spoils the water,

BO-PEEP: Look at the smoke that fouls the air,

CHILDREN: In the woeful world that people made.

JILL: Look at the dump that clutters the land.

JACK: Look at the slime that spoils the water,

BO-PEEP: Look at the smoke that fouls the air,

CHILDREN: In the woeful world that people made. (MAIDEN *and* MAN *enter.*)

MAIDEN (*Coughing*):

I am the maiden all forlorn,
Who coughs and chokes with the smoke each morn,
But I'll write to my Congressman, sure as you're born.
(*She waves stamped letter.*)

CHILDREN: To clean up the world the people made.

MOTHER NATURE (*Taking off her mask*):
I'm tired of the litter all tattered and torn,

MAN (*Holding out newspaper*):
And I'll help the maiden all forlorn,
I'll put trash in the basket, that's what I've sworn,

CHILDREN: To clean up the world the people made.
(MOTHER NATURE *removes goggles.* WATER COMMISSIONER *enters.*)

COMMISSIONER:
I'm the Water Commissioner, shaven and shorn,
Phosphates and foam deserve my scorn,
I'll clear up that water this very morn.
(*He turns sign on well around. It now reads:* 100% PURE.
MOTHER NATURE *takes off canteen and helmet.*)

CHILDREN: To clean up the world the people made. (FROG *hops in and squats next to well. He carries little banner reading,* PURE WATER SAVES FROGS. BOY BLUE, *on tricycle, with muffler on horn, crosses to center.*)

BOY BLUE:
I'm the boy who clamored each morn,
But I've put a muffler on my horn.
(MOTHER NATURE *takes off her earmuffs.*)

CHILDREN: To quiet the world the people made. (MOTHER NATURE *removes duster, revealing green gown with chain of daisies.* BO-PEEP *crowns her with daisies.*)

MOTHER GOOSE: Why, Mother Nature, you are your old self again.

MOTHER NATURE: I never thought I'd wear Spring again. Thank you, Mother Goose. Thank you, children.

CHILDREN (*Standing*):

People can undo, what people have done.
Turn off the smokestacks; turn on the sun.
Clean up the lily ponds; green-up the grass,
Hush up the hubbub where traffic must pass.
Then we'll sing as we wander through meadow and
glade . . .

MOTHER NATURE: What a wonderful world the people have made!

ALL (*Together*): What a wonderful world the people have made! (*Curtain*)

THE END

On Camera, Noah Webster!

Characters

LEX LEXICON, *an announcer*	CHORUS
JOE JARGON, *a newscaster*	LI'L LARRY
HAUNTED MAN	LARRY'S MOTHER
THREE SPELLING DEMONS	MR. LINGO
WHICH DOCTOR	PENELOPE PATOIS
MARY MISNOMER	VIRGINIA VERBAL
MOTHER TONGUE	CAMERAMAN
SINGING GROUP (6 SOLOS)	

SETTING: *A television studio. A large sign on rear wall reads:* CHANNEL 26—ENTERTAINMENT AND EDUCATION FROM A TO Z. *A desk and chair are down left; a washing machine is at center; and down right are a table and chair, with a small cart holding cooking utensils nearby.*

AT RISE: LEX LEXICON, *carrying a dictionary, enters down right, followed by* CAMERAMAN, *pushing a TV camera. As* CAMERAMAN *positions camera near desk,* LEX *speaks to audience.*

LEX: Have you ever noticed what a neglected book the dictionary has come to be? Oh, people open it now and then, but there are literally thousands of words gathering dust on their hyphens, never to be uttered by a single human voice. For instance—when was the last time you mentioned the muntjac, or barking deer? Why, I'll bet you didn't even know there was a barking deer. (*Points to dic-*

tionary) It's right there—in the dictionary. Now, some of us feel that there should be equal time for the dictionary. We have come to the conclusion that the dictionary should have its own television channel and sponsors. So here, without further ado, is Channel 26—your doorway to a better vocabulary. (*He smiles and adjusts his tie.* CAMERAMAN *moves in for a close-up of* LEX.) Good morning, Word Watchers of the World. This is Lex Lexicon, your staff announcer, welcoming you to Channel 26, operating on 50,000 megasyllables. Now we switch you to Joe Jargon with his summary of the news. Take it away, Joe . . . (JOE JARGON *enters on the run, down left, a bulletin in his hand, and sits at desk. Sound of teletype clicking is heard.* CAMERAMAN *directs camera toward* JOE. NOTE: CAMERAMAN *follows each act with camera as it appears.*)

JOE: Morning, Word Watchers, this is Joe Jargon, your anchorman on the news front. Flash! An important bulletin has just come over the wires. Flash! Explorers report that they have found an area containing peace, harmony, brotherhood, health, wealth and happiness. Don't everybody rush to buy a ticket, however. These items exist together only in one place—the dictionary! Take it away, Lex Lexicon. (*He runs off left.*)

LEX: And now . . . a message from our sponsor.

HAUNTED MAN (*Running in down right and falling to his knees in supplication*): Help me! Somebody help me! They're haunting me! The Spelling Demons! Here they come. (THREE SPELLING DEMONS *enter and dance around* HAUNTED MAN, *jabbing at him with their tridents.*)

DEMONS (*Ad lib*): A spell. A spell. We have you under a spell. (*Etc.*)

1ST DEMON: Spell "there." Is it (*Spelling*) t-h-e-r-e?

2ND DEMON: Or is it (*Spelling*) t-h-e-i-r?

HAUNTED MAN: I don't know! I don't know!

3RD DEMON: Maybe it's (*Spelling*) t-h-e-y-apostrophe-r-e.

HAUNTED MAN: Apostrophes are catastrophes! Please, somebody . . . help me! (WHICH DOCTOR *dances on, waving a dictionary at* DEMONS, *who shriek and cover their eyes.*)

DEMONS: No, no! Take it away! You'll break our spell! (*They retreat fearfully.*)

WHICH DOCTOR: Begone, Spelling Demons. I have the antidote for you. I am the Which Doctor and I bring this magical book. (*He waves the dictionary at them. They exit right.*)

HAUNTED MAN: You have saved me. But why are you called the Which Doctor, and what is this wonderful book of magic?

WHICH DOCTOR: I am called the Which Doctor because I tell you *which* way to spell words correctly, by *using* this dictionary.

HAUNTED MAN: Dictionary!

WHICH DOCTOR: Pick a word. Any word at all. This book will show you how to spell it in one easy glance.

HAUNTED MAN: Oh, where has this dictionary been all my life?

WHICH DOCTOR: You will find it in your local bookcase. Remember—the dictionary is the all-time best speller. Now, I must be off to rescue more unfortunates. You'd be surprised how many poor souls are caught between double r's and double t's. Farewell. That's (*Spelling*) f-a-r-e-w-e-l-l. (*Exits*)

HAUNTED MAN: I will run right down to my local bookcase and find a dictionary. Those Spelling Demons haven't seen the last of me! (*He runs off down right.*)

LEX: And now . . . Channel 26 presents the moving story of the girl-next-door's fight for truth, happiness and the presidency of her class. Let's look in at the language laundromat where Mary Misnomer is trying to brighten her campaign speech. . . . (MARY MISNOMER *enters up left, a laundry basket full of crumpled papers under her arm. She takes out a paper and tries to smooth it out.*)

MARY: Just look at that dull, lifeless speech. "Fellow whatchamacallits, please vote for me for class thingamajig because . . . and also . . . and in conclusion. . . ." I can't give a speech like this. Oh dear, why is my prattle always tattle-tale gray? (MOTHER TONGUE *enters down left, a dictionary in her hand.*)

MOTHER TONGUE (*Crossing to* MARY): Did I hear you say your speeches were dull and lifeless, dearie? Let Mother Tongue, the little old linguist, help you. Let me introduce you to the dictionary. Just toss your dingy speech into the language laundromat. (MARY *puts crumpled papers into washing machine. Sound of a noisy washing machine is heard.* MOTHER TONGUE *drops dictionary into machine.*) Now let's add a few words to the wash. You know, the dictionary contains five active ingredients to clarify your thoughts: synonyms for sparkle, antonyms for action, homonyms and heteronyms for humor, and metonyms for magnificence. Now, dearie, your speech is ready. Try it on for size. (MARY *takes fresh piece of paper from machine and reads it.*)

MARY: "Fellow students: As your candidate for president of this class, I request the honor of your vote. If I am elected, as your faithful president, I will guarantee you all a two-hour lunch period, a reduction in the homework load, and a field trip to Disneyland." (*Looks up*) My goodness, what a difference a dictionary makes!

MOTHER TONGUE: All the difference in the word. Don't forget, dearie—

If your speech needs a bleach,
Help for you is right in reach.
Do not fume and do not rage.
Let your fingering do the lingering

On the dictionary page!

Get the giant, unabridged size—today!

(MARY *and* MOTHER TONGUE *exit down left.*)

LEX: And now, a few words from our sponsor. . . . (SINGING GROUP *enters up right and strikes a pose.*)

SINGING GROUP (*Singing to tune of "All God's Chillun Got Shoes"*):

I love soup,

You love soup,

Everyone's children love soup. (*Humming*)

Hm-m-m-m.

(LI'L LARRY *runs in down right.* LARRY'S MOTHER *follows, holding out bowl and spoon.*)

LI'L LARRY: I hate soup!

MOTHER: But, Li'l Larry, soup is good for you. Now take a spoonful for Mother. (*He sits at table, arms folded stubbornly.*)

LI'L LARRY: I wouldn't take a spoonful even for Superman. (MR. LINGO *zooms across stage from up right. He crosses to* LI'L LARRY.)

MR. LINGO: Man-from-Word. Man-from-Word. What seems to be the problem here?

MOTHER: Why, it's Mr. Lingo, the Man-from-Word. Oh, Mr. Lingo, Li'l Larry won't eat his nice soup.

LI'L LARRY: Aw, it tastes like dishwater.

MR. LINGO (*Sipping soup*): Hm-m-m. So it does. (*He takes out bowl from his briefcase.*) Here, Li'l Larry—try a bowl of Adjective Soup.

MOTHER *and* LI'L LARRY: Adjective Soup? (LI'L LARRY *tastes it doubtfully, then downs it with gusto.*)

LI'L LARRY: Oh, boy! Savory . . . delectable . . . toothsome . . . gusty . . . scrumptious . . . yummy. . . .

MR. LINGO (*Patting his head*): That's enough, Li'l Larry. See —he's getting the benefit of all those healthful adjectives already.

LI'L LARRY: Flavorful—mouthwatering—piquant. . . .

MR. LINGO: Enough, Li'l Larry. (*To audience*) When you feel that life is one long bowl of dishwater, spice up your soup and soup up your spice with adjectives like—

LI'L LARRY: Peppery . . . nippy . . . snappy . . . gingery.

MR. LINGO (*Putting hand over* LI'L LARRY'*s mouth*): And others too numerous to mention. All these adjectives come to you prepackaged, alphabetized and ready to use in this handy, easy-to-open package—the dictionary! (*He zooms off up right, with* LI'L LARRY *and* MOTHER *following.*)

SINGING GROUP (*Singing*):

I love words,
You love words,
Everyone's children love words. . . . (*Humming*)
Hm-m-m.

(*They exit down right.*)

LEX: And now . . . for you lovers of gourmet glossaries, here is your favorite queen of the cuisine, Miss Penelope Patois. What's cooking, Penelope? (PENELOPE PATOIS *enters up right with large bowl. She goes to table.*)

PENELOPE: Hello there, food-for-thought fans. Today we're going to make a really exciting international dish: Polyglot Pie! All ready? All righty. Take your chopping boards and half a cup of assorted Greek epithets. Now, mince your words well. (*She pours out wooden Scrabble letters and pretends to chop them. Then she returns them to bowl and tosses them as she speaks.*) Then take several finely parsed Chinese sentences and combine with some well-aged Sanskrit roots. Stir rapidly. Add a little French phrase here, and a little Spanish phrase there, turning the phrases well. There's nothing like a well-turned French phrase, is there? Now toss in several salty Siamese sayings, and a couple of Norwegian notions. Garnish prettily with asterisks and a dash of a dash. All ready? All righty. Now bake in a moderate oven for at least forty minutes. We don't want any half-baked notions, do we? Now, take your pie out of the oven. (*From cart she takes a pie decorated with flags of all nations.*) If you have followed instructions, your Polyglot Pie should look just like this one. (*She sniffs it, then vigorously shakes a pepper shaker over it.*) It needs just a little more Italian accent. There, isn't that heavenly? You can eat your words in twenty-seven languages. Now, if you want my recipe, all you have to do is print the word "Dictionary" on a large piece of paper and present it to your neighborhood librarian. Tune in next week, won't you? We're going to learn to make Swedish Idioms on the Half-Shell. Toodle-oo. (*She shakes pepper shaker at audience, and exits down right.*)

LEX: It's time now for Channel 26 to sign off. But before we do, here is our Thought for the Day, brought to you by the pensive Virginia Verbal. (VIRGINIA VERBAL *enters with dictionary.* CHORUS *enters, forms a semi-circle behind her, and hums "Home, Sweet Home" as she speaks.*)

VIRGINIA (*Crossing down center*):
    Feeling kind of sad and low?
    Feeling mighty blue?
    Somewhere in this great big world,
    A good word waits for you.
    (*She points to the open dictionary.*)

CHORUS (*In unison*):
    Open up your dictionary,
    Look upon each page,
    Happy words await your glance.
    From every clime and age.

VIRGINIA (*As* CHORUS *hums*):
    So take a word that's cheery;
    If they are small, take two.
    For somewhere in this great big world,
    A good word waits—for you.

LEX: A good word . . . that's what we all need. But suppose

for a moment that all the words that ever were written or spoken vanished like bubbles.

SINGING GROUP: We'd be speechless . . .

1ST SOLO: Dumb . . .

2ND SOLO: Incommunicado.

VIRGINIA: Oh, dear! We couldn't say "Good morning" or "How are you?" Oh, dear! We couldn't say "Happy Birthday" or "Merry Christmas." Oh, dear! We couldn't even say "Oh dear!"

2ND SOLO: I couldn't write my private thoughts in my diary.

3RD SOLO: I couldn't write a letter to the editor.

4TH SOLO: Well, it wouldn't matter if you could—there wouldn't be any newspaper to print your letter.

5TH SOLO: What about radio and television? You'd turn the switch and there would be—

CHORUS (*Whispering*): Deep . . . dead . . . silence.

6TH SOLO (*To* 5TH SOLO): Say, I heard a funny joke this week—

5TH SOLO (*Shaking head*): Sorry. You can't tell a joke without words.

1ST SOLO: Books, books, what about books?

2ND SOLO: No words—no books. Just blank, bleak pages. No Dickens. No Kipling.

3RD SOLO: No Louisa May Alcott. No encyclopedias. No atlases. No cookbooks. No song books.

4TH SOLO: Not even Peter Rabbit?

CHORUS (*Together*): Not even Peter Rabbit.

VIRGINIA: I suppose we could use pantomime.

5TH SOLO: Pantomime? Well, how about this—All the world's a stage, and all the men and women merely players . . .

6TH SOLO: Try to say that with a wave of your hand!

LEX: Yes, there's no substitute for words. Why, I can't even imagine a world without words—because I even *imagine* with words. Words are the indispensable building blocks of our minds. We ought to take care of them.

1st Solo: How do you take care of words?

Lex: Why, Channel 26 gave us a clue. We take care of words by knowing their meanings, by using them effectively, and by spelling them correctly. Don't use the same tired old words all the time.

6th Solo: I know a tired word. *Interesting.* That word should be retired!

5th Solo: But if you take away *interesting*, what will I use in my composition when I want to talk about people and places and things?

Li'l Larry (*Running in, followed by* Mr. Lingo): I know. I know. Try stimulating . . . inspiring . . . rousing . . . electrifying . . . (Mr. Lingo *leads him offstage.*)

Lex: Yes, folks, take care of your words, and your words will take care of you. Keep them polished and ready and they'll trip off the tip of your tongue.

Chorus: You said a mouthful!

Lex: Now, Channel 26 bids you adieu, adios, and so long. We sign off with our last word of the day: the motto of Noah Webster himself . . .

All (*Slowly*): A word to the wise—is sufficient. (*Curtain*)

THE END

The Care and Feeding of Mothers

Characters

NARRATOR	BOY TWIN
SENIOR BABY	GIRL BABY
NURSE	BOY BABY
GIRL TWIN	JUNIOR BABY

BEFORE RISE: NARRATOR *enters through curtains, center.*

NARRATOR: Have you ever wondered what goes on in the head of a newborn baby as he—or she—gazes around at a totally new world? What do you suppose that he—or she—thinks about that all-important person—Mother? By a strange coincidence, we just happen to have a hospital nursery behind the curtains. In the nursery are a number of babies who are willing to give their opinions on things in general, and mothers in particular. Shall we join the babies? (NARRATOR *exits. Curtain opens. Recording of Brahms' "Lullaby" is heard from offstage.*)

SETTING: *A hospital nursery. There are six chairs downstage, draped with sheets or cheesecloth so that each resembles a bassinet.*

AT RISE: SENIOR BABY, *in kimono and mortarboard, sits in bassinet at right.* NURSE *enters, her arms around* GIRL *and* BOY TWINS. NURSE *seats* GIRL TWIN *in bassinet next to* SENIOR BABY. BOY TWIN *sits in third bassinet, beside* GIRL TWIN. NURSE *exits and re-enters at once with* GIRL BABY *and* BOY

BABY. NURSE *seats* GIRL BABY *in bassinet next to* BOY TWIN, *and* BOY BABY *beside* GIRL BABY. *One bassinet at left remains empty.*

NURSE: There now, you precious itty-bitty lambs. There'll be one more itty-bitty lamb to join you in just a minute. (NURSE *exits left.* SENIOR BABY *leans over and shakes hands with* GIRL *and* BOY TWINS, *then nods gravely to* GIRL BABY *and* BOY BABY.)

SENIOR BABY: Good morning, new arrivals.

TWINS *and* BABIES (*Together*): Who are you? Who are we?

GIRL TWIN: I know. We're lambs.

TWINS *and* BABIES: Lambs. We're lambs. Ba-a-a!

SENIOR BABY: You are not lambs. You are babies.

BOY TWIN: Babies! Who would have guessed? How do you know so much?

SENIOR BABY: I'm the Senior Baby of this nursery. I'm going home today with my mother. I know the ropes around here—so if there's anything you want to know, ask me. (NURSE *re-enters with* JUNIOR BABY, *who is crying loudly. She seats him in bassinet at left, patting his shoulder.*)

NURSE: There, there. Everything will be just fine. Don't cry. I'm going to see your mother now. (*She exits left.*)

JUNIOR BABY: Wah!

SENIOR BABY: Oh, boy. Just our luck. A crybaby. You should have been here with the last bunch. They yelled day and night.

GIRL BABY: What's day?

BOY BABY: What's night?

SENIOR BABY: Don't you know anything? Oh, well. Your mothers can explain day and night to you, when you go home.

TWINS *and* BABIES: What's a mother? (JUNIOR BABY *continues to sniffle.*)

SENIOR BABY: What's a mother? You mean you haven't even met your mothers yet?

TWINS *and* BABIES: No.

SENIOR BABY: Well, a mother is—well, she is—look. I'll show you your mothers. See that empty window in front of you? (*Points down center*)

TWINS *and* BABIES: Yes.

SENIOR BABY: When I count to three—

GIRL TWIN: What's "three"?

SENIOR BABY: Never mind. When I say "go," everybody yell and scream and kick your feet. Ready? Go!

TWINS *and* BABIES (*Crying loudly and kicking*): Wah! Wah! (NURSE *rushes in left. They extend their arms to her.*) Mother!

SENIOR BABY: No, no, no! That's not your mother. That's the nurse. Keep your eyes on the empty window. (*Smiling,* NURSE *takes* TWINS *by the hands and leads them down center.*)

TWINS: Where are we going?

SENIOR BABY: The nurse is showing you to your mother.

TWINS (*Pointing*): We see her! We see her!

GIRL TWIN: She's beautiful.

BOY TWIN: She's a little wrinkled, but she has nice ears.

SENIOR BABY: Don't just stand there, wave your fists. Make her smile!

GIRL TWIN: Aw. She's smiling. Isn't she sweet?

BOY TWIN (*Waving his hands*): Hey, Mother! Look at me! (*To* SENIOR BABY) What's her name, by the way?

SENIOR BABY: How would I know? She's your mother. She'll tell you. (NURSE *takes* TWINS *back to bassinets and brings* GIRL BABY *center.*)

GIRL BABY: Oh, I'm so excited. There she is! (*She waves.*) Oh, she's crying. What shall I do?

SENIOR BABY: They all cry the first time they see you. I think we must look funny to them. Don't worry, she'll soon stop. Do something funny. Yawn or something. That always makes mothers stop crying.

GIRL BABY: Mother, look. I'm yawning. See baby yawn. (*Yawns*) She stopped crying. (NURSE *leads her back to bassinet*) Goodbye, Mother. (*Waves.* NURSE *brings* BOY BABY *down center.*)

BOY BABY: Hey, I'm up front now. Where is my mother? I don't see her. Oh, there she is. Aw—she's nice. She's wearing a cute little derby hat and smoking a cute little cigar.

SENIOR BABY: That's your father!

TWINS *and* BABIES: What's a father?

SENIOR BABY: One thing at a time. Get acquainted with your mothers first. (NURSE *leads* BOY BABY *back to bassinet.*)

JUNIOR BABY: Wah! Wah!

NURSE (*Shaking her head*): I'm sorry, ducky, but your mother can't come out and play just yet. (NURSE *exits.*)

GIRL TWIN (*Pointing down center*): Look. The mothers went away. Where did they go?

SENIOR BABY: I don't know. They come when we cry, and disappear when they feel like it.

BOY BABY: What do I do with my mother when I get home? I'm afraid I'll be all thumbs with her.

JUNIOR BABY: Wah!

SENIOR BABY: For one thing, don't be like crybaby over there. (*Points to* JUNIOR BABY) Be patient. When your mother can't feed you right away, don't scream and kick. Wait a while.

GIRL BABY: How do you tell your mother that you like her?

SENIOR BABY: Very simple. Smile and coo.

GIRL TWIN: Smile?

BOY TWIN: Coo?

SENIOR BABY: Boy, are you green! Now, pay attention. Lesson One: How to Smile at Your Mother.

TWINS *and* BABIES (*Except* JUNIOR BABY): Lesson One. How to Smile at Your Mother.

SENIOR BABY: This is a smile. (*Smiles*)

GIRL BABY: I see. The mouth goes up. (*She smiles lopsidedly.*)

SENIOR BABY: Both corners of the mouth, please.

BOY TWIN: I've got it! (*He grins broadly.*)

SENIOR BABY: Good. Now, everybody try. (*All smile, except* JUNIOR BABY.) Very good. Now along with the smile, let's hear a coo. Gurgle-gurgle-coo. Got that?

TWINS *and* BABIES (*Except* JUNIOR BABY): Gurgle-gurgle-coo.

SENIOR BABY (*To* JUNIOR BABY): How about a coo from you, crybaby?

JUNIOR BABY: Wah!

SENIOR BABY: Oh, well. Do the rest of you have any questions?

GIRL TWIN: Yes, please. What should I do if my mother won't eat?

SENIOR BABY: That's a good question. What you should do is see that your mother gets some interesting food. She should eat such things as shrimp newburg, *filet mignon,* and strawberry shortcake. Next question?

BOY TWIN: How should mothers be dressed?

SENIOR BABY: Mothers should wear nice clothes, because it makes them feel good. But, when they go outside, they should wear warm coats and galoshes.

GIRL BABY: When should you take a mother outside?

SENIOR BABY: Mothers need lots of air. Watch their eyes. When their eyes get red around the rims, take them out for air. You can take them out for a walk, but mothers like to ride, too. Especially in nice new cars.

BOY TWIN (*Waving his hand*): Me next. Suppose your mother is sleeping. Shouldn't you wake her up now and then, to make sure she is all right?

SENIOR BABY: Never, never, wake up a sleeping mother. Let sleeping mothers lie.

GIRL TWIN(*Waving her hand*): I have an important question. Do you think that mothers can be spoiled?

SENIOR BABY: I'm glad you asked that question. After five

days of observing all kinds of mothers very closely, I have come to this conclusion.

TWINS *and* BABIES: Tell us!

SENIOR BABY: Mothers cannot be spoiled. They need all the love and attention they can get. Repeat that after me.

TWINS *and* BABIES (*Reciting together*): Mothers cannot be spoiled. They need all the love and attention they can get.

SENIOR BABY: Keep that engraved on your minds. Now, let's practice cooing again. A little heavier on the gurgles this time.

TWINS *and* BABIES (*Except* JUNIOR BABY): Gurgle-gurgle-coo. (NURSE *enters.*)

NURSE: Listen, everybody, I have good news for you. We're all going home today. Our mothers are waiting for us. We're going to take our mothers home! (SENIOR BABY, TWINS, BOY *and* GIRL BABIES *stand.* SENIOR BABY *takes off his mortarboard and leaves it on a bassinet.*)

JUNIOR BABY: Wah!

NURSE: Oh. All except you, precious. (*She leads* JUNIOR BABY *to* SENIOR BABY'S *bassinet at right.*) You're going to be the Senior Baby now. (*Others join hands with* NURSE *and she leads them offstage, leaving* JUNIOR BABY *alone.*)

JUNIOR BABY: Me? I'm the Senior Baby now? (*Puts on mortarboard, crosses to center, and squints at audience.*) Where is she? Where's my mother? (*Waving*) There she is! Hello, Mother! I wonder if her name is Jane. She looks like a Jane. Ah-h-h, look. She has my eyes. She's a little skinny, but she'll grow out of it. Look, Ma. I'm smiling. (*Grins broadly*) Gurgle-gurgle-coo! (*Curtain.*)

THE END

Hotel Oak

Characters

LIZARD

BLACK BEETLE

BLUE BEETLE

GREEN BEETLE

POLKA DOT BEETLE

THREE BIRDS

THREE SQUIRRELS

CHIPMUNK

THREE RABBITS

AX MAN

SAW MAN

BEAVER

FISH

DEER

CATERPILLAR

SETTING: *A forest glade. At center stands a huge oak tree, with large branches extending outward on each side. There are bushes at left and right, and a stream flowing down left around tree and ending in a beaver dam.*

AT RISE: CATERPILLAR *is asleep on large branch at right. From offstage comes sound of chopping and sawing.*

AX MAN (*From offstage*): Timber! (*There is sound of crash offstage.* LIZARD *enters right, crawling on all fours.*)

LIZARD: Twenty! Twenty trees brought down to earth. Ah, it won't be long now. I'll just wait here.

SAW MAN (*From offstage*): Timber! (*Another crash is heard.*)

LIZARD (*Gloating*): Twenty-one. (BLACK BEETLE *tiptoes in from behind tree, followed by* BLUE BEETLE. *Then,* GREEN BEETLE

225

and POLKA DOT BEETLE *tiptoe in from behind tree. They all stand in front of tree, hands on antennae, as if listening.*)

BLACK BEETLE: Bz-z-z. What's that sound? Is that sound what I think it is?

BLUE BEETLE: Bz-z-z. I think it is. A chopper is chopping.

GREEN BEETLE: Bz-z-z. It's coming closer. (*Sounds of chopping and sawing grow louder, followed by sound of tree falling.*)

LIZARD: Twenty-two.

BEETLES (*With hands on hips*): Ugh! A lizard. A slippery-slimy-gritty-grimy-lizard. (*They surround him.*)

BLACK BEETLE (*Pointing at* LIZARD): State your business, Lizard.

BLUE BEETLE (*Pointing at* LIZARD): Why did you leave the desert, Lizard?

GREEN BEETLE (*Pointing at* LIZARD): Why have you come to our forest, Lizard?

POLKA DOT BEETLE (*Pointing at* LIZARD): Why are you grinning at our tree, Lizard?

BEETLES (*Pointing to tree*): Why are you grinning like a crocodile, Lizard?

LIZARD (*Airily*): I'm just biding my time. Biding my time.

BEETLES (*Folding their arms*): For what?

LIZARD: I'm waiting for the sand to blow in, and the dust to cover everything. I'm waiting for the desert.

BLACK BEETLE: You have the wrong forest. There will never be a desert here.

LIZARD: I beg your pardon, but the desert is coming any day. Any day. As soon as the choppers chop down this old tree. (*From offstage there are loud chopping sounds.* BEETLES *tremble.*)

BEETLES: They're coming! They're coming closer and closer. (*They join hands and run to tree. Facing front, they form chain around tree.*)

BLACK BEETLE: If only our tree had legs, it could run away!

BLUE BEETLE: If only our tree had wings, it could fly away!

LIZARD: Ha, ha. It has no legs. It has no wings.

GREEN BEETLE: If only our tree had a brain, it could think of a way to save itself!

POLKA DOT BEETLE: If only our tree had a voice, it could tell us what to do!

LIZARD: Tsk, tsk. Too bad. Trees can't think, and trees can't speak.

BLACK BEETLE: Trees can't think—but beetles can. Four heads are better than one. Let's put our antennae together. (BEETLES *huddle together, nodding their heads and buzzing.*)

BEETLES: Bz-z-z. Bz-z-z. Bz-z-z. That's it. Call a meeting. Call everybody.

BLACK BEETLE: I'll bring the birds. (*He exits, buzzing, up left.*)

BLUE BEETLE: I'll fetch the squirrels and chipmunk. (*He exits down left, buzzing.*)

GREEN BEETLE: I'll round up the rabbits. (*He exits, buzzing, behind tree.*)

POLKA DOT BEETLE: Wait. Whom shall I bring? (CATERPILLAR *raises himself, rubbing his eyes.*)

CATERPILLAR: What's all the buzzing? What's the matter?

POLKA DOT BEETLE: Choppers are coming to chop down Hotel Oak. We're having a meeting. (CATERPILLAR *yawns.*) Look alive! (POLKA DOT BEETLE *shakes* CATERPILLAR.)

CATERPILLAR: I'll try. But I'm not supposed to be awake until next June. (BIRDS *fly on up left and stand in a row.* BLACK BEETLE *follows them and sits crosslegged at center.*)

BIRDS: This is dreadful! What shall we do, Beetles? (SQUIRRELS *enter down left, followed by* CHIPMUNK *and* BLUE BEETLE. *They stand in front of tree, next to* BIRDS. BLUE BEETLE *sits crosslegged next to* BLACK BEETLE.)

SQUIRRELS: We must have a plan, Beetles, a plan! (RABBITS

enter from behind tree. They kneel in front of BIRDS *and* SQUIRRELS. GREEN BEETLE *and* POLKA DOT BEETLE *join other* BEETLES.)

RABBITS: We must save our tree. Save our tree, Beetles.

CATERPILLAR: Save me. Save me, Beetles.

BLACK BEETLE: We know what to do.

BLUE BEETLE: We have a plan.

GREEN BEETLE: We will simply explain to the choppers that this is our home.

POLKA DOT BEETLE: After all, even the choppers have a home. I think . . .

LIZARD (*Scoffing*): Dumb animals! Talk. Explain. Men don't understand. (*Looking off*) Well, here come the choppers now. Go ahead. Talk and explain. See how much good it does. You dumb animals! (AX MAN *and* SAW MAN *enter down right.*)

AX MAN (*Pointing to tree*): That one. Let's take that old oak.

SAW MAN: Wait! Look! Look at all the animals around the tree. Why, it's a regular Noah's ark—with bark! (AX MAN *crosses to animals, motioning them off.*)

AX MAN: Go away. Get out. We're cutting this tree down! (*He stands left.*)

SAW MAN: They aren't moving. (*He brandishes his saw.*) Shoo! You're in the way. Scat!

CATERPILLAR: They mean business. Somebody start explaining. (BIRDS *cross center.* AX MAN *and* SAW MAN *back off, nervously.*)

1ST BIRD: How do we address them?

CATERPILLAR: Try "dear sirs."

1ST BIRD: Dear Sirs: We birds have lived in Hotel Oak for generations.

2ND BIRD: We have rested here and nested here. And here we have spent our sunny summer days.

3RD BIRD: We cordially invite you not to cut down our tree.

We thank you. (BIRDS *cross back, as* SQUIRRELS *and* CHIPMUNK *take center stage.*)

1ST SQUIRREL: Dear Sirs: Let us present some facts and figures.

2ND SQUIRREL: It is a fact that there are fifteen lady squirrels and fifteen gentleman squirrels and six baby squirrels living in the East Wing of Hotel Oak.

CHIPMUNK: And one chipmunk. We thank you. (*They cross back, as* RABBITS *stand.* RABBITS *thump their feet three times.*)

1ST RABBIT: Dear Sirs: Important rabbits live in the basement apartment of Hotel Oak.

2ND RABBIT: Our tunnels go down ten feet, and we have over twenty-one apartments in our burrow.

3RD RABBIT: Mother rabbits and father rabbits, rabbit aunts, and rabbit uncles live under Hotel Oak. Not to mention rabbit grandmothers and rabbit grandfathers. We even have one old, old, great-grandfather rabbit.

CATERPILLAR: You wouldn't cut down a tree with a great-grandfather rabbit living under it, would you? (RABBITS *kneel again.*)

AX MAN: Birds twittering. Squirrels chattering. Rabbits thumping and a caterpillar jumping around. What is this? What do they want?

SAW MAN: I don't know. But this tree is coming down right now. Go ahead, start chopping.

AX MAN: Oh, no. After you.

SAW MAN: I know. I'll start to saw the trunk, just a little— not enough to hurt the animals. Then they'll high-tail it. (*He crosses to tree, and animals back away fearfully. He puts saw against trunk. Animals groan.*)

ANIMALS (*Ad lib*): No! No! Stop! Don't touch our tree! (*Etc.*)

1ST BIRD: If you cut down the tree, the birds will fly away.

2ND BIRD: If the birds fly away, the song of the forest will vanish.

1ST SQUIRREL: If you cut down the tree, the squirrels will scamper away.

2ND SQUIRREL: If the squirrels leave the forest, who will scatter the acorns?

3RD SQUIRREL: There will be no new trees. The forest will vanish.

1ST RABBIT: If you cut down the tree, the rabbits will run away.

2ND RABBIT: The roots of the tree will let go of the hill.

3RD RABBIT: The whole hillside will slide into the stream. What will become of the beaver and fish?

BEAVER (*Raising his head from behind dam; alarmed*): I'll tell you. I'll tell you what will happen to the beaver. The beaver will move away, and the stream will dry up.

FISH (*Looking out from behind dam*): I'll tell you what will happen to the fish. The fish will glide to the river, and the stream will become a path of dust. Dust and sand.

LIZARD (*Gloating*): Dust and sand. (DEER *runs in down right.*)

DEER: Run! Run! Run out of the forest before the fire comes.

CHIPMUNK: What fire? Where?

DEER: Fire will come, when the tree falls. When the tree falls, the hillside will slide into the stream. The stream will dry up, and the bushes will turn brown in the sun. The sky will darken and lightning will streak down, like a torch from the sky. (*There is sound of thunder from offstage.*) The bushes will burn, and there will be ashes, ashes everywhere.

LIZARD: Ashes, ashes, everywhere.

DEER: Follow me. Run! Run! (*He trots off down right, followed by* BIRDS, SQUIRRELS, *and* RABBITS, *with* BEETLES *and* CHIPMUNK *at rear, followed at a distance by* CATERPILLAR *inching along.*)

CATERPILLAR: Wait for me! (*They exit down right.*)

BEAVER: To the river!

FISH: To the river! (BEAVER *and* FISH *exit.*)

LIZARD: And now, number twenty-three, coming right down. (*He moves down left.* AX MAN *and* SAW MAN *look at each other.* AX MAN *stands right of tree, ax raised.* SAW MAN *stands left of tree, saw held against it.*)

AX MAN: After you.

SAW MAN: Weird, wasn't it? All those animals running away. Wonder if they were trying to tell us something.

AX MAN: Funny you should say that. I was thinking the same thing. Maybe there's something the matter with the tree. (*Puts down ax.*)

SAW MAN: Let's have a look. (*Puts down saw.*)

AX MAN (*Looking up, shading his eyes*): Tall, isn't she? Like the mast of a big ship. It must have taken a hundred years to grow this tree.

SAW MAN: And it'll only take three minutes to cut it down. Now that's a shame!

AX MAN (*Feeling bark*): Bark seems all right. Say, I see little holes in the bark. Beetles must live here.

SAW MAN (*Looking at top of branch, left*): Acorns. Hundreds of acorns. This must be the First National Acorn Bank.

AX MAN (*Looking at top branch, right, through binoculars*): It's a regular hotel. There are birds living in the penthouse. I see a nest.

SAW MAN: Let's have a look at the roots. (*He bends down and looks carefully at bottom of tree.*) Hey. There's a rabbit burrow down there. (AX MAN *puts down ax and crosses center and sits down.* SAW MAN *leans saw against tree and follows him, sitting down.*)

AX MAN: You know, I never really looked at a tree before. I always used to chop first and look afterward.

SAW MAN: I know what you mean. A tree was just so many board feet of lumber before. Now, it's a hotel.

AX MAN: Maybe that's what the animals were trying to tell us.

SAW MAN (*Rising*): Maybe. Well, anyway, we have to get started. (*He walks to tree and picks up saw, then stands left of tree. Ax* MAN *follows him, picks up ax and stands right of tree.*) All right, begin chopping.

AX MAN: No, you start first.

SAW MAN: After you.

AX MAN (*Uneasily*): Well, I would, but I keep thinking: how would I like it if a couple of rabbits came to my hotel with a wrecking ball and started to knock down my room without even asking!

SAW MAN: I wouldn't like that. Not at all.

AX MAN: Neither would I. What's more, I'm sure that's what all the twittering and chattering and thumping and jumping were about.

SAW MAN: "Save our hotel." That's what they were saying, but we were too stupid to understand.

AX MAN: What shall we do? We're supposed to cut down twenty-three trees today.

SAW MAN: Hm-m-m. Twenty-three *trees,* did you say? Ah, but nobody gave us permission to cut down a *hotel.*

AX MAN (*Relieved*): That's right. We can't cut down a hotel. What do you say we call it a day?

SAW MAN: Wait, now. Before we call it a day—what about tomorrow?

AX MAN: What about tomorrow?

SAW MAN: There'll be no tomorrow for this forest, if we're not careful. We don't have to cut every tree in sight. We can cut what we need and still protect the forest.

AX MAN: Right. (*With sweeping gesture*) Here then, Hotel Oak—here's a gift from us to you and the forest. We'll take only twenty trees from a grove. And we'll leave three to renew the forest.

SAW MAN: Goodbye, Hotel Oak. You have a lease on life for another hundred years. (*They exit down right, as* CHIPMUNK *hops on from up right.*)

CHIPMUNK: My acorns! I can't go away without my acorns! (*He covers his eyes.*) Oh, poor Hotel Oak. I can't look. I can't . . . (*He peeks a little.*) Look! It's still here. (*He calls offstage excitedly*) Listen, everybody. Hotel Oak is here! We can all come back! (LIZARD *starts to cross slowly.*) Hello, you slippery-slimy-gritty-grimy Lizard. Where are you going?

LIZARD (*Moving to front of stage*): I'm moving along, just moving along. (*Curtains begin to close; as* LIZARD *goes forward, other animals move behind him. He speaks to audience.*) You think I've lost my desert, don't you? You just wait. Wherever men are careless about trees, you'll find me. I'm going to look for the loggers who slash the forest bare. I'm going to look for the campers who leave campfires glowing. I'm going to look for the builders who leave the hillsides raw and brown. Will you be there? If you are, I hope you like dust and sand, dust and sand . . . and lizards! (*He chuckles wickedly and exits left.*)

THE END

The Search for the Sky-Blue Princess

Characters

VROUW ANNA VAN DYKE
KLAUS VAN DYKE, *her husband*
PETER VAN DYKE, *their son*
GRETCHEN
KATRINA
INGA
OSWALD, *a palace guard*
PRIME MINISTER
KING WILHELM
HERALD
TWO ROWDIES
TWO SOLDIERS
CHORUS, *boys and girls*

SCENE 1

SETTING: *A street in Holland. The scene may be played in front of curtain.*

AT RISE: VROUW VAN DYKE *enters from right, followed by her son,* PETER, *who carries a basketful of rolls.* PETER *is yawning.*

VROUW VAN DYKE: Come, Peter, get the sleep out of your eyes! You must look sharp if you expect to sell my rolls, these sad days. (GRETCHEN, *carrying tray of cheeses, enters left, followed by* KATRINA, *who wears a yoke from which a milk pail is hanging, and* INGA, *who carries a market basket of vegetables. They stand in a row from right to left, downstage.*)

GRETCHEN, KATRINA *and* INGA: Good morning, Vrouw Van Dyke. Good morning, Peter.

VROUW *and* PETER: Good morning, girls.

GRETCHEN: Did you sell many rolls yesterday, Peter?

PETER (*Boasting*): Thousands! People bought our rolls all day.

VROUW (*Sharply*): Peter!

PETER: Well, we sold several—

VROUW: The truth, Peter.

PETER: Several dozen.

GRETCHEN: Several dozen? That's pretty good, isn't it, Katrina?

KATRINA: It's very good. I stood in this place all day yesterday, and I didn't sell one dipperful of milk.

INGA: It's because the King is ill. People haven't wanted to buy so much food.

VROUW: Perhaps some fresh-baked rolls will give them an appetite. (*Turns to go*) I'll leave you in charge, Peter. But there's one thing . . .

PETER: I know. Tell the truth.

VROUW: Just don't boast. Boasting is going to get you into trouble one fine day. (OSWALD, *a palace guard, enters right.* VROUW *crosses to him.*) Good morning, Mynheer Oswald. How is the King this morning?

OSWALD (*Touching his cap to her*): He is low, Vrouw Van Dyke, very low. The doctors say good King Wilhelm will not be with us when the tulips bloom.

VROUW (*Dismayed*): That cannot be! What will become of Holland without King Wilhelm?

OSWALD: What will become of us, indeed? There are thousands of Spanish soldiers at our borders just waiting to answer that question.

VROUW: We shall have to pray that King Wilhelm recovers.

(*She exits left.* OSWALD *stands at attention, down left. He does not hear following dialogue.* PETER *faces right, arranges rolls in basket.* TWO ROWDIES *enter left, look around, then slip behind* OSWALD *and approach girls.*)

1ST ROWDY (*Pointing to* INGA): Well, well! Look what I see—girls!

2ND ROWDY (*Mischievously*): We ought to inspect their wares. (*He grabs cabbage from* INGA's *basket. He holds cabbage in one hand and wiggles forefinger of other hand over the top, as if it were a worm.*)

1ST ROWDY (*Pointing to cabbage*): Girl! Girl! You are selling rotten cabbages. Look—there's a worm on this one.

2ND ROWDY: We are market inspectors, girl. I'll keep this cabbage for evidence. (*Puts cabbage behind his back*)

INGA: Give that cabbage back, you thief!

GRETCHEN: Peter! Help us! (PETER *turns, sees* ROWDIES.)

PETER: Hey, there! Leave the girls alone! (*Puts down basket of rolls*)

1ST ROWDY (*Crossing to* PETER, *insolently*): Why, it's Peter Van Dyke—the son of old laughingstock Van Dyke.

PETER (*Putting up his fists, furious*): Don't you dare call my father a laughingstock!

2ND ROWDY (*Crossing to* PETER, *tauntingly*): Laughingstock! Laughingstock! Everyone laughs at your father and the crazy things he invents!

PETER: Stop it! My father is the most brilliant man in the world. Some day he'll invent something so grand that even the King will stop to look at it.

2ND ROWDY: Your father—invent something grand? He can't even earn a living! (PETER, *enraged, tackles* 2ND ROWDY, *but* 1ST ROWDY *holds* PETER's *arms. They scuffle.* GRETCHEN *and* KATRINA *watch in horror.* INGA *runs to* OSWALD *and tugs at his sleeve.*)

INGA: Please, sir, come quickly! There's a terrible fight, and

Peter is getting the worst of it! (OSWALD *turns, sees fight and crosses right with* INGA.)

OSWALD: Here! Stop that! Go away, now! (ROWDIES *run off right. As he exits,* 1ST ROWDY *turns over* PETER'S *basket of rolls.*)

KATRINA: Oh, the rolls! (*She picks up rolls, putting them into basket.*)

PETER: Look at that. Now they're all dirty. I can't sell them.

OSWALD: That's a shame. Still, the royal horses aren't fussy about a little dirt. I'll just take the rolls to them. (*Taking a coin from his pocket*) Will half a crown do?

PETER (*Taking coin*): Very well! Thank you, Mynheer Oswald. (*Gives basket to* OSWALD)

GRETCHEN: Please, sir, we have all been so worried about the King. Do you have any news? (*Girls and* PETER *gather about* OSWALD.)

OSWALD (*Confidentially*): I'm not supposed to say, but the fact is, he's low, children, very low. The only thing that gives him any pleasure is the picture of a blue tulip that hangs on his wall.

KATRINA: A blue tulip? There's no such thing as a blue tulip.

OSWALD: You know that. I know that. But His Majesty's feverish mind fancies that somewhere in the world there is a blue tulip. He calls the tulip his "sky-blue princess." (TWO ROWDIES *sneak onstage, down right, eavesdropping.*)

GRETCHEN: "Sky-blue princess." That's a pretty name.

INGA: What a pity there's no such thing as a real blue tulip. It might give the King hope.

PETER: How do you know there's no such thing as a blue tulip? I'll bet my father could raise a blue tulip if he tried.

GRETCHEN (*Putting finger to her lips*): Sh-h-h! Peter, don't boast!

OSWALD: Could your father raise a blue tulip? Hm. . . . a

real blue tulip. Excuse me, children. I have an urgent message for someone in the palace. (*He crosses left, carrying basket of rolls, and speaking to himself.*) The King must know of this. (*Exits*)

GRETCHEN (*Shaking her head*): Oh, Peter, I wish you hadn't boasted about that blue tulip. Nothing good will come of this. I just know it! (PETER *and girls exit left.* ROWDIES *cross to center.*)

1ST ROWDY: Did you hear that little windbag? Blue tulips!

2ND ROWDY: It might be true. Last year Van Dyke bred striped tulips. If he does grow a blue tulip, it will be worth a lot of money.

1ST ROWDY: I see what you mean. Why should old Van Dyke have all the tulips, eh? What's one more tulip to him?

2ND ROWDY: You're right. When the tulips bloom, we're going to pay Van Dyke a visit.

1ST ROWDY: We'll take the blue tulip, and sell it at the festival, to the highest bidder! Now, let's get out of here before old Oswald comes back. (*They exit.*)

* * *

SCENE 2

SETTING: *The Van Dyke kitchen. There is a Dutch door center, and windows up left and right. A Dutch fireplace is at right, and left is a large cupboard. There are a kitchen table and small benches downstage center.*

AT RISE: VROUW VAN DYKE *stands at table, kneading dough in a bowl.* KLAUS VAN DYKE *sits in a captain's chair near fireplace, counting coins into a sugar bowl.*

VAN DYKE: Only a few crowns left, Anna. I thought that surely the great coach company would buy my idea for a horseless carriage. Instead, they laughed at me.

VROUW: It was a fine idea. I still think so. And don't worry about the money. When the new tulips bloom, people will buy many, many bulbs. Only, Klaus—

VAN DYKE: Yes, Anna?

VROUW: Try to restrain your generosity. Don't give all the bulbs away this year. (PETER *bursts through door, center.*)

PETER: I sold them! I sold all the rolls!

VAN DYKE: You sold a whole basket of rolls? Good boy! Did you hear that, Anna? He'll make our fortune yet.

VROUW: Just a minute. How did you sell a whole basket of rolls so fast?

PETER: Oh, I was such a salesman! You should have seen me. People came from all over town—

VROUW (*Sternly*): The truth, Peter.

PETER: Well, the truth is—two rowdies came by and spilled the rolls on the ground. Old Oswald was kind enough to buy them for half a crown.

VROUW: That was nice of him. What will he do with a basket of rolls, I wonder?

PETER: Feed them to the King's horses. (VAN DYKE *laughs heartily.* VROUW VAN DYKE *is horrified.*)

VROUW: Feed my beautiful rolls to horses? Oh, Peter!

VAN DYKE: Now, Anna, you must admit—they'll be the best-fed horses in Holland. (*There is a knock on door.*)

VROUW (*Wiping her hands on her apron*): Who can that be? (*She crosses to door and opens it.* PRIME MINISTER *and* OSWALD *enter.* VAN DYKES *all bow, astonished.*)

VAN DYKE: Mynheer Prime Minister!

OSWALD: The Prime Minister is here for a most important reason. Peter knows, eh, Peter? (*He winks at* PETER.)

VROUW: Peter? What have you done, Peter?

PETER (*Frightened*): Me? I don't know.

PRIME MINISTER: I must come to the point quickly, Mynheer Van Dyke. Our King is gravely ill. His mind is full of a strange blue tulip.

PETER (*Alarmed*): Oh! The blue tulip!

PRIME MINISTER: Oswald, here, tells me that you, Mynheer Van Dyke, have bred a blue tulip.

VAN DYKE (*Bewildered*): A *blue* tulip?

PRIME MINISTER: When this tulip blooms, in two weeks, I shall take the flower for the King. It is all he lives for now. You, Van Dyke, will be rewarded handsomely, for you will have saved the life of your monarch—and your country. Come, Oswald, we must return to the palace. Farewell, Van Dyke—until the tulips bloom. (*He exits center.* OSWALD *pauses, beaming at* PETER.)

OSWALD: There. Aren't you proud of yourself, Peter? (*He exits.*)

VROUW *and* VAN DYKE: Peter!

VROUW: I always told you boasting would get you into trouble.

VAN DYKE: My son, whatever possessed you to tell such a lie? A blue tulip—ach!

PETER: It wasn't a lie, Father. I only said you could raise a blue tulip if you tried. I didn't know Oswald would pay attention to me.

VAN DYKE: But don't you know that to breed a blue tulip, I would have had to start years and years ago? The tulips are about to bloom. How could I possibly breed a blue tulip in two weeks?

PETER (*In a small voice*): I don't know, Father.

VROUW: Peter, you will go immediately to the palace and confess the truth to the Prime Minister. You will beg his pardon, and the pardon of the King. Oh, shame, shame!

VAN DYKE: Wait, please, Anna. The King's very life depends upon this imaginary blue tulip. We cannot disappoint him now.

PETER: Could we paint a tulip, Father?

VAN DYKE: No, that would be an insult to the King. This

tulip must be blue as a summer sky. A perfect cup of azure, radiant and pure.

VROUW: Ach, Peter. Why didn't you boast that your father could make tulips of gold? That would have been easier.

VAN DYKE: Tulips of gold? Hm-m-m. Once I met a gardener who changed a yellow tulip into an orange tulip just before it bloomed. He used all sorts of expensive chemicals and dyes in the soil. We have some common purple tulips—I wonder . . .

PETER: Try, Father. You can do it.

VAN DYKE: I don't know. I will have to force tulips to bloom in the window, there. We will have to live tulips, and breathe tulips. We will have to tend them like delicate babies. It will be tulips morning, noon and night. We will see tulips in our sleep.

PETER: And then—?

VAN DYKE: And then, if we are very lucky, we will have a royal tulip for His Royal Majesty.

PETER: A sky-blue princess.

VAN DYKE: Ja, a sky-blue princess.

VROUW (*Shaking her head*): A sky-blue princess! Ach, Peter, if only you had kept your mouth shut! (*The curtains close.*)

* * *

SCENE 3

TIME: *Early morning two weeks later.*

SETTING: *The same as Scene 2.*

AT RISE: *At the upstage windows are three small wooden boxes with transparent blue paper over the tops. In the side of each box is a small peephole.* KLAUS VAN DYKE *is sleeping in chair at fireplace.* PETER *is dozing on a stool near window boxes, center.* PETER *stirs and yawns, then opens his eyes and stands.*

PETER: Dawn. I almost slept through that last feeding. I seem to be feeding tulips all night. (*He takes a medicine bottle and eyedropper from one of the window boxes, and drops some plant food through the peephole in each box*). Come on, babies. Soak it all up. (*He squints through peephole, then calls out in great excitement.*) Mother! Father! Come quickly. The tulips have bloomed!

VAN DYKE (*Rubbing his eyes, then standing and crossing to window boxes*): What's that? They've bloomed? (*He looks through peepholes. VROUW VAN DYKE enters from down left with two bowls, spoons, and a jar of honey.*)

VROUW: You're dreaming again, Peter. You thought they bloomed yesterday, too. Come, eat your porridge and honey. (*She sets bowls down on table.*)

VAN DYKE (*Turning*): It's true! They must have unfolded just at dawn. We must be very careful. There are only three left, out of seven dozen. Ready? (*Picks up first box.*)

PETER: Oh, yes, Father.

VAN DYKE: Here comes the first one.

VROUW: My heart is beating like a drum. (VAN DYKE *carefully takes paper from first box, lifting out tulip. It is gray.*)

ALL (*Sadly*): Oh . . .

PETER: It's gray. Like rain clouds.

VAN DYKE: There are still two more. Here comes the second one. (*He lifts out tulip from second box. It is purple.*)

VROUW: Ach, purple. It might be anybody's tulip. Everyone has purple tulips.

VAN DYKE: One left. Well, let's have the bad news quickly. Here's the last tulip. (*Picks up third box.*)

VROUW (*Closing her eyes*): I can't bear to look.

PETER: Neither can I. (*He covers his eyes.* VAN DYKE *takes tulip from third box. It is sky-blue and larger than the others. An arpeggio may be played offstage.*)

VAN DYKE: Oh . . . how wonderful. Open your eyes, everybody! (*He puts blue tulip on table.*)

VROUW and PETER (*Opening their eyes*): It's blue!

VROUW: Bright blue. . . .

PETER: Beautiful blue. . . . (*They join hands and dance about kitchen in excitement.*)

ALL (*Chanting*): A tulip, a tulip! We bred a bright blue tulip! (*Urgent knocking is heard at door.* GRETCHEN *bursts into room, frightened.*)

GRETCHEN: Mynheer Van Dyke—has your blue tulip bloomed?

PETER: Yes! Come and see it!

GRETCHEN: Hide it, quickly! Two rogues in black masks are coming this way. I overheard them say they're going to steal the blue tulip!

VROUW: Oh, how wicked! Klaus, give me the tulip. I'll hide it in the linen closet. (*There is heavy knock on door.*)

1ST ROWDY (*From offstage*): Open up in there. (VROUW *takes rolling pin from cupboard. She stands in front of door.*)

VROUW (*Loudly*): Go away. We're not receiving visitors. Go away, or I'll give you a taste of my rolling pin!

2ND ROWDY (*From offstage*): We're coming in. Open up, or we'll break the door down.

VAN DYKE: There's no time to hide the tulip now.

PETER: Oh, how I wish all the tulips had been gray!

VAN DYKE: All gray—that's it! Peter, take the petals from the gray tulip and give them to Gretchen. Hurry. Gretchen, smear the blue tulip with honey.

PETER: Father—have you lost your wits?

VAN DYKE: Do as I tell you. Hurry. (PETER *takes petals from gray tulip as* GRETCHEN *puts honey on blue tulip. Loud knocking and battering is heard at door.* VROUW VAN DYKE *shakes her rolling pin at door.*) Now, Gretchen, cover the blue tulip with the gray petals. Don't worry—the honey won't hurt the blue tulip. (GRETCHEN *puts gray petals over blue tulip, camouflaging it.*)

2ND ROWDY (*From offstage*): Let us in—or we'll grind you to liverwurst.

VAN DYKE: Let them in, Anna. (VROUW VAN DYKE *steps away from door.* TWO ROWDIES *enter.* 1ST ROWDY *searches cupboard.*)

1ST ROWDY: Where is the blue tulip?

2ND ROWDY: Give us the blue tulip, or we'll slice you like sausages.

VAN DYKE (*Calmly*): You will find no blue tulip here.

1ST ROWDY: He's right. It's not here.

2ND ROWDY: He's hidden it in the garden. Come, we'll look there. (*To others*) Stay where you are, or we'll chop you to hamburger. (ROWDIES *exit, center.*)

PETER: He should have been a butcher. (GRETCHEN *goes to window up right, fearfully. Then she begins to laugh.*)

GRETCHEN: Oh, look. It's the palace guard, Oswald. He's caught those rogues by their coat collars. We're saved! We're saved! (VAN DYKE *crosses to table and removes gray petals from blue tulip.* OSWALD *opens top half of Dutch doors. He holds unmasked* ROWDIES *by their coat collars.*)

OSWALD: Mynheer Van Dyke—look. Look what I found trampling through your tulips. Two tulip tramplers. If you don't mind, I'll take them to the dungeon.

VAN DYKE: We don't mind!

OSWALD (*Pointing to blue tulip*): Ah, there she is. I came especially to see her. The sky-blue princess herself.

1ST ROWDY: Do you see what I see? A blue tulip!

2ND ROWDY: But we searched high and low. It's magic.

1ST ROWDY: Dumbhead. You didn't use your little beady eyes.

2ND ROWDY: Don't call me dumbhead, you blunderer. The tulip was under your big red nose all the time.

OSWALD: Now, now. Let's get along. You can blame each other all you want—in the King's lowest dungeon. (*They exit.* INGA *and* KATRINA *appear at door.*)

INGA: Peter! Gretchen! Hurry! The tulip festival is beginning in the palace courtyard.

KATRINA: The King himself is going to be there. Hurry! (*They exit.*)

VAN DYKE: How very strange. My son boasts about a tulip that does not exist. That boast goes all the way to the ears of the King. Boasting is a bad thing, and yet, out of that boast comes a miracle.

PETER: But, Father, it wasn't a boast. It was a belief. A boast is a something you know inside is not true. But a belief is something you know inside *is* true. I believed that you could do anything with tulips. And so you can. (*Curtains begin to close.*)

VAN DYKE: Oh, Peter, Peter. How can I scold you? But promise me this—Don't put me to the test too often.

PETER: I promise, Father. (*Curtain*)

*   *   *

SCENE 4

BEFORE RISE: CHORUS, *with* GRETCHEN, KATRINA *and* INGA, *march on from left and right* (*or march down aisles*), *carrying potted tulips, and singing.*

ALL (*Singing to tune of "Come to the Fair"*):

Oh, tulips, oh, tulips, from here and from there.
Tu-lips! From everywhere.
Red ones and yellow ones, dark ones and fair;
Tu-lips! From everywhere.
For it's Festival Day, and there's such happy news,
Come in Spring linens, and new wooden shoes—
Oh, it's come, then, everyone come,
To the Festival here in the morning.
Oh, tulips, oh, tulips, from here and from there.
Tu-lips! From everywhere.

(Repeat, slowly)
Tu-lips! From everywhere.
(Curtains open.)

* * *

TIME: *Later that day.*

SETTING: *The palace courtyard.*

AT RISE: *A throne is at center. The picture of the blue tulip hangs above throne. Banners hang on rear curtain.* CHORUS, GRETCHEN, KATRINA *and* INGA *march to throne and place their tulips on each side of throne. They stand left and right of throne. Fanfare is heard from offstage.* HERALD *enters.*

HERALD: His Royal Highness, King Wilhelm. *(He stands up left.* CHORUS *applaud and cheer as* KING WILHELM *enters right. He raises his hand in greeting, sits on throne.* CHORUS *bow and curtsy.)* Presenting the most original and unusual tulip of the realm. Presenting the blue tulip, now named "the sky-blue princess."

1ST CHORUS MEMBER: A blue tulip? Impossible.

CHORUS *(Together)*: Impossible. *(They laugh heartily. Another fanfare is heard and* KLAUS VAN DYKE *marches in, proudly holding blue tulip in pot. Behind him march* VROUW VAN DYKE *and* PETER. *They are followed by the* PRIME MINISTER, OSWALD, *and* TWO SOLDIERS. CHORUS *exclaim at tulip and bow and curtsy as tulip passes them.* VAN DYKE, VROUW *and* PETER *kneel before* KING.)

PRIME MINISTER: The sky-blue princess, Your Majesty. *(*VAN DYKE *hands tulip to* KING. TWO SOLDIERS *stand left and right of throne.)*

OSWALD: Just as I promised, Your Majesty.

KING *(Holding tulip out to admire it)*: She is even more beautiful than I imagined her. She is worth every moment of my struggle against the powers of darkness. She has saved me, and now she will save Holland. For the sky-blue princess will be our emblem. She will be emblazoned on every banner as we march against Spain. Stand, Mynheer Van Dyke. Ask what you will of your king.

VAN DYKE (*Standing, embarrassed*): Oh, well . . . I don't know what to ask.

VROUW (*Standing*): I do. Please, Your Majesty. Everyone knows that Klaus Van Dyke is the best gardener in all Holland. If I may be so bold—could you, would you write him a recommendation?

KING: I will do better than that. Klaus Van Dyke, from this time forward you shall be the royal gardener. The palace grounds with all the trees and gardens shall be yours.

VAN DYKE: Thank you, thank you, Your Majesty.

OSWALD: Three cheers for Klaus Van Dyke. Three cheers for His Majesty!

CHORUS: Hurrah! Hurrah! Hurra-a-ah! (*They wave their hands and cheer as music begins, then sing, to tune of "Come to the Fair."*)

GRETCHEN (*Singing, skipping forward*):
Oh, tulips, oh, tulips, from here and from there.

CHORUS:
Tu-lips! From everywhere.

KATRINA (*Singing, skipping forward*):
Red ones and yellow ones, dark ones and fair;

CHORUS:
Tu-lips! From everywhere.

INGA (*Singing, skipping forward*):
For it's Festival Day, and there's such happy news,

GRETCHEN, KATRINA *and* INGA (*Singing*):
Come in Spring linens, and new wooden shoes.
Oh, it's come, then, everyone come,
To the Festival, here in the morning.

ALL:
Oh, tulips, oh, tulips, from here and from there.
Tu-lips are everywhere!

(*Repeat, slowly*)
Tu-lips are everywhere!
(*Curtain*)

THE END

Next Stop--Spring!

Characters

Four Subway Riders	Ice Cream Man
Conductor	Stickball Players
Umbrella Man	Three Hopscotchers
Boy	Three Rope Jumpers
Grocer	Mother
Hat Shop Owner	Policeman
Three Housewives	Four Ladies

Time: *Just before spring.*

Before Rise: Four Subway Riders *enter down right through turnstile and take places in front of curtain. They wear overcoats, and shiver as they stand with arms upraised, as if holding straps.* 2nd Rider *carries newspaper. As he rides, he holds newspaper so headline faces audience:* winters are getting colder. *Other* Riders *read over his shoulder.*

Riders: Br-r-r-r! (Conductor, *carrying small stool and megaphone, enters left.*)

Conductor (*Speaking through megaphone*): We are departing through the February Tunnel. This subway will make stops at March Avenue, April Junction, and all points South. (*He sets stool down at left, sits, pantomimes driving subway. He pulls an imaginary cord, and steam whistle sounds.* Riders *jog up and down, as if in motion. They sway over to right,*

249

and then over to left, as if going around turn. CONDUCTOR *pulls a brake.* RIDERS *jerk as if stopping suddenly.* CONDUCTOR *crosses to* RIDERS.) March Avenue. All off for March Avenue. Transfer at the Equinox Exit. (RIDERS *take off their heavy overcoats, draping them in unison over their left arms.* 2ND RIDER *turns page, revealing another headline in larger type:* FAIR AND WINDY. *Other* RIDERS *cluster about and read over his shoulder again.*)

RIDERS: Oh-h-h! (CONDUCTOR *pulls whistle cord. Steam whistle is heard.* CONDUCTOR *pantomimes driving.* RIDERS *jog up and down.* CONDUCTOR *pulls brake again. They jerk to stop, and* CONDUCTOR *crosses right.*)

CONDUCTOR (*Calling out*): April Junction. April Junction. Change here for Shower Street and Flower Street.

UMBRELLA MAN (*Entering right, carrying black umbrellas*): Umbrellas. Get your umbrellas here! (*Each* RIDER *takes an umbrella, hangs it from left wrist.* UMBRELLA MAN *crosses left and exits.* 2ND RIDER *turns page. Headline reads:* RUMORS OF SPRING!)

1ST RIDER (*To* 2ND RIDER): Did you see?

2ND RIDER: I saw. (*To* 3RD RIDER) Could it be?

3RD RIDER: Should be! About time.

4TH Rider: Confidentially—a little bird told me—spring's definitely coming.

RIDERS: What bird? What bird?

4TH RIDER: A real, live, bright-eyed, olive-feathered, red-breasted robin!

RIDERS (*Ad lib*): Robins are back. Robins! Did you hear that? Robins are back! (*Etc.* CONDUCTOR *brakes to stop. All jerk to stop.* 2ND RIDER *turns page. Headline takes up full page:* SPRING IS HERE!)

CONDUCTOR (*Putting flower in his lapel*): May Terminal. End of the line. May Terminal. Everybody off. (*He takes his stool and exits down left.*)

RIDERS (*Reading paper*): *Spring* is here.

1ST RIDER: Spring is *here.* If the paper says so—

2ND RIDER: It must *be* so.

3RD RIDER: Must tell somebody.

4TH RIDER: Must tell *everybody.*

RIDERS: Somebody had better know. Everybody had better know. (1ST *and* 2ND RIDERS *exit down right, and* 3RD *and* 4TH RIDERS *exit down left. Curtains open.*)

* * *

SETTING: *A street. Three houses with doors and steps leading to side-walk are up center. Each has shuttered window with flower box. Flower box of first house has petunia in it, middle one has geranium, and third has rubber plant. At right is grocery store with sign in window reading:* HOT CEREAL. HOT POTATOES. HOT DOGS. *At left is hat shop with sign reading:* SALE: FUR HATS. WOOL CAPS. PARKAS. *Hopscotch diagram is chalked on floor, center.*

AT RISE: BOY, *bundled up in jacket and holding football, stands at center.* 1ST *and* 2ND RIDERS *enter right wearing spring clothes.*

1ST RIDER: Hey, there, Grocer. It's time for a change. Spring is here. (GROCER *enters from grocery store. He stands with hands on hips in doorway.*)

GROCER: Who says so?

2ND RIDER (*Showing* GROCER *paper*): Paper says so.

GROCER: Oh. Well, if the paper says so, it must be so. (*He turns sign in window around. It now reads:* SPRING MENU. FRESH SALADS. FRESH STRAWBERRIES. FRESH LEMONADE.)

2ND RIDER (*Crossing to* BOY): Boy! Did you hear about spring? Spring, here in the paper. See? (*Shows paper to* BOY.)

1ST RIDER: Put away the football. The game's over. Time for a new game.

BOY (*Kicking football, as he exits left*): Spring. The paper says spring. Goodbye, football. (*He returns, in shirt sleeves, with stickball bat and ball.*) Hello, stickball. (*He crosses to center and*

stands with bat slung across his shoulders.) Hello, stickball!
(3RD RIDER *enters up left, wearing straw hat, crosses to hat shop, knocks on door.*)

3RD RIDER (*Calling*): Hello, in there. Haven't you heard? I have the word. Fur is out. Wool is out. Parkas are out. Spring is in, in, in!

HAT SHOP OWNER (*Coming out from hat shop*): What? What? Is it that time of the year already? Is it straw time? Bow and brim time? Lazy-daisy trim time? Fancy-foolery whim time? Time for bluebonnets on the blue bonnets?

3RD RIDER: Yes, ma'am. Read it in the paper.

HAT SHOP OWNER: If the paper says so, it must be so. (*She turns her sign, which now reads:* SPRING CHAPEAUX HAVE ARRIVED. 4TH RIDER *enters and shouts at closed windows of houses.*)

4TH RIDER: Open the windows! Spring is here! (*Shutters open, and* THREE HOUSEWIVES *in kerchiefs pop their heads out of windows.*)

HOUSEWIVES: Spring? Here? Who said so?

4TH RIDER: A little bird. A robin.

HOUSEWIVES: A robin. (*They nod to each other.*) Ah, right from the robin's bill. (*They shake dustcloths out windows and dust around sills.*)

    Open the windows.
    Let out the darkness.
    Dust off the winter snow.
    Let in the sunshine,
    Let in the Springtime.
    Give the robin a big hello!

(*They wave dustcloths in air.*) Hello, robin! (*They remain watching from windows.* RIDERS *exit, as* BOY *swings bat.*)

BOY: Hey, where is everybody? Where's the team? Where are the hopscotchers? Where are the jump ropers? Where *is* everybody? (ICE CREAM MAN *riding tricycle ice cream truck enters left. Behind him are* STICKBALL PLAYERS *in polo shirts and blue jeans.*)

ICE CREAM MAN: Here's everybody. Here's everybody. Here are twenty-eight different flavors of everybody. Can't be spring without the old ice cream wagon. (*Hands popsicles to* PLAYERS)

PLAYERS (*Chanting*): A penny a lick. A penny a bite. Chocolate-covered springtime. That's all right.

BOY: Come on, team. Street's getting crowded. Everybody over to the next street! (*They exit right.*)

ICE CREAM MAN: Next street. Next street. More ice cream for the next street. Must bring spring to the next street. Bring a little spring to the next street. (*He pedals off right.* HOPSCOTCHERS *hop on. They stand center, on diagram drawn in chalk on stage*)

1ST HOPSCOTCHER (*Holding up finger to wind*): The wind is right.

2ND HOPSCOTCHER (*Putting hand up to feel sun*): The sun is right.

3RD HOPSCOTCHER (*Putting hand on ground*): The ground is right.

HOPSCOTCHERS: Right weather. Right day. We declare the Hopscotch Season is officially open! (1ST HOPSCOTCHER *throws token on first space. Others line up behind her. Recording of polka is heard.* HOPSCOTCHERS *perform polka on diagram. At conclusion,* HOUSEWIVES *applaud.* ROPE JUMPERS *skip on.*)

1ST JUMPER: Our turn. Our turn.

JUMPERS (*Together*): Our turn. Our turn.

2ND JUMPER: The sidewalk is not a wide walk.

3RD JUMPER: So hop along. Hop along.

JUMPERS: It's our turn. Our turn. (HOPSCOTCHERS *sit on steps.* HAT SHOP OWNER *sits left, and* GROCER *joins her.* JUMPERS *begin to jump, performing actions described.*)

    Look what you can do with a little length of rope,
    With a little length of rope,

And a pair of jumping shoes.
Oh, look what you can do,
Come and look what you can do!

1ST JUMPER:

You can skip and never trip,
With a little length of rope,
With an over and an under,
You will never make a blunder.

2ND JUMPER:

That is what we surely hope—
With a little length of rope.
(*They skip in unison.*)
Backwards, backwards you can go,
With a little length of rope.
Turning 'round the wrong way . . .

3RD JUMPER:

Or turning 'round the long way,
Practice hard, till you can cope,
With a little length of rope.

(*They jump backwards, then fasten two ropes together.* 1ST *and* 3RD JUMPERS *turn, while* 2ND JUMPER *shows off several fancy ways of jumping.*)

1ST JUMPER:

You can jump all by yourself,
With a little length of rope.

1ST *and* 2ND JUMPERS:

Or invite a friend or two,
To come get in step with you.
(*To* 3RD JUMPER)
Come along now. Do not mope.
Bring your little length of rope.

(3RD JUMPER *hands rope to* 1ST JUMPER, *who jumps alone.* 2ND JUMPER *jumps in, then* 3RD JUMPER, *and all skip together three times*)

JUMPERS:

> Faster, faster, you can go,
> With a little length of rope.
> Make it whip and make it whir,
> Till the jump rope's but a blur,
> And you spin so fast around,
> That your toes don't touch the ground!

(JUMPERS *jump "hot peppers" until* HOUSEWIVES, *wagging their fingers, call out.*)

HOUSEWIVES: Stop! Stop! Enough! Enough!

1ST HOUSEWIFE: You'll get overheated.

GROCER: True. I heard of a girl once who never stopped jumping from sunup to sundown. She finally melted just like a wax candle, down to a grease spot. They never did find her. Only her jump rope!

ALL: Oh-h-h!

2ND HOUSEWIFE: Sit for a while. Enjoy the spring sunshine. Come, watch the world go by. (JUMPERS *sit on steps. All hold their heads in their hands and watch, as* MOTHER, *pushing baby carriage, enters and crosses stage.*)

MOTHER: Good morning.

ALL: Good morning.

MOTHER: Fine day.

ALL: Fine day.

MOTHER: Bye-bye.

ALL: Bye-bye! (*As she exits right,* POLICEMAN *enters right, and tips his hat.*)

POLICEMAN: Good morning.

ALL: Good morning.

POLICEMAN: Nice day.

ALL: Nice day.

POLICEMAN: So long.

ALL: So long! (*As he exits left,* FOUR LADIES, *in wild spring hats, enter through hat shop door, crossing up right. They carry hand mirrors, glancing into them*)

LADIES: Heavenly morning!

ALL: Heavenly morning.

LADIES: Lovely, lovely day. Lovely, lovely *us*. (*They preen in mirrors.*)

ALL: Lovely, lovely day. Lovely, lovely you.

LADIES (*Posing*): Toodle-oodle-oo. (*They exit up right.*)

ALL: Toodle-oodle-oo. (*As* LADIES *exit,* UMBRELLA MAN, *carrying black umbrella, enters down left and crosses to right.*)

UMBRELLA MAN (*Glumly*): Bad morning.

ALL: Bad morning?

UMBRELLA MAN: Terrible day.

ALL: Terrible day?

UMBRELLA MAN: Hope it rains!

ALL: Hope it rains?

UMBRELLA MAN: No sale!

ALL: No sale?

UMBRELLA MAN (*Opening umbrella and walking off right; defiantly*): Goodbye!

ALL: Goodbye!

1ST HOUSEWIFE: Hot. Getting hotter. (*She picks up watering can and waters her flower in box.*) Wake up, little petunia. Time for a nice drink of water, dearie. (*To* 3RD HOUSEWIFE) Oh, Missus, did I tell you what my little petunia did yesterday?

3RD HOUSEWIFE: No. Tell me, what did your little petunia do yesterday?

1ST HOUSEWIFE: She put out a brand-new leaf, she did!

3RD HOUSEWIFE: Growing like a weed, eh?

1ST HOUSEWIFE: I'll thank you not to use that word about my little petunia. She is not a weed!

2ND HOUSEWIFE (*To* 1ST HOUSEWIFE): Pardon me, but I see you still use an old-fashioned watering can. All the best botanists tell you to use an eye-dropper. Pure plant food, that's the secret. I never use a drop of water on my geranium. Look at his healthy, glossy petals. Pure plant food. That's the secret.

3RD HOUSEWIFE: Oh, poppycock! You're just coddling your plants. There's nothing worse than a spoiled flower. Now, I just let nature take its course, and you should see my plant. A fine, bouncing rubber plant.

ALL: Rubber plant?

3RD HOUSEWIFE: That's right. A rubber plant. Now, be quiet. My plant is about to produce its yearly crop of spring fruit.

GROCER: Fruit? I never heard of a rubber plant giving fruit.

3RD HOUSEWIFE: Well, just where do you think all the rubber balls come from in the spring? (*She gives ball to* 1ST HOPSCOTCHER)

1ST HOPSCOTCHER: Look, a tiny ball for ball and jacks. (*She pantomimes playing jacks*)

3RD HOUSEWIFE: That's only the first crop. Look. (*She gives handball to* GROCER.)

GROCER: A handball! That's a grand ball! (*He pantomimes throwing handball against wall.*)

3RD HOUSEWIFE: They get better and better. How about this one! (*She gives large bouncing ball with design on it to* 1ST JUMPER.)

1ST JUMPER: A bouncing ball! (*She bounces it.*)

3RD HOUSEWIFE: I told you I had a bouncing rubber plant. You haven't seen anything yet. (*She hands volleyball to* HAT SHOP OWNER.)

HAT SHOP OWNER: A volleyball! That's a jolly ball. (HAT SHOP OWNER *pantomimes making overhead shots with volleyball.*)

3RD HOUSEWIFE: Wait. There's one more. (*She brings out beach ball, as* CONDUCTOR *enters left with his megaphone.*)

ALL: A beach ball. A beach ball. A peach of a summer beach ball!

CONDUCTOR (*Through megaphone*): Your attention, please. The subway is now leaving for the Island of June, with stops at July Resort and the Shores of August. There is immediate seating. Step lively, if you please. (CONDUCTOR *takes beach ball and faces left, as all line up to follow him. Curtain slowly begins to close, as all march in place behind* CONDUCTOR.) Form your line in columns of two and follow me to the Island of June! (*Curtain closes.* GROCER *steps through curtain with sign on an easel:* ON VACATION. SEE YOU IN THE FALL. *He exits center through curtain, as* UMBRELLA MAN *rushes in right. He carries beach umbrella and parasols, and wears flowered shirt, sunglasses and pith helmet.*)

UMBRELLA MAN: Wait for me! Hold the doors! Beach umbrellas. Get your beach umbrellas! Sunshades! Parasols! Hey, wait for me! (*He runs off left.*)

THE END

Who Will Bell the Cat?

Characters

AESOP
MAYOR MOUSE
CHEESE SELLER
TAILOR
FURRIER

GRAIN VENDOR
PHILO, *the philosopher*
VALIANT, *the constable*
CAT

BEFORE RISE: AESOP *enters in front of curtain. He carries a scroll, from which he reads his fable.*

AESOP: My lords, my ladies. I am Aesop, a wandering story-teller. I have told you about mighty elephants and noble lions. Now I shall recite a fable about something small. For even the tiniest beasts have lively stories to tell. Today, I shall tell you about a town whose citizens were mice. (*He reads from scroll.*) ". . . In a certain human village with plenty of grain and cheese, there was a hidden town in which lived many happy, well-fed mice." (*Curtains open.*)

* * *

SETTING: *Mouse Town. There is a backdrop of houses, whose entrances are large, cut-out mouseholes through which characters can enter. A tree and a bench are down right. In front of each shop-owner's hole are a table and sign advertising his wares.*

AT RISE: AESOP *comes downstage.*

259

AESOP: There was a Mayor, who made speeches and gave out medals . . . (MAYOR *enters.*)

MAYOR (*Crossing down center*): My beloved fellow mice . . . The sun has appeared on yon mountain. Come forth from your holes. I smell a fine, profitable day.

AESOP: There was a cheese seller (CHEESE SELLER *enters and crosses to his table of wares.*) who was very clever at stealing cheese from mousetraps. . . .

CHEESE SELLER: Cheese. Cheese. I have white cheese, yellow cheese, blue cheese and mellow cheese. Choose, please, your cheese, please. And don't sneeze at my cheese.

AESOP: There was a grain vendor who borrowed a little wheat here, a few oats there, and a lot of barley everywhere. Ah, yes, he borrowed the grain but he never remembered to put it back.

GRAIN VENDOR (*Entering*): Fresh wheat, so sweet. New oats, only two groats. Barley corn, brought this morn!

AESOP: Of course, we mustn't forget the tailor. Now in Mouse Town, a tailor does not cut and fit clothes. He attends to tails. He clips them, and curls them and crimps them . . .

TAILOR (*Entering*): Get your tail curled here. Stylish curls for all occasions.

AESOP: And the furrier. He was a kind of mouse barber. He fluffed and groomed his mice friends until they were as sleek as water rats.

FURRIER (*Entering*): Hey, now . . . come in for a combing. Rush down for a brush down. Greet the world neatly. Hey now!

AESOP: Last, and I am afraid, least, there was the town philosopher—Philo. (PHILO *enters and sits by his mousehole.*) He thought deep thoughts and gave forth grand ideas. But he was the poorest mouse of all, for everybody was too busy for deep thoughts and grand ideas. (VALIANT, *the constable, enters, polishing his sword. He is enormously fat, with several pillows under his coat.*) Ah, wait. There was one more important member of the town. Constable Valiant. He kept the peace. But Mouse Town was so quiet and so happy that there was nothing whatever for a constable to do . . . but polish his sword. (VALIANT *polishes his sword again.*)

MAYOR: Good morning, Constable Valiant. How goes the town?

VALIANT: Good morning, Mayor Mouse. Not a peep. Not a scuffle. It's another sleepy day, I fear. (*He yawns.*)

CHEESE SELLER: Come, taste my yellow cheese today, Constable. Tell me how it suits you.

VALIANT (*Nibbling and wiggling his nose*): It's nice enough. Just a trifle salty.

GRAIN VENDOR: Try my barley, Constable. It's very choice.

VALIANT (*Nibbling again*): Hm-m-m. Well, it's the slightest bit tough.

TAILOR: May I freshen up the curl in your tail, Constable? (*He holds out a curling iron.*)

VALIANT: If you don't mind. It does drag a bit. (TAILOR *curls tail around iron.*)

FURRIER: Smooth your fur, Constable? (*He holds out large brush.*)

VALIANT: Just give it a quick once-over. (FURRIER *brushes* VALIANT.)

PHILO: Ah, Constable Valiant. Will you share a deep thought or two with me? It's a bargain today. Six original ideas for a penny.

VALIANT: Not today, Philo. Deep thoughts always put me to sleep. (*He yawns.*) You see? Even thinking about deep thoughts makes me sleepy. I shall catch forty winks under yonder tree. (*He crosses to tree down right, and sits. His head immediately drops to side, and he snores softly.*)

AESOP: Did I say the town was peaceful and happy? Ah,

that was in the time B.C. Before Cat. For the people who lived in the village grew tired of having their fine cheeses stolen, and their ripe grains borrowed. So, they hired a cat. He was the largest, hungriest, wickedest cat in all of Greece. Perhaps in all the world. (CAT *stalks in unseen, crosses to* VALIANT, *takes sword from him and goes offstage with it, returning at once and crossing to* VALIANT.)

CAT (*Tapping* VALIANT *on shoulder*): Wake up, fat mouse. I can't eat you while you sleep.

VALIANT (*Crossly*): Who dares disturb my slumber? (*Seeing* CAT) A cat! He-e-lp! (*Cowers*)

CAT (*Threateningly*): Take this message to Mouse Town: Cat is here. Before sundown, I will make a meal of each and every mouse. (*He claws the air.*) Go. Tell them. (VALIANT *begins to run across stage right,* CAT *bounding after him, grinning.*)

VALIANT (*Shouting*): It's a cat! Hide! (*Mice run into their holes. Only* PHILO *keeps his head out of his hole. He watches with interest, as* CAT *chases* VALIANT *off left. Offstage* VALIANT *removes a pillow, so that each time he is chased off he "loses weight."*)

CAT (*Ready to pounce*): Come back, fat little mouse. This is fun. (VALIANT *tiptoes onstage.* CAT *chases him from left to right. He goes off, removes pillow, and staggers onstage, breathing heavily.* PHILO *beckons to him.*)

PHILO: Quickly—in here. (VALIANT *scuttles upstage and hides behind* PHILO, *in his hole.* CAT *swaggers center.*)

CAT: I let you get away that time. But I'll be back to finish you off. All of you. (*He slinks off right.*)

AESOP: And that dreadful beast was as good as his word. The next morning, when the merchants crept out of their holes (*Mice creep cautiously out of their holes, crossing downstage.* CAT *leaps out from up right, snarling.*), there was the Cat, like a shadow of evil. (*Mice run back to holes, shrieking.* CAT *brushes his fur with the* FURRIER's *brush.*)

CAT (*Grinning*): Don't I make a handsome mouse? (*He picks up curling iron and curls his tail.*) There. I'm right in style. (*He snoops around grain and cheese tables.*) What have we here? Cheese. Grain. I'll just help myself to a little snack. (*He takes cheese and basket of grain, then exits right.* PHILO *crosses downstage after him, with* VALIANT *clinging to* PHILO'S *tail fearfully. Other mice follow* PHILO. MAYOR *points scornfully at* VALIANT.)

MAYOR: What kind of a constable are you? Why didn't you stop that Cat?

ALL (*Ad lib*): Why didn't you stop the Cat? Yes! Why didn't you? (*Etc.*)

VALIANT: He took my sword. Besides, he is never there when I look for him. And when I do not look for him, there he is.

MAYOR: What shall we do? Has anyone an idea?

ALL (*Shaking their heads*): Not I.

PHILO (*Crossing center*): I have an idea. (*They form semicircle around* PHILO.)

ALL: You have an idea? Let us hear your idea.

PHILO (*Surprised*): You really want to hear my idea?

ALL: We implore you.

PHILO: Well, since you implore me, I will tell you. If we could hear the Cat coming, we could hide from him. If we could hide from him, he could not catch us. If he could not catch us, he would become discouraged. Then he would leave us alone.

ALL: Ah, if he would only leave us alone.

PHILO: Now, listen well. In order to hear the Cat coming, we must put a bell around his neck.

ALL: A bell? Of course. A bell.

MAYOR: A fine idea. I will present you with a medal.

PHILO: Now, the question is: Who will bell the Cat?

ALL: Who? (*Pointing to each other*) Why don't you?

MAYOR: Any volunteers? (*No one speaks.*) I will present a medal for cat-belling. (*No one speaks.*) I will give a banquet for the one who bells the Cat.

VALIANT: A banquet!

MAYOR: Did I hear you volunteer, Constable Valiant?

VALIANT: I—I volunteered to come to the banquet, your honor.

PHILO: *I* will volunteer to bell the Cat.

ALL: At last, a volunteer.

PHILO: There is, however, a price.

MAYOR: Anything—within reason.

PHILO: If I am able to bell the Cat, everyone in the town must come to my lectures between the hours of two and four o'clock each afternoon. I'm tired of being a philosopher without an audience.

MAYOR: It shall be done.

PHILO: Bring me a bell and a collar, then leave me alone. (FURRIER *brings bell and collar from table. Mice retreat to their holes, watching* PHILO. VALIANT *shares* MAYOR's *hole.* PHILO *sits cross-legged on stage. He holds up collar, admiring it. He carefully polishes bell.* CAT *sneaks onstage, watching* PHILO. PHILO *sees him out of corner of his eye, and smiles gently.* CAT *pounces, and sits next to* PHILO. PHILO *snatches collar away, hiding it behind his back.*)

CAT: What are you doing?

PHILO (*Pretending fear*): You startled me, friend Cat.

CAT: What was that thing you hid from me?

PHILO: Nothing, friend Cat. Pray, do not eat me.

CAT: Pah. I don't eat philosophers. They're much too dry for my taste. Let me see that thing.

PHILO: It wouldn't interest you. (*He makes bell tinkle.* CAT *cocks his head.*)

CAT: I heard it ringing. Show it to me.

PHILO: Oh, very well. But I was going to present it to the prince. (*He holds out collar reluctantly.* CAT *grabs it.*)

CAT: It's for a prince, eh? What is it?

PHILO: The latest fashion for princes. Everyone wears them in Athens. It's a collar with a bell.

CAT (*Holding it up to his neck*): A collar with a bell? Everyone wears them in Athens, you say? How does it look on me?

PHILO: I hate to say it, but it makes you look—princely.

CAT: Princely, you say? I'll take it.

PHILO (*Pretending distress*): Oh, please. Don't take my fine collar and bell!

CAT: You should be happy I don't take you, too. Fasten it. (*He turns his head.*)

PHILO: Must I?`

CAT: You must. (*Feigning a sigh,* PHILO *fastens collar.*)

PHILO: There. But I warn you, once this collar is fastened, you won't be able to remove it.

CAT (*Sneering*): Now, why should I ever want to take off such a fine collar? (*He struts off right, preening.*) Goodbye, philosopher. Better luck next time.

PHILO: Farewell, Cat. And the same to you. (*When* CAT *exits,* PHILO *beckons to other mice. They join him downstage.*)

MAYOR: Has he gone?

VALIANT: Have you—done it?

PHILO: He has gone, and I have done it. I have belled the Cat.

ALL (*Jubilant*): Hurrah! He has belled the Cat!

PHILO: Now we must test our theory. Listen. (*All cup their ears. Off right is heard tinkle of bell, coming closer. Mice stroll back to their holes, and stand in them, laughing, as* CAT *leaps onstage.*)

CAT: I have you! (*He looks around.*) Well, I *had* you. Where did you go, you silly mice? (*To himself*) Perhaps they saw my shadow. I'll give them my never-fail left-handed lethal leap. (*He tiptoes left, turns and bares his claws. Mice scuttle forward, out of their holes.* CAT *stalks them. Bell tinkles; mice put their hands to their ears, and run into their holes.* CAT *fingers his bell.*) They can hear me coming. Me! The silent stalker. It's this cursed bell. (*Pointing to* PHILO) *He* did this to me. (*He calls to* PHILO, *who stands beside his hole, warily.*) Oh, philosopher. Come here.

PHILO: What do you wish, friend Cat?

CAT: This collar you gave me. It doesn't suit me. Take it off.

PHILO: I told you. I won't take it off.

CAT (*Snarling*): Take it off, or I'll—

PHILO: You'll do what?

CAT (*Sighing*): I'll make a bargain with you.

PHILO: You have nothing to bargain with. We can hear you coming now. Your teeth are useless. Your claws are useless. You, friend Cat, are useless.

CAT: Useless? But I am Cat, the terror of the countryside. Haven't you any idea what I can do now?

PHILO: Ah, you're in the market for an idea. It just so happens I *have* an idea. Why don't you become a pet—a house cat.

CAT: Me a house cat? Never. Why, I'll starve first. They'll never make a purring, pussyfooting, pussycat out of me! (*He stalks off right.*)

AESOP: But the more the Cat railed, the more he realized that Philo was right. With the bell around his neck, his hunting days were over. So, off he went, to the village to look for a house in need of a pet. Poor, foolish Cat. Philo understood very well that cats are vain, curious, and just a bit greedy. As for Philo, the Mayor kept his promise. (PHILO *crosses down center, holding up his hand, as if illustrating a point. Mice gather about him, seated as if listening.*) Every day from two o'clock until four o'clock, the mice gathered around Philo to hear his lecture. And the Mayor presented Philo with two medals. (MAYOR *hangs two medals around* PHILO's *neck.*) Did I say all the mice attended Philo's lecture? All the mice, that is, except Constable Valiant. He was very busy, doing nothing. (VALIANT *takes piece of cheese, and exits left, nibbling it. Offstage he restuffs himself with pillows, and enters again, crossing right to bench where he sits, falling asleep and snoring gently.*) The town had again become so peaceful and so happy that there was really not much for the good constable to do. And it wasn't very long until he was the largest, fattest, sleekest mouse in the whole country of Greece, and perhaps—the whole, wide world. (*All hold their poses;* AESOP *bows. Curtain.*)

THE END

Pepe and the Cornfield Bandit

Characters

SEÑOR GRANJERO
JUAN ⎫
PEDRO ⎬ *brothers*
PEPE ⎭
SAPO, *the toad*
IXLANDA, *the enchanted bird*
CHORUS, *six boys and girls*
DANCERS

TIME: *Many years ago.*
SETTING: *A hacienda in Mexico.*
BEFORE RISE: CHORUS, *wearing Mexican costumes, enter in front of curtains. Boys carry bongo drums; girls have maracas.*

CHORUS: Olé! Olé! Olé! (*They beat drums and shake maracas. Girls sit down right, on apron of stage. Boys kneel behind them.*)
Many, many years ago in Old Mexico,
Where the mountains are taller than anywhere else,
And the skies are bluer than anywhere else . . .
1ST BOY (*Fanning himself*): And the sun is hotter than anywhere else . . .
CHORUS: There was a rich farmer. . . .

*   *   *

AT RISE: *Curtains open, disclosing backdrop of purple mountains, cactus, and straw-thatched cottage. Down center is a well, behind which* SAPO, *the toad, hides. Down left are three rows of corn; two rows have tassels.* JUAN, PEDRO, *and* PEPE, *three brothers, are in front of cottage.* JUAN, *the eldest brother, sits with his sombrero pulled down over his eyes.* PEDRO *stands next to him, combing his drooping moustache and gazing admiringly at himself in hand mirror.* PEPE, *the youngest brother, holds a broom.*

SEÑOR GRANJERO (*Entering from up right*): Buenos días.

CHORUS: This rich farmer was called Señor Granjero.

1ST BOY: Ah, but he was rich.

1ST GIRL: He had two fat oxen.

2ND GIRL: He had a house with a roof.

3RD GIRL: And windows in the front and windows in the back.

2ND BOY: But best of all, he had a cornfield full of corn.

CHORUS: Corn for tortillas. Corn for tostadas. Corn for tamales. Corn for enchiladas. Ah, but he was rich!

3RD BOY: He also had three sons. First, there was Juan Ramon Luiz Estaban.

SEÑOR GRANJERO: Wake up, Juan. (JUAN *pulls sombrero further down over his eyes.*)

CHORUS: Wake up, Juan. (JUAN *yawns.*)

SEÑOR GRANJERO: He is a little lazy—but he is a good boy.

2ND BOY: Next, there was Pedro Carlo José Francisco.

SEÑOR GRANJERO (*As* PEDRO *continues to admire his moustache*): That's enough, Pedro. You are handsome enough. After all— do you not take after me?

CHORUS: That's enough, Pedro. (PEDRO *continues to stroke his moustache.*)

SEÑOR GRANJERO: He is a little vain—but he is a good boy.

1ST BOY: And then there was Pepe—just—Pepe.

CHORUS: Ah, Pepe.

SEÑOR GRANJERO: Poor Pepe. I could not think of one more

name for Pepe. What can I tell you about my youngest son? He is a very good boy. That's all. (PEPE *sweeps floor*.)

1ST BOY (*As* SEÑOR GRANJERO *crosses down left, examining corn*): One fine Mexican day, Señor Granjero visited his cornfields. The first row of corn was full of fat, waving corn tassels.

SEÑOR GRANJERO: *Magnífico!*

CHORUS: The second row was full of fat, waving corn tassels.

SEÑOR GRANJERO: *Magnífico!*

CHORUS: But the third row had not one single fat, waving corn tassel. Not one.

SEÑOR GRANJERO: Oh! A corn-snatcher! A bandit! (*He runs across stage to his sons.* JUAN *stands up.* PEPE *puts down broom.*) My sons, listen.

JUAN, PEDRO, PEPE (*Together*): We hear you, Father.

SEÑOR GRANJERO: A bandit has stolen the corn from the cornfield. You must be good sons and bring me that bandit. Whichever one of you brings me the corn-snatcher— he shall have all my riches.

PEPE (*Eagerly*): I don't want all your riches, my father, but I will go and get the bandit.

JUAN (*Scornfully*): You? You are only the third son. I am the first son. I will go, my father. Next week. (*He yawns.*)

SEÑOR GRANJERO (*Sternly*): Next week there will be no corn at all. You will go tonight.

JUAN: Tomorrow night. (*He yawns again.*)

SEÑOR GRANJERO (*Loudly*): Tonight! (*He hands* JUAN *his gun.*)

JUAN: *Sí. Sí.* Tonight.

CHORUS: When the sun went down behind the mountain, it was night. (SEÑOR GRANJERO *and his sons sit cross-legged up center, holding their heads in their hands.*)

1ST BOY: It was a wonderful, cool Mexican night.

1ST GIRL: There were more stars crowding the sky than anywhere else. (JUAN *stands, crosses left.*)

3RD BOY: Juan walked a little way. Then he rested. (*He sits.*)

2ND GIRL: He walked a little way more. Then he rested.

JUAN (*Crossing down to well, sitting down*): What a long walk! I'll just rest here by the well. (*He begins to nod.* SAPO, *the toad, hops out from behind well. Short drum roll is heard.*)

SAPO: Wake up! Wake up!

JUAN (*Sitting up*): Ay-yi-yi! An ugly old toad. Vamoose! Get away!

SAPO: Close your eyes, if you don't like what you see. But listen. I may be an ugly old toad, but I can help you.

JUAN (*Hitting him with his sombrero*): Go away. Go back in the well where nobody can see you. Vamoose!

SAPO: Very well. But you are making a big mistake. (*He hops back behind well.* JUAN *lies down and sleeps.*)

2ND BOY: When the sun came up from behind the mountains, it was another fine Mexican day. Who should visit the well but Juan's father, and Juan's brothers. (SEÑOR GRANJERO, PEDRO *and* PEPE *cross to well, stand with arms folded, shaking their heads at* JUAN.)

PEDRO: Wake up, Juan.

CHORUS: Wake up, Juan. (JUAN *wakes with a start.*)

JUAN (*Foolishly*): Buenos días, my father. Buenos días, my brothers.

SEÑOR GRANJERO: Did you catch the bandit?

JUAN: The bandit? (*Slyly*) Ah—he was quick as a jaguar and clever as a monkey. How I wrestled with him! But, alas, I did not catch him.

PEDRO: Ha! All Juan has caught is forty winks.

PEPE: Please, my father, let me try this time.

PEDRO (*Scornfully*): You? Keep your place, little brother. You know very well it is my turn. (*To* JUAN) Give me the gun, you bandit-bumbler. (JUAN *gives him gun.*)

SEÑOR GRANJERO: Good luck, my son.

PEDRO: I do not need luck, my father. I have brains. Brains

will catch the thief. (SEÑOR GRANJERO, JUAN, *and* PEPE *return upstage. They again seat themselves, resting their heads on their arms.*)

1ST BOY: Again, the sun went down behind the mountain. It was a more beautiful night than the last. That is the way it is—in Mexico! (PEDRO, *pointing gun here and there, nervously, guards corn.*)

PEDRO: Nothing here. Nothing there. Well, I'm thirsty. I'll have a drink. (*He bends over well, scooping water with his hand.* SAPO *pops up on other side of well. Short drum roll is heard.*)

SAPO: Good evening, friend.

PEDRO: Ugh! A toad. An ugly old toad.

SAPO: I was afraid you'd say that. Well, as I always say, if you don't like what you see, close your eyes. But listen to me. I can help you.

PEDRO: Ha! You don't fool me. I have too many brains. I know that toads don't talk.

SAPO: They don't? Then who is speaking to you, may I ask?

PEDRO: Nobody. It's all in my mind. Go away now, and don't pretend to talk to me.

SAPO: Very well. But you are making a big mistake. (*He hops behind well.* PEDRO, *his gun ready, crosses to cornfield. He kneels, then cocks his head. Sound of maracas, shaken softly, is heard.*)

PEDRO: I hear wings. What can it be? (IXLANDA, *dressed as enchanted bird, dances in from down left. She flutters back and forth.*) A bird! More beautiful than the quetzal. (IXLANDA *takes ear of corn.*) Oh, no you don't. Beautiful or not—I'll shoot you. (*He takes aim, and fires. Sound of drum beat is heard.* IXLANDA *laughs, and tosses him feather, then she flutters off left.* PEDRO *picks up feather, runs upstage to his father and brothers.*) The bandit! I've shot the bandit! (*All wake up.*)

SEÑOR GRANJERO: Where is the bandit? Show me!

PEDRO: Here. (*He holds out feather.*)

JUAN: That's not a bandit. That's a feather.

SEÑOR GRANJERO: Is this all you have to show for yourself?

PEDRO (*Sulking*): Isn't it enough? I risked my very life for this feather. The bandit was an eagle—tall as a yucca tree. He sounded like thunder as he beat his wings.

SEÑOR GRANJERO: Why, the bandit won't even miss that feather. He will come back again and again, unless someone catches him.

PEPE: Please, my father, let me go. It is my turn now.

JUAN: You? You are too little. What could you do?

PEDRO: You? You have no brains. I'll bet you even think toads can talk, eh, Juan?

JUAN: Toads talk? Never.

SEÑOR GRANJERO: Very well, little Pepe. Go and try your luck. Take the gun. (PEDRO *gives gun to* PEPE. SEÑOR GRANJERO, JUAN *and* PEDRO *cross upstage, sitting down with their heads on their arms.* PEPE *crosses to well.*)

CHORUS: Once again, the sun went down behind the mountains.

2ND GIRL: It was night—the third night.

3RD GIRL: The third night is always the magical night.

2ND BOY: Especially in Mexico.

PEPE: Ah, the old well. It is as good a place as any to eat my tortilla. (*He takes tortilla from inside his sombrero. Sound of short drum roll.* SAPO *hops out from behind well.*)

SAPO: Good evening, friend.

PEPE (*Politely*): Good evening, Señor Toad.

SAPO: *Señor* Toad? How polite! Aren't you going to tell me how ugly I am, as your brothers did?

PEPE (*Looking closely*): I don't think you're ugly. You should see some of the lizards I've caught.

SAPO: Really? How kind! You're much kinder than your brothers.

PEPE: Would you like to share my tortilla, Señor—

SAPO (*Happily*): Señor Sapo. Nobody ever asked my name

before. Yes, I'll have a bite of your tortilla. (*He munches.*)
Do you believe I can talk?

PEPE: Of course. I hear you with my ears.

SAPO: Quite right. What would you say if I offered to help
you catch the bandit?

PEPE: I'd say, *sí, sí.* I can't have too much help.

SAPO: Wise boy. Now, do as I ask you. Bend over the well.

PEPE (*Leaning over well*): Like this?

SAPO: Quite right. What do you see?

PEPE: The stars in the sky reflected in the well.

SAPO: What else?

PEPE: A gleaming white stone far beneath the water.

SAPO: That white stone is magic. It will give you three
wishes.

PEPE: Three wishes? Why not? Wish number one. I wish
that I may catch the bandit who carries off the corn each
night. Wish number two. I wish that I may marry a
beautiful wife. Wish number three. I've never seen a real
fiesta. I wish that I might see a fiesta when I return home.

SAPO: Let's be off now. To the cornfield! (*They cross down left.*
PEPE *keeps his gun ready. Sound of maracas shaken softly is
heard.*)

PEPE: Listen. I hear wings. (IXLANDA *enters down left. She flutters beside cornstalk.* PEPE *raises his gun.*)

SAPO: No—no. Don't shoot. Don't shoot or you will lose
your first two wishes. (PEPE *puts gun down.* SAPO *begins to
croak.*) Ker-rivet. Ker-rivet. Enchanted bird who comes in
the night. Stop, I pray you. Stop in your flight. (IXLANDA
remains motionless, arms outstretched.)

PEPE: I've caught the bandit bird. My first wish came true.

SAPO: Of course. Now for wish number two. (*He croaks
again.*) Ker-rivet. Ker-rivet. Enchanted bird, who comes
from afar, show us, I pray, who you really are. (*Sound of
maracas.* IXLANDA *takes off her helmet. She shakes out her long
hair.*)

PEPE: A bird with long hair! (IXLANDA *takes off her feathered cloak. She is dressed in the costume of an Aztec princess.*) Why—there is a girl inside that bird.

IXLANDA: I am Ixlanda. A thousand years ago, a wicked sorcerer changed me into a bird. Please forgive me. I took your corn only because I was starving. (*She hands* PEPE *ear of corn.*)

PEPE: No, no. Please. You take it, Señorita Princess.

SAPO: Here. I'll take it. (*He takes corn.*) Well, go on—ask her to marry you. After all, she is your second wish come true.

PEPE: But I didn't expect her so soon. (*He puts his head down.*) I'm too bashful.

SAPO: Jumping iguanas! After a thousand years the poor princess has no one but you. Ask her!

PEPE: Señorita Princess, if you have nothing better to do—

SAPO (*Holding his head*): Popocatepetl! Must I be a matchmaker, too? My dear princess, what this stammering boy means is—his heart is on fire with your beauty. His mind is aflame with your charm. Will you do him the great honor of becoming his wife?

IXLANDA (*Lowering her eyes*): It's the least I can do.

SAPO: Quivering quetzals! What the poor princess means is —you are her knight in shining armor, her noble defender. She begs you to accept her as your wife. Now—for once and for all—will you marry each other?

PEPE *and* IXLANDA (*Hands on their hearts*): We will.

CHORUS: And they did.

2ND BOY: Together they set out for the hacienda of Señor Granjero.

1ST GIRL: What rejoicing there was then!

2ND GIRL: Even Juan woke up, at last.

JUAN (*Wide-eyed*): Qué? Pepe has caught the bandit? Little Pepe?

PEDRO: Pepe has brought home a wife? Little Pepe?

PEDRO *and* JUAN: Well done, little brother.

SEÑOR GRANJERO: Well done, my son. Ah—there is too
much happiness for one small hacienda. We must invite
all Mexico to share this day. I declare—a fiesta!

PEPE: A fiesta! Why—that's my third wish.

CHORUS (*Beating bongos and shaking maracas*): Fiesta! Fiesta!
Come from the hills and the valleys of Mexico.

2ND BOY: Come from the Baja and Chihuahua, and Cam-
peche.

1ST BOY: Come from Hidalgo and Jalisco and Guerrero.

1ST GIRL: Come from Tabasco and Durango and Sonora.

CHORUS: Fiesta! (DANCERS *enter from up right and left, and down
right and left. They stand in two groups on each side of the well,
down center. A Mexican folk song may be sung, after which
DANCERS form circle around well. SAPO sits on box in middle of
well, a large sombrero on his head. PEPE and IXLANDA stand
down right. SEÑOR GRANJERO, JUAN and PEDRO cross down
left. DANCERS perform Mexican Hat Dance. At conclusion, SAPO
hops out of well, still wearing sombrero. He hops onto apron of the
stage, as the curtains close behind him.*)

SAPO: And that is the story of Pepe and the cornfield bandit.

2ND GIRL: It was told to us by a very old silvermaker in
Taxco.

1ST BOY: He heard it from a very old fisherman in Vera-
cruz.

1ST GIRL: And he heard it from a grandmother in Oaxaca.

CHORUS: And she heard it from . . .

SAPO: Why—from me, of course. Who else? (*He tips his hat to
audience and hops off right*) Ker-rivet! Ker-rivet!

THE END

A Song Goes Forth

Characters

FOUR NARRATORS
COMMENTATOR
KING BASSO
QUEEN CONTRALTO
SUSANNA SOPRANO

PRINCE BANJO KNEE
CHORUS (*various members take parts of* 1ST SOLO, 2ND SOLO, DUET, TRIO *and* QUARTET)

BEFORE RISE: 1ST NARRATOR *enters in front of curtain, and stands center.*

1ST NARRATOR: There's a song in the air, and music in our theme today. Now, everybody knows what a "song" is. The birds invented it, and people improved on it. Songs are feelings gift-wrapped in melody and special-delivered to the heart. But we're very practical, so we ask, "What can a song do? What is a song good for, besides sounding pretty?" Well, here to help us find out about songs and put them through their paces are some people who sing together. They call themselves a chorus. (1ST NARRATOR *signals for curtains to open.*)

* * *

AT RISE: CHORUS *is seated at center.* 2ND NARRATOR *is sitting down left, next to empty chair.* 3RD *and* 4TH NARRATORS *are sitting down right.*

277

CHORUS (*Standing*):

> Did you send for us?
>
> We are the chorus.

1ST NARRATOR: We have our singing people. Now all we need is a song. Any suggestions, Chorus? (*All shout out various song titles.* 1ST NARRATOR *holds up hand.*) Wait! Wait a minute! (CHORUS *stops shouting.*) You don't sound like a chorus. You sound like a mob. I'll tell you what. Since there's music in the air, let's just reach up and pull out a song. (1ST NARRATOR *reaches up, pantomimes plucking song out of air, and hands imaginary sheet to member of* CHORUS, *who pantomimes handing it to others.*) There you are. The song is "Oh! Susanna." Do you know it?

CHORUS (*In unison*): We do! (1ST NARRATOR *sits down left as* CHORUS *sings quick, straight version of "Oh! Susanna," then sits.*)

2ND NARRATOR (*Coming to center*): That's fine, but that isn't the way they used to sing "Oh! Susanna" when Stephen Foster wrote the song, way back in the 1840s. Right away, it became the number-one hit of the Old West. Everybody was a-singing it, and those who couldn't warble a note whistled it. On wagon trains and clipper ships, up mountain trails and down valley roads, "Oh! Susanna" was the folk song that echoed everywhere. Right, chorus?

CHORUS: Right! (2ND NARRATOR *sits, as* CHORUS *puts on straw hats or stetsons and sunbonnets, then sings "Oh! Susanna" country-style, accompanied by guitar, harmonica, or accordion, if desired. At conclusion, they remove hats and sit.* 3RD NARRATOR *comes forward.*)

3RD NARRATOR: Now, we've heard everything. Well, not quite everything. We haven't heard *everything* until we've heard an opera. An opera is just one long song with a story. Everybody sings and sings and sings. Except the audience. They listen, and listen, and listen. In an opera, sometimes a person sings alone, sometimes with other people. (*To* CHORUS) Why don't you explain it to us?

CHORUS: Delighted.

1ST SOLO (*Standing*): The person who sings alone is a soloist. (*Sits*)

DUET (*Standing; speaking in unison*): Two people who sing together are a duet. (*They sit.*)

TRIO (*Standing; in unison*): Three people who join in melody are a trio. (*They sit.*)

QUARTET (*Standing; in unison*): Four people in sweetest harmony are a quartet. (*They sit.*)

CHORUS: And please do not forget the chorus!

3RD NARRATOR: Thank you. Now all we need is the commentator. Is there an opera commentator in the house? (COMMENTATOR, *wearing cutaway and top hat and carrying cane, enters, comes to center, and bows to* 3RD NARRATOR *and audience.*) Excellent! Please begin. (*As* COMMENTATOR *bows again to audience,* 3RD NARRATOR *sits.*)

COMMENTATOR: Good evening, ladies and gentlemen. Today we are privileged to hear a new opera titled "Oh! Susanna," performed by the Imaginary Opera Company. The story of the opera is called the libretto. Our libretto is very exciting, I assure you. It is full of baleful bassos and cunning contraltos, triumphant tenors and sensitive sopranos! (*Fanfare is heard.*) And here come two of our singers now. (KING BASSO *and* QUEEN CONTRALTO *enter.*) The wicked King Basso (KING *bows theatrically.*) and the evil Queen Contralto. (*She curtsies deeply, then both stand down center.*) Naturally, in good opera fashion, they are keeping someone prisoner. And who else but a soprano? They make wonderful prisoners. Nobody else can scream in high C and still sound beautiful. (SUSANNA *enters, weeping and wringing her hands.*) Here she is, our heroine, Susanna Soprano! (COMMENTATOR *stands to one side, as* SUSANNA *goes up to* KING.)

KING (*Shaking fist at* SUSANNA, *as he sings to the verse of "Oh!*
Susanna"):

Never leave Louisiana,
Never pass the palace gate,
Never try to thus escape us,
Worse than death will be your fate.

QUEEN (*Also singing to same tune*):

We will store you in the tower,
We will stash you in a cell,
We will tie you to the bucket,
We will wind you down the well.

(KING *and* QUEEN *laugh evilly, as* SUSANNA *falls on her knees
before them.*)

KING *and* QUEEN (*Singing duet to chorus of "Oh! Susanna"*):

No, Susanna, you never shall be free,
We will keep you here forever,
In the dungeon, you shall be!

CHORUS (*Singing softly*):

No, Susanna, you never shall be free.
They will keep you here forever,
In the dungeon you shall be.

COMMENTATOR: Now Susanna gets her chance. She sings an
aria. An aria is a melody the audience goes home humming. You don't have to know the words. Even the soprano doesn't have to know the words. Listen! (SUSANNA
gets to her feet.)

SUSANNA (*Gesturing dramatically*): Oh! (*She sings single syllable
"Oh" to tune, adding trills as desired, and ending on high note. At
conclusion, she puts her hand to her forehead and holds pose.*)

CHORUS (*Singing excitedly*):

Oh, Susanna!
Oh, weep, oh, weep no more.
For your own true love is coming, coming,
Coming through the door.

(PRINCE BANJO KNEE *enters with great flourish, riding on stick horse. He rides center and doffs his hat to* SUSANNA, *to* KING *and* QUEEN, *to* CHORUS, *and to* COMMENTATOR, *who shakes his hand and takes stick horse.*)

COMMENTATOR (*To audience*): Applause, please. If you haven't already guessed, this is our hero, the tenor— Prince Banjo Knee the First. You always greet a hero with applause, and if you happen to think of it, you shout "Bravo!" even before he sings. Bravo! Bravissimo! (SUSANNA *extends her arms to* PRINCE, *who embraces her, as* KING *and* QUEEN *cower together at one side.*)

SUSANNA (*Singing a single high note*):
Oh-h-h-h-h . . .
(*She sustains note as* PRINCE *sings.*)

PRINCE (*Singing*)
    . . . Susanna! Oh, don't you cry for me,
    For you'll come to Alabama,
    As the bride of Banjo Knee!
(KING *and* QUEEN *go over to* SUSANNA *and* PRINCE *and stand with them. All four sing at once in a quartet.*)

KING *and* QUEEN (*Singing*):
    No, Susanna, you never shall be free,
    We will keep you here forever,
    In the dungeon you shall be!

PRINCE (*Singing at same time as* KING *and* QUEEN):
    Oh, Susanna! Oh, don't you cry for me,
    For you'll come to Alabama,
    As the bride of Banjo Knee!

SUSANNA (*Singing at same time as* KING, QUEEN *and* PRINCE):
Oh-h-h. . . .
(*Holds single high note until others finish singing, adding trills as desired. At end of song* PRINCE *points dramatically offstage, and* KING *and* QUEEN *exit as* CHORUS *sings jubilantly.*)

CHORUS (*Singing*):
    Oh! Susanna! Oh, happy jubilee!

She will go to Alabama

As the bride of Banjo Knee!

(SUSANNA *and* PRINCE *embrace, then run off hand in hand, as* CHORUS *waves pompons.*)

COMMENTATOR: Everything ends well at the opera. The basso is vanquished, the contralto is conquered, and the tenor and soprano go to live in the land of the hemidemi-semiquaver. (*He exits.*)

4TH NARRATOR (*Coming forward*): Before we sing a final fare-well to Susanna, there is one more form a song can take. We present—the oratorio. The oratorio is very serious, so pray do not smile. The oratorio is very profound, so pray think deeply. Listen well, for the words and music are long and complicated. Ladies and gentlemen, the world premiere of an oratorio based on the legend of Susanna. (4TH NARRATOR *stands down right.* CHORUS *sits primly, hands folded*)

1ST SOLO (*Standing and singing recitative-fashion, on one note*):

I have recently departed from my native territory,

With my musical apparatus borne upon my articu-lated patella . . .

2ND SOLO (*Standing and singing on higher note*):

He is sojourning in a southerly state,

Commonly referred to as Alabama,

In order to observe his donna bella . . .

CHORUS (*Rising and singing solemnly*):

Oh! Susanna, be not so lachrymose,

For he cometh, yea, he cometh,

Yea, he cometh very close.

GIRLS IN CHORUS (*Singing*):

For he cometh, yea, he cometh . . .

BOYS IN CHORUS (*Singing*):

Yea, he cometh very close.

DUET (*Singing*):

For he cometh, yea, he cometh.

QUARTET (*Singing*):
>   Yea, he cometh very close.

CHORUS (*Singing*):
>   For he cometh, yea, he cometh,
>   For he cometh, cometh, cometh,

1ST SOLO (*Singing*):
>   Yea, he cometh, cometh, cometh,

CHORUS (*Singing*):
>   For he cometh, yea, he cometh,

2ND SOLO (*Singing*):
>   Yea, yea, yea, he cometh,
>   He cometh . . . very . . . close.

CHORUS (*Singing*):
>   Hallelujah!
>   He cometh . . . very . . . close!

4TH NARRATOR: And now, I think we have heard everything.

1ST SOLO: No, wait. There are more kinds of songs.

CHORUS (*Singing to verse and refrain of "Oh! Susanna"*):
>   There are serenades and lullabies,
>   Songs of war and art,
>   Ballads, blues and madrigals,
>   And croons that stir the heart.
>   Dream songs, theme songs,
>   Plain songs and chants,
>   Rondeaus, trolls and canticles,
>   And lieder and descants!

4TH NARRATOR: Stop. Music may go on forever, but we can't. Isn't there a song to end all songs?

2ND SOLO: Of course!

CHORUS: A swan song.

1ST SOLO: Won't you all join us in the chorus. (*All sing refrain of "Oh! Susanna" with audience, as curtain closes.*)

THE END

Melinda's Incredible Birthday

Characters

MELINDA

INSPECTOR TROVER

TIMEKEEPER

DELIVERY BOY

AUTOGRAPH SEEKER

REPORTER

FAN

FLOWER GIRL

ONLOOKER, *a girl*

BALLOON MAN

CAKE VENDOR

MAYOR

COMMENTATOR

TWO CHEERLEADERS

TOWNSPEOPLE

SCENE 1

TIME: *A day in January.*

BEFORE RISE: MELINDA *enters in front of curtain. She carries calendar. She is crying, and from time to time, wipes her eyes.*

MELINDA: I've lost it. I've lost my birthday. It's gone. Disappeared. Vanished. How could such a thing happen? Oh, please, somebody. Help me find it. (INSPECTOR TROVER *enters right, blowing whistle.*)

INSPECTOR: All right now, miss. Dry your tears. Inspector Trover is here. (*Flashes badge*) Bureau of Missing Matters. What have you lost? You name it. I'll find it.

MELINDA (*Showing him calendar on which January 17th is missing*): My birthday, January 17th. See? January 17th is nowhere on this calendar. What's worse, nobody wished me happy birthday this morning.

INSPECTOR: That's disappointing. (*He scribbles in notebook.*)

MELINDA: Nobody sent me a present.

INSPECTOR: That's a shame.

MELINDA: And it's not just me, either. Lots of people have birthdays on January 17th—even Benjamin Franklin. (*She begins to cry again.*) And if I don't find my birthday, I might have to go on being the same age forever and ever!

INSPECTOR: That's tragic. Now, don't cry. I know I can help you. I can find anything. When Shakespeare couldn't find the right word—who found it? Trover. When Napoleon lost his temper—who found it? Trover. Suppose you describe your birthday to me.

MELINDA: It's a wonderful birthday. I always have a party. I always have a whipped cream cake, and pink and white streamers. I always have exactly eight friends wearing their best dresses and patent leather shoes. And, oh, yes, don't forget the balloons. I have a whole room full of pink and white balloons.

INSPECTOR (*Writing*): Pink and white balloons. Yes, that wraps it up. Your birthday shouldn't be hard to find. By the way, what's your name?

MELINDA: Melinda. But how will you find a day? Where will you look for January 17th?

INSPECTOR: I'll find it in Time, Melinda. Yes, somewhere in Time. (*He takes large magnifying glass from his pocket and paces back and forth on stage examining floor, as if for footprints.*) I'll follow the footprints on the sands of Time. Goodbye, Melinda. Wait for me at the crossroads of Monday and nine o'clock. (MELINDA *waves goodbye and exits right.*) Aha, the footprints are getting clearer. Up the path of the seconds. . . . (*He crosses left and turns, crossing right again.*) Down the lane of the minutes. . . . (*He crosses left, stands center.*) Turn right on the Avenue of the Aeons, and here I am. The Hall of Time. (*Calling*) I say, in there. Let me in. Open up, in the name of the Lost. (*Curtains open.*)

* * *

SETTING: *The Hall of Time.*

AT RISE: TIMEKEEPER *is busy up center at blackboard marked* ARRIVALS. *Next to blackboard is large wheel, like a fortune wheel, marked with time zones from minutes to years. As he writes with one hand,* TIMEKEEPER *turns wheel with the other.* DELIVERY BOY, *loaded down with gift-wrapped packages, runs in left.* INSPECTOR TROVER *crosses to him and helps him steady his load, and unpack it onto table up left marked* JANUARY BIRTHDAYS.

DELIVERY BOY: More January birthdays, whew!

TIMEKEEPER (*Bothered*): Sh-h-h. I have to keep a running tally. (*He counts on his fingers.*) One billion, one million, one thousand and one third. One third? One third of a person? I've goofed. I knew I would.

DELIVERY BOY: It's a pygmy, that's what. You haven't goofed. They always come in thirds.

TIMEKEEPER (*Throwing up his hands*): No, maybe I haven't goofed yet, but I will. I can't keep up with this board. Write down arrivals! Keep a tally. Turn the wheel of time. Help!

DELIVERY BOY: That's what we need—help. There's too much work for the two of us. Sometime, somewhere, we're going to make a mistake and somebody will complain. (INSPECTOR *blows whistle.*)

INSPECTOR: I wish to complain.

DELIVERY BOY: See what I mean?

TIMEKEEPER (*Exasperated*): A complaint? Well, if it's about that stitch in time I dropped, take it up with somebody else. I'm busy, busy, busy.

INSPECTOR: Hold on, Timekeeper. This is much more serious than a stitch in time. A whole day is missing—January 17th, to be exact. A birthday, to be exact.

DELIVERY BOY: A whole day—a birthday! We're in trouble.

TIMEKEEPER: We're in deep trouble. (*He examines wheel.*) January 13—14—15—16—18? Oh-oh. I goofed. No January 17.

DELIVERY BOY: Yipes! Twelve million and one people including Benjamin Franklin did not get a birthday this year.

INSPECTOR: What are you going to do about it?

TIMEKEEPER: I'll just turn the Wheel of Time back a day. Cover your ears. Time doesn't go backward without a big fuss. (*He turns wheel. There is a grinding of gears. Brakes squeal, then there is a whining and a bang.*) It is now officially January 17th.

INSPECTOR (*Holding up pink and white package*): Thank you. We have to keep the records straight, you know. Hm. So these are what birthdays look like before they begin. Very pretty. (*He examines package.*) Ha! What an astonishing coincidence! This is my client's birthday. May I take it to Melinda in person? I'm going that way.

DELIVERY BOY: Sure. It'll save me a trip. Now I'll only have twelve million birthdays including Benjamin Franklin's to deliver. (INSPECTOR *crosses to barrel of stars. He picks out large gold star and pastes it onto package, admiring it.*)

INSPECTOR: Very pretty! (DELIVERY BOY *gapes at him in horror.*)

DELIVERY BOY: What have you done?

TIMEKEEPER: Why did you do it?

INSPECTOR: Do what? I only put a bit of a star on the package. To dress it up.

DELIVERY BOY: To dress it up! Oh, no! Not with a *star.*

TIMEKEEPER: Never with a *star.* Do you know what those stars are for? (*He advances on* INSPECTOR.)

DELIVERY BOY: We use those stars only for birthdays which

are destined to be (*Fanfare. He takes off his cap solemnly.*)—national holidays.

TIMEKEEPER: You have just made Melinda's birthday into a (*Fanfare*)—national holiday.

INSPECTOR (*Holding his head*): How am I going to explain this to Melinda? Melinda, I have something a little out of the ordinary to tell you. It's about your birthday. Sit down, Melinda. Melinda, your birthday is about to become (*He takes off his hat and holds it against his chest. Fanfare*)—

ALL: A national holiday! (*Curtain*)

*   *   *

SCENE 2

BEFORE RISE: *Appropriate party songs may be played, concluding with "Happy Birthday" played like a national anthem.* MELINDA *runs in from left in front of curtain, calendar in hand.* INSPECTOR *slinks in from right, looking dismal.*

MELINDA (*Gaily*): You found it! Thank you, Inspector Trover! Oh, you *are* clever. See? It's right here on the calendar.

INSPECTOR: Sh-h-h. Not so loud.

MELINDA: But I'm going to have a birthday this year after all. Will I have a party, too? Did you find my party?

INSPECTOR: Oh, you'll have a party all right. Oh, what a party. Melinda, I have something a little out of the ordinary to tell you. Sit down, Melinda. (CHEERLEADERS *enter through curtain at center.*) Ahem. Melinda, your birthday is about to become a—

CHEERLEADERS: Happy Birthday!

MELINDA (*Surprised*): Thank you. How do you know it's my birthday?

1ST CHEERLEADER: Everybody knows about your birthday.

2ND CHEERLEADER: We've come to escort you to your party.

(AUTOGRAPH SEEKER, FAN, *and* REPORTER *enter center, excitedly.*)

AUTOGRAPH SEEKER: Oh, here she is. In person. Oh, isn't she just wonderful! (*She thrusts autograph book and pencil at* MELINDA.) Please sign my book. Just a few words.

REPORTER (*Flipping open notebook*): Will you answer a few questions for the school newspaper? (*Firing questions rapidly*) What was the most important moment in your life? Do you have any advice for the younger generation? Do you like chocolate cake or angel food best? How do you spell Melinda?

FAN (*Adoringly*): Would you shake my hand? (*She grabs* MELINDA'*s hand and pumps it vigorously.*) Oh! She touched me! The great Melinda touched me. (*Holding up limp hand*) I'll never wash this hand again.

MELINDA (*Baffled*): What? What? What on earth are you all doing? There's been a mistake. Will somebody please explain?

1ST CHEERLEADER: Not now.

2ND CHEERLEADER: We have to hurry.

CHEERLEADERS: The whole town is waiting. (*Curtains open behind them.*)

* * *

SETTING: *An auditorium. There is a rostrum up center draped in pink and white bunting, with huge banner above it, on backdrop, reading,* HAPPY BIRTHDAY. *Three folding chairs are in front of rostrum. Rows of chairs are at right and left.*

AT RISE: TOWNSPEOPLE *are sitting on chairs right and left. In front row are* ONLOOKER *and* FLOWER GIRL, *holding large bouquet of pink and white flowers.* MAYOR *stands at rostrum, holding large pink and white key to city, and wearing pink shoulder sash.* TOWNSPEOPLE *wear pink shoulder sashes and some hold balloons.* BALLOON MAN *stands down left, with balloons.* CAKE VENDOR *stands at small table down right, selling whipped cream cake.*

COMMENTATOR, *holding microphone, stands center. As he speaks,* AUTOGRAPH SEEKER, REPORTER, *and* FAN *enter and sit in front row of seats at right.* INSPECTOR *crosses and sits up left in folding chair. He pulls up his collar and tries to look inconspicuous.* MELINDA *and* CHEERLEADERS *turn and enter set.*

COMMENTATOR: Ladies and gentlemen of the radio audience, we are greeting you from the home town of one of our great National Heroines. In the distance you can hear the Balloon Man and the Cake Vendor selling their traditional wares. Listen.

BALLOON MAN (*Calling*): Balloons. Pink and white balloons. Get your balloons before the celebration begins. Rosy pink and pearly white balloons. Our National Heroine's favorite balloons.

CAKE VENDOR (*Calling*): Whipped cream cake. Buy a heaping hunk of hearty, healthful whipped cream cake. Get your cake here, folks.

ONLOOKER (*Pointing to* MELINDA): Oh, there she is! I see her. I see Melinda. (*All cheer.*)

COMMENTATOR: Did you hear that cheer, folks? You guessed it! She's right here. (*He holds microphone out to* MELINDA.) Ladies and gentlemen, I have the honor of speaking to Melinda. Melinda, will you give us a few pearls of wisdom on this great occasion?

MELINDA: Who, me?

COMMENTATOR: You heard her, folks. That was actually Melinda herself speaking with her actual voice and saying the actual words, "Who, me?" (FLOWER GIRL *presents bouquet to* MELINDA, *curtsying as she does so*) Ah, here's a Flower Girl with a speech of welcome for Melinda.

FLOWER GIRL: Gracious Melinda, on behalf of the Mayor and the people of this town, I present you with this bouquet of flowers. Happy Birthday.

MELINDA: Who, me? (*She accepts flowers, and is led up center by* CHEERLEADERS.)

1ST CHEERLEADER: This way, please.

2ND CHEERLEADER: His honor, the Mayor, wishes to greet you officially.

MELINDA: Who, me?

COMMENTATOR: Melinda, our great National Heroine, appears overcome by this demonstration. The Mayor now extends his hand. And Melinda extends her hand. The two are now shaking hands. (MELINDA *and* MAYOR *pantomime shaking hands.* CHEERLEADERS *take places right and left of rostrum.* MAYOR *presents* MELINDA *with key to city.*) And the Mayor presents Melinda with the key to the city. (*All applaud.*) And now the Mayor appears to be going to speak. Listen.

MAYOR: Fellow citizens of this fair town, I am about to introduce someone who needs no introduction.

MELINDA (*Looking around*): Who?

MAYOR: A great person. A famous person. A person who has put civic duty above all else. Let us rise and sing the birthday anthem to the one, the only, the original—Melinda. (*All rise and sing "Happy Birthday" solemnly, applauding at conclusion.*)

MELINDA (*Dumbfounded*): Who, me? There's been a terrible mistake. I'm not great at all.

MAYOR: Such modesty. I'm overcome. Such genuine modesty.

ALL: Hooray for modesty!

MAYOR: Of course you are great, my dear. We wouldn't celebrate your birthday throughout the nation if you weren't a great heroine.

MELINDA: Heroine! The only thing I ever did was to rescue an old alley cat from a tree.

ALL: Hooray for alley cats!

MAYOR: Tut, tut. We have all heard of your fantastic scientific achievements.

MELINDA: My *what?* You mean that time I mixed glue with shampoo and gave myself a permanent permanent?

ALL: Hooray for glue!

MAYOR: But you must have done something remarkable. Ah—I know. You've given away huge sums of money to charity!

MELINDA (*Sighing*): The most I ever gave was eighteen cents to my needy little brother. You see, I'm very ordinary. I'm sorry you went to all this trouble for me, Mr. Mayor. I'm only Melinda. Not great. Not famous. At least, not yet. It's terribly embarrassing to have a national holiday for a national nobody. And all I ever wanted was just a quiet party with my eight best friends. Oh, I wish I could give this holiday to somebody who really deserves it.

INSPECTOR: But that's it. Of course. The perfect solution! (*He whispers in* MELINDA's *ear.*)

MELINDA: Yes. Yes. I'll do it. Mr. Mayor—Fellow Townspeople: Would you like to celebrate the birthday of someone who really put civic duty above all else?

ALL: We would.

ONLOOKER: What did he do—for example?

MELINDA: For example, he started the first fire department, the first post office, the first public library and in his spare time he built a fort, and drafted a constitution, and founded a debating society.

ALL: Hooray for civic duty!

MELINDA: Would you like to honor the birthday of somebody who really made great scientific achievements?

ALL: We would.

ONLOOKER: What did he do, for example?

MELINDA: For example, he invented swim fins, and bifocals, and a stove and a musical instrument and a sea anchor. For example, he discovered that electricity and lightning were the same. And in his spare time he charted the Gulf Stream, experimented with heat, and that isn't all . . .

MAYOR: One moment, please. Who are these six people you wish to honor?

MELINDA: Not six people. One person. Today is his birthday, too. So if you please, I wish to donate the 17th of January to (*First bars of "Yankee Doodle" are heard.*)—Mr. Benjamin Franklin.

MAYOR: Benjamin Franklin?

ALL: Benjamin Franklin!

MAYOR: Yes, indeed. Very fitting. Well spoken, Melinda. On behalf of this town, I hereby accept the 17th of January as Benjamin Franklin Day. All banks, post offices and libraries shall remain closed.

ONLOOKER: What about schools?

MAYOR: Schools, too. (*All applaud.*) We shall have kite flying at the town park. Let us rise and sing our Happy Birthday Anthem. (*All sing "Happy Birthday" to Benjamin Franklin. They turn pink sashes over, disclosing red, white and blue stripes.* BALLOON MAN *takes balloons off left, returning with red, white and blue kites.* CAKE VENDOR *takes his tray off right, returning with teapot and cups.*)

BALLOON MAN: Kites! Get your handmade Franklin kites here. Every one guaranteed to discover electricity. Kites. Come and get your kites.

CAKE VENDOR (*As curtains start to close*): Tea. Get your hot tea here. Every pot made on a Franklin stove. Get your hot tea here. (*Curtains close, to indicate passage of time.* INSPECTOR *steps out in front of curtain, his magnifying glass in his hand.* MELINDA *enters down left, a pink balloon in her hand.*)

INSPECTOR: Ah, there you are, Melinda. I'm still looking for your missing birthday party—the one you have at home, I mean.

MELINDA: Why, thank you very much, but I've just had my party.

INSPECTOR: What? With whipped cream cake and pink and white streamers?

MELINDA: Yes. It was right there waiting for me when I came home. With just exactly eight friends in their best dresses and patent leather shoes. It was an elegant party. I'm sorry I don't have any money to give you for all your trouble, but I saved you a pink balloon. (*She puts balloon in his hand.*) Goodbye. (*She runs off left.* INSPECTOR *ties balloon to his wrist.*)

INSPECTOR: Remarkable. In every way remarkable. In fact, quite the most remarkable case I have ever solved. (*He writes in notebook.*) Lost: one ordinary birthday. Found: one national holiday. (*He shakes his hand.*) Congratulations, Inspector Trover, you've done it again. (*He puts away notebook and follows trail of invisible footprints with his magnifying glass.*) And now—back to the trail again. You name it—I'll find it! (*He exits right, with his eye to magnifying glass.*)

THE END

Production Notes

TAKE ME TO YOUR MARSHAL

Characters: 4 male; 2 female; 3 male and 1 female for television voices.
Playing Time: 20 minutes.
Costumes: Everyday, casual clothes for all except Zanthus, who wears a green space suit and space hat with two antennas.
Properties: Knitting needles and yarn, newspaper, slide whistle for Zanthus, gun belt with six-shooters, Stetson with two holes.
Setting: The living room of the Reed house. A television set down left faces away from audience. There is a large window right. Exit up right leads outside, exit at left leads to the rest of house. There is a sofa at left center, with an armchair at right. Bookcases are up center and left. A large rug may be placed in front of the television set.
Lighting: Lights flash, dim, go off and on, as indicated in text.
Sound: Footsteps, doorknob rattling, beeping sound, dramatic music, as indicated in text.

HOW TO CHOOSE A BOY

Characters: 9 male; 5 female.
Playing Time: 12 minutes.
Costumes: All dog characters wear beanies with ears. Bowser wears white jacket, collar, and spectacles. Madame Fideaux and Fifi wear tutus and leotards, ankle frills, have curly hair, and wear jeweled collars.

Major Beagle wears hunting jacket and high boots. Mr. Rover wears business suit, tie, and collar. Mrs. Rover wears a housedress and collar, and Sporty wears blue jeans, T shirt and collar. Nancy wears a simple dress and a bow in her hair. Emily wears fancy party dress, and an elaborate hair-do. Hunter wears pith helmet, safari jacket and toy gun over his shoulder. Boxer wears polo shirt, trunks and sneakers. Greyhound wears blue bus driver's uniform. Husky wears sweatshirt padded with "muscles," a parka and dungarees.
Properties: Pad, pencil, telephone, jump rope, 2 leashes, whistle, auto horn, set of toy barbells.
Setting: Woofington T. Bowser's People Shop. A counter with telephone, leashes, collars and other pet store items is up center. Signs on curtains or counter read: PEDIGREED PEOPLE SOLD HERE, A DOG'S BEST FRIEND IS A MAN, and THIS IS BE KIND TO HUMANS WEEK. A chair is down right. Exit at left leads to back of shop, and right exit leads outside.
Sound: Telephone ringing, as indicated in text.

LADY MOON AND THE THIEF

Characters: 6 male; 1 female; 7 boys or girls for fishermen, xylophonist, gong player, property boys; as many actors as desired for Villagers.
Playing Time: 20 minutes.

Costumes: Chinese costumes. Lord Sun wears gold armor, and carries round gold shield. The front of Lady Moon's kimono is silver and the back is black. She carries two fans, silver on one side and black on the other. Bow-Low wears silk robe and carries scroll. Nid-Nod wears bright kimono, and is made up as an old man. Others wear kimonos or short Chinese jackets, trousers, sandals, and coolie hats. Property Boys are dressed in black.

Properties: Fans for Villagers, fishing poles, cardboard fish, basket containing rice shoots, dark cloak, long-handled fan for Ah Me, fishnet on pole, pillows, gong, xylophone, tea table set with teapot and cups.

Setting: Ting-a-ling, a village in ancient China. A blue pagoda, large enough to hide Lord Sun behind it and with steps to climb it on both sides, is on a platform at center. Day Screens, painted with scenes of trees, sky, clouds, etc., are on either side, and behind them are Night Screens, painted black. A bridge over a pond is at left, and up right is a hill painted to resemble a terraced rice paddy. A twisted pine tree with a tea table set with teapot and cups is down right. Exits are at right and left, and behind pagoda, if desired.

Lighting: No special effects.

Sound: Gong and xylophone, Oriental music, as indicated in text.

The Book That Saved the Earth

Characters: 6 male; 1 male offstage voice. If desired, parts may be taken by girls.

Playing Time: 20 minutes.

Costumes: Historian wears cap and gown, and has long white beard. Think-Tank wears robe decorated with stars and circles. He has huge, egg-shaped head, and around his neck he wears pair of huge goggles

on chain. Noodle and spacemen wear tunics, tights, and beanies with antennas. Spacemen have silver belts with small boxes containing pills, and Omega has a disc on a chain around his neck.

Properties: Hand mirror; large book with *Mother Goose* on cover in large letters, containing a picture of Humpty Dumpty which resembles Think-Tank; microphone; books; pills.

Setting: Down right, in front of curtain, are a table and chair. A movie projector is on the table. Beside table is an easel with a sign: MUSEUM OF ANCIENT HISTORY: DEPARTMENT OF THE TWENTIETH CENTURY. Down left, in front of curtain, are a raised box and an elaborate switchboard with knobs and levers. A sign on an easel reads: MARS SPACE CONTROL. GREAT AND MIGHTY THINK-TANK, COMMAND-ER-IN-CHIEF. BOW LOW BEFORE ENTERING. At back of stage is backdrop of library shelves. A sign reads: CENTERVILLE PUBLIC LIBRARY. A card catalogue is at center and bookcases containing books are at right and left. On one shelf is large copy of *Mother Goose.*

Lighting: Spotlights on Historian and Martians, as indicated in text.

Sound: Electronic buzzes and beeps.

Beware the Genies!

Characters: 7 male; 5 female; as many male and female as desired for Dusters, Swabbers, and Paper Pickers.

Playing Time: 20 minutes.

Costumes: Lucy, Wendy, and Dan wear everyday dress. Genies wear Oriental robes, turbans and slippers with curved toes. Cave family wears appropriate primitive dress. Underground family wears coveralls and miners' hats with lights. Dusters wear aprons and carry dustcloths; Swabbers may be dressed as sailors, and they have mops; Paper Pickers wear park uniforms and caps.

Properties: Brass bottle, locket, fishing line, rubber boot, flint, bow and arrow, animal skin, wooden bowl, basket containing cans, book, dustcloths, mops, border of flowers, beach umbrella, signs, as indicated in text.

Setting: The city dump. Backdrop shows city skyline with smoking chimneys. (Smoke can be erased to show blue sky and sun at end.) A large rock is down left. Overflowing trash cans are scattered about. In scene with Cave family, a campfire is at right, and rock is at left. In scene with Underground family, table stands at center, and rock at left. Exits are right and left.

Lighting: Lights flash as Genies enter.

A ROMAN ROMANCE

Characters: 4 male; 5 female.

Playing Time: 20 minutes.

Costumes: Ancient classical dress. Pomona may wear gold Grecian-style dress and tiara of autumn leaves. Maidens and Venus wear long dresses, and Venus may have gold accessories. Marcus wears rough toga and sheepskin cape. Quintus has a blue smock and battered felt hat. Galba wears leather apron and headband. Septimus has a long cloak with hood.

Properties: Water jars, shepherd's crook, basket of fruit, basket of barley ears, pruning shears, staff.

Setting: Pomona's orchard. The backdrop shows an orchard with trees laden with fruit. Down left is an apple tree with a bench and a bucket and dipper. Down right is an elm tree with a grape vine twined around it. Across stage is a low wall, with a gate in it with a scroll: POMONA'S ORCHARD. ABSOLUTELY NO ADMITTANCE. Exits are at right and left.

Lighting: No special effects.

Sound: Flute music may accompany romantic action, if desired.

THE LONG TABLE

Characters: 7 male; 2 female principals. Tableau Families may include as many members as desired. Chorus may be as large as desired, or Tableau members may double as Chorus and Property Boys.

Playing Time: 25 minutes.

Costumes: Narrator, Pilgrim costume. Sarah Josepha Hale, full-skirted dress, reticule containing papers, shawl, bonnet, parasol. Dr. Antiquarius, frock coat, cravat, top hat, spectacles. Henry Gideon, farm clothing. Adelaide Pruitt, long full-skirted dress, cape, hat. Secretary, frock coat, vest, wing collar, cravat. Guards, Union uniforms. President Lincoln, frock coat, shirt with wing collar, bow tie. Pilgrim Family, men, women and children in Pilgrim costume. Indian, skins, beads, feathers in hair. Northern and Southern Families: women, full-skirted dresses; girls, pinafores and pantaloons; boys, short jackets, long trousers, wing collars and cravats. Northern Father, Union uniform. Southern Father, Confederate uniform. Plantation Family, farm clothing. Messengers from the Future, blue uniforms with star clusters on the shirts, silver boots, silver caps. Astronaut, space suit.

Properties: Letters, reticule, crystal ball, appointment book, tattered letter, pocket watch, documents, quill pen, blotting sand, inkstand, clicker, wooden bowl with apples and nuts, floral centerpiece, lamp, telephone, atom model, toy auto, airplane, globe model of the moon.

Setting: Before rise, a long bench is placed in front of curtain to represent President Lincoln's waiting room. In Mr. Lincoln's office, two flags up center, a desk at center, and a visitor's chair at right. The Long Table is fitted together in three sections and placed across stage from right to left. Chorus stands to one side.

Sound: Musical selections are played or hummed in background, then sung by Chorus, as indicated in text. Spoken choral parts may be divided and assigned to individuals, if desired.

Lighting: Blackouts, as indicated in text.

JACK JOUETTE'S RIDE

Characters: 10 male; 3 female; 6 or more male and female for Chorus.

Playing Time: 20 minutes.

Costumes: Colonial costumes and British and Continental army officers' uniforms.

Properties: Poker, tray with mugs and teapot, polishing cloth, ragged coat and hat, map, tray with plates of food and silverware, mug.

Setting: Scene 1: The Cuckoo Tavern in Louisa County, Virginia. There is a brick fireplace up center, with skillets and pots hanging from mantel. Fire tools are on the hearth. A sign reading THE CUCKOO TAVERN hangs above fireplace. Upstage left and right are mullioned French windows covered with closed curtains. There are two tables with benches downstage left and right. Scene 2: Dining room in the Walker house at Castle Hill. Basic set is the same as Scene 1, but decor has been altered. Draperies replace curtains at windows, and windows are flung open. Sideboard stands in front of window, right. Pots and skillets have been taken down from mantel; candles now stand on mantel. Landscape painting hangs over fireplace, replacing tavern sign. One table and bench have been removed. Remaining table stands at right, covered with a white tablecloth. Candelabra stand on table.

There are three ladder-back chairs at table. In both scenes, exit left leads to interior of building and back door, and exit right leads outside.

Lighting: No special effects.

HONORABLE CAT'S DECISION

Characters: 14 male; 4 female.

Playing Time: 20 minutes.

Costumes: Emperor, Scribe and Court wear kimonos. Shoji, happy coat or short kimono, sandals, white trousers, coolie hat. Okusan, brown kimono, obi, sandals. Shubo, happy coat, white trousers, sandals. Carvers, bandanas tied around foreheads, kimonos, sandals. Honorable Cat wears cat costume, gloves with claws.

Properties: Gong; bowl; skeins of thread; pillow; rice bowl; individual bowls; chopsticks; tea cups; hibachi; tea kettle; screen; low table; pillows for kneeling; butterfly net; small scroll; very long scroll; spectacles; bag with gold pieces; hobo bundle on a stick; cloth rat; white rat, wood rat, stone rat on cushions; wooden box containing shapeless fish-rat; tray with mound of rice and other dishes; large bowl of flowers.

Setting: A backdrop of Oriental scenes, if desired. Up center is a dais of four tiers on which kneel the court and the Emperor. Down right is a screen in front of which are table, hibachi and pillows for Shoji and his family.

Lighting: No special effects.

THE TALL-TALE TOURNAMENT

Characters: 9 male; 5 female; as many male and female as desired for Jug Band and Chorus.

Playing Time: 20 minutes.

Costumes: Oregon Smith wears overalls, checked shirt, straw hat. Mary Anne wears summer dress and hat. Others wear outfits appropriate to the legendary characters they represent.

Jug Band and Chorus wear jeans and checked shirts or old-fashioned long dresses and sunbonnets.

Properties: Gavel, chalk, booklet, hammer, flag, knapsack, pitcher, hoe, cardboard rifles and ax, lariat, pole.

Setting: A town square in Bloomington, Indiana, decorated with gaily-colored pennants and bunting. A banner across the back reads: WELCOME! NINETY-NINTH ANNUAL TALL-TALE TOURNAMENT. Down right is a rostrum with a gavel; at center are a bench for the jury and chairs for Chorus and Jug Band, placed in a semicircle across stage. Down left is a gilded and sequinned bench. Exits are at right and left.

Sound: Offstage chimes, bus horn.

Lighting: No special effects.

How Mothers Came To Be

Characters: 2 male; 2 female; 10 spirits and animals, which may be played by either male or female actors; 10 male or female for Chorus; 3 Musicians (non-speaking parts).

Playing Time: 15 minutes.

Costumes: Musicians, Chorus: headbands, fringed tunics, trousers, moccasins. Manitou: full headdress, white tunic, buckskins, white moccasins. Kiwa: headband, tunic, buckskins, moccasins. Kiwi: headband, Indian dress, moccasins. Air: blue tunic, blue chiffon scarves, blue beaded headdress. Fire: red tunic, red chiffon scarves, red beaded headdress. Water: white tunic, white scarves, white or silver headdress. Owl: Indian costume, wings, spectacles, cap with tufts and beak. Deer: Indian girl costume, brown cap with ears. Turtle: green Indian costume, green shell. Squirrel: gray Indian costume, bushy tail, ears. Beaver: brown Indian costume, broad tail, large front teeth. Bee: yellow Indian costume with black bands. Head-band with stinger, wings. Spider: black Indian costume, black headdress with six prongs.

Properties: Tom-tom, rattles, bells, owl's headband, small Indian blanket, turtle's small shell, acorn necklace, bundle of sticks, flower, spiderweb.

Setting: Backdrop of the sun, with sun and stylized Indian symbols of trees and brooks painted on it. A riser or wooden box up center. Blanket down right.

Lighting: No special effects.

Sound: Tom-tom, rattle and bells, as indicated in text.

Destination: Christmas!

Characters: 20 male; 13 female. As many Carolers and Cheerleaders as desired. Additional children for extras. One set of Dancers may play all three groups, if desired.

Note: Music and most spoken parts are handled by Carolers and Cheerleaders. These parts may be carried onstage in choir folders. Other parts are primarily non-speaking roles. Thus, young groups can perform this special Christmas program with little difficulty.

Playing Time: 30 minutes.

Costumes: Ticket Agent, Pilot and Customs Agent wear appropriate uniforms in red and green motifs. Stewardesses wear appropriate national costumes. Scandinavian Stewardess wears St. Lucia costume, with long white gown, red sash, crown of fir with seven candles. Julenisse wears an elf costume with red pointed cap, gray beard. Old Befana wears a black dress, shawl, and black shoes. Wise Men wear Magi costumes. Ethiopian boys wear short-sleeved white shirts, white shorts, sandals, short black capes, and later put on shepherd's robes. Angel wears white wings, robe, and shining halo. Mary, Joseph and Innkeeper wear festive

Mexican costumes. Cheerleaders wear dark skirts and trousers, white sneakers, red 'and green scarves. Carolers wear red choir robes and green bows. Dancers wear appropriate national costumes.

Properties: Red and green pompons, sign reading, THIS VEHICLE CLEARED FOR A MERRY CHRISTMAS!, tray with coffeepot and coffee cups, small bowls, small Christmas tree, Yule log, switch, broom, large bag of gifts, smaller sack of gifts, wrapped gifts, sticks, clubs, balls, shepherds' crooks, piñata on pole (paper flowers inside), cardboard door, blindfolds.

Setting: Double rows of chairs up left and up right, as in airplane. Backdrop may be decorated with appropriate airplane signs and cutout windows.

Lighting: No special effects.

Sound: Sleigh bells, triangle, tambourine, bongo drum, castanets, to be played as indicated by Carolers.

Music: Carols may be found in *A Treasury of Christmas Songs and Carols,* edited by Henry W. Simon (Houghton Mifflin); Mexican songs may be found in *A Treasury of Mexican Folkways,* by Frances Toor (Crown Publishers).

ONE HUNDRED WORDS

Characters: 5 male; 5 female.

Playing Time: 20 minutes.

Costumes: Helga wears Danish schoolgirl's costume, Hans a work cap, white shirt with flowing tie, a sleeveless bolero, and black trousers with boots. Girl with the Red Shoes wears a Danish costume and red ballet shoes, and the Ballerina a frilly dance costume with ballet shoes. Ducks have caps with bills, capes with wings, tights, and yellow webbed feet. Ugly Duckling has straggly wings and very large red webbed feet. Soldier is dressed in Grenadier uniform. Street Lamp Spirit wears black frock coat and trousers, black stocking cap and carries cane.

Properties: Slate, chalk, dustcloth, stick with bundle tied to it.

Setting: A park in Copenhagen. Backdrop may depict a blue sky, trees and flowers, and a duck pond. Left stands a bench with a street lamp next to it.

Lighting: No special effects.

NUMBER ONE APPLE TREE LANE

Characters: 4 male; 2 female; 3 male or female for baby robins; 8 or more male and female for Chorus.

Playing Time: 15 minutes.

Costumes: Chorus and Boy wear everyday dress. Boy carries toy rifle, and Chorus members have binoculars. Birds and animals wear appropriate masks or costumes.

Properties: Binoculars, cardboard ear of corn, collar with bells, toy rifle.

Setting: A nest in an apple tree. A circle of cardboard represents nest. The backdrop shows branches of apple tree and sky.

Lighting: No special effects.

THE LITTLE RED HEN

Characters: 6 male; 6 female; as many boys and girls for Chorus as desired.

Playing Time: 20 minutes.

Costumes: Narrators and Chorus wear farm clothes. Little Red Hen is dressed in red, and chicks wear yellow. Tabitha, Quacker, and Percival wear appropriate animal masks or costumes. Farmer and Miller wear overalls, and Scarecrow wears tattered clothes.

Properties: 5 hoes, 5 cardboard scythes, grindstone, flour sacks, table, bowl, spoons, egg, milk bottle, cardboard oven, bread pans, plates, 7 chairs, bread knife, eating utensils, 3 large dinner napkins.

Setting: A farmyard. A pile of hoes and scythes is at one side. Backdrop shows fields and red barn. Exits are at right and left.

Lighting: No special effects.

Sound: Offstage bell, piano accompaniment for songs, if desired.

MAY BASKET FANTASIA

Characters: 11 male; 11 female; 2 male or female for Child and Walking May Basket.

Playing Time: 20 minutes.

Costumes: Bright spring clothes for Narrators, Modern Girls, boy Maybasketeers, 3rd girl Maybasketeer, and Child. Old-Fashioned Girl and 1st girl Maybasketeer wear crinolines. 2nd girl Maybasketeer wears mod outfit. Secret Agent wears trench coat, beard and spectacles; Phantom wears sheet. John Alden may have on Pilgrim outfit. Cowboy, Eskimo, and Florida Girl wear appropriate costumes. Western Union Messenger wears uniform, and Martian's costume has antennas. First girl of Many-Armed Goddess wears gold outfit with Oriental make-up. The other two girls wear gold sleeves. Walking May Basket carries or wears a huge May basket.

Properties: May baskets, including one filled with candy, one filled with balloons, and one containing several smaller baskets, lollipop, whistle, pad, pencil.

Setting: Three flowered archways representing doors are at center. Behind each is a flowered chair.

Lighting: No special effects.

Sound: Music to accompany pantomimes, if desired, as indicated in text.

THE WILD RABBIT CHASE

Characters: 14 male; 6 female; 2 boys or girls for Property Boys (non-speaking parts).

Playing Time: 20 minutes.

Costumes: Boys wear baseball uniforms. Mother Rabbit, Twins, Peter, Flopsy, Mopsy and Cottontail wear brown rabbit costumes with white tails. Jack Rabbit, March Hare and Cane-Cutter also wear brown; Jack has very large ears, and Cane-Cutter wears diving mask and snorkel. March Hare wears fancy waistcoat, vest, and large bow. Arctic Hare, White Rabbit, Magician's Rabbit, and Easter Rabbit wear white rabbit costumes. Arctic Hare has on Eskimo parka, White Rabbit wears frock coat, Magician's Rabbit wears turban and carries top hat, and Easter Rabbit has on straw hat, striped coat, and sequinned bow tie. Pooka wears blue rabbit costume with large gold shamrock on the front.

Properties: Baseball, bat, gloves, saltshaker, butterfly net, waterlily pad, fan, large Easter basket.

Setting: A forest. At the beginning of the play, a large tree is at left, a rocky hill with a cave is at center, bushes are at right, and a border of tall grass runs across stage at center. Backdrop shows blue sky. Later the tree, bushes, etc., are turned around to show opposite sides painted in pink, blue, and yellow. Cave is silver, and a rainbow is on the backdrop. For the scenes in front of the curtain, Property Boys bring on hollow log, igloo, and signs, as indicated in text.

Lighting: If desired, lights may dim after Arctic scene.

PANDORA'S PERILOUS PREDICAMENT

Characters: 9 male; 5 female; 4 or more male or female for Citizens; 2 male or female for Copycat and Pretzel Bird.

Playing Time: 25 minutes.

Costumes: Pandora and Gracie wear everyday modern clothes. Gax and

Timix wear sorcerers' hats and robes. Sky-Watcher and Detector are dressed in long silver capes with hoods; under them they wear policemen's uniforms and caps. Citizens and Salesmen wear polka-dotted tunics, butterfly wings, caps with antennas. Robots wear silver boxes with dials painted on them, and antennas. Pets wear appropriate fantastic costumes.

Properties: Silver hoop, coins, dollar bill, flashlight, chiming wand, muffs, jars, chain, leash, featherduster, gavel, shells, bag, computer card, broom, whip, signs as indicated in text.

Setting: Scene 1 and last episode (played before curtain) are in a park. Two park benches and sign are placed on stage, as indicated. For the marketplace of Ultimate City, there is a backdrop showing a large red sun and a small yellow sun, jagged blue mountains and a city of mushroom-shaped buildings. There is a gaudy awning with sign and several tables under it. The scene in Helica's house is played before the curtain, with Household Robot bringing on blow-up chair, table with exotic-looking plant.

Sound: Buzzer, chimes. If desired, computer music may be played between scenes.

Lighting: No special effects.

Snowflake

Characters: 9 male; 8 female; male and female extras for Villagers and Snowflakes.

Playing Time: 20 minutes.

Costumes: Russian peasant costumes. Spring and Summer wear elaborate holiday costumes with ribbons, green for Spring and yellow for Summer. Autumn wears red and gold Cossack costume. Boy and Girl Snowflakes wear white costumes, and carry white scarves. Frost King wears white cloak trimmed with sequins, white astrakhan-style hat, white boots and white gloves. Snowflake wears full-length white robe, boots, gloves, and hat like Olga's. Children wear winter caps and scarves; Olga gives her hat to snow figure. Later Snowflake re-enters with tall white and silver crown.

Properties: Flower baskets, hatchets, wooden whistle, sleigh bells; for snow figure, four white balls in graduated sizes, of Styrofoam or papier-mâché, with eyes, nose and mouth on smallest ball; "sleigh," wagon or carriage body on wheels with cardboard sides painted white, and a riser for Snowflake to sit on so she is raised above the sleigh body.

Setting: Russian village near a clearing. Backdrop of cloudy sky, hills and forest. Row of fir trees runs across rear of stage. An exit is between two large trees up center. Thatched cottage, painted on flat, is at left.

Lighting: No special effects.

Sound: Sleigh bells; flute or ocarina for bird; and rising wind, rooster, and echo which may be done offstage by Snowflakes. The Russian folk tune, "Minka," also known as "Yes, My Darling Daughter," is used as running theme throughout the play. This tune appears in *Voices of the World*, by Wolf, Crane and Fullerton (Follett Publishing Company). Piano accompaniment may be used, and accordion, guitars, chimes or xylophone would also enhance the music.

Ah See and the Six-Colored Heaven

Characters: 10 male; 4 female. Narrators and Property Boys may be played by girls. Musicians are non-speaking parts.

Playing Time: 20 minutes.

Costumes: Musicians wear colorful Chinese robes and matching pillbox hats. Ding Ling, Ming Ling and Sing Ling wear satin or brocade robes, and Chinese crowns. They add gray cloaks later in play. Ding Ling may wear moustache and goatee. So Low, dressed as the wind, wears silver robes, white demon mask which may be suspended around his neck, dark coolie coat and hat. He adds a gray robe when he is in gatekeeper's disguise. Three Princes wear gray mandarin jackets, gray queues and pillbox hats, slit trousers and slippers. Ah See has ragged trousers, straw sandals, blue coolie coat and straw hat.

Properties: Large, brightly-colored cutouts of the sun, clouds, and large rainbow; hand-mirror; fans; fan with hole in center; three bags of gold; Chinese lantern with flashlight inside; sunglasses; Chinese crown for Ah See; baskets of bright-colored paper flowers; gong; wood blocks; slide whistle; flute; tambourine.

Setting: Long ago in China. The stage is bare, and set pieces are used, consisting of a pagoda (red on one side, gray on the reverse), willow tree, and gray Torii gate (two upright posts connected at the top by two horizontal crosspieces).

Lighting: No special effects.

Sound: Sound effects are provided by Musicians onstage, as indicated in text, or may be dubbed from offstage.

WHAT EVER HAPPENED TO MOTHER NATURE?

Characters: 7 male; 7 female.

Playing Time: 15 minutes.

Costumes: Appropriate storybook costumes. Mother Nature wears long green gown with daisy chain under gray duster. She also wears earmuffs,

goggles, helmet, mask, and canteen. Frog wears green tights and shirt and frog mask. Spider wears black trousers and shirt, black streamers to represent legs. Water Commissioner may wear yellow sou'wester and hat.

Properties: Signs, broomstick decorated to look like goose, tricycle with horn, telescope, pail, coil of wire, green rope, spray can, large stamped letter, newspaper, muffler for horn, banner, daisy crown.

Setting: Before Rise, a large door frame and sign are down left. At Rise, backdrop shows deteriorated landscape, with a backdrop of smoking factories. There are crates and old boxes scattered about stage. Down right there is a dilapidated wishing well, down left a pile of trash. Exits are at right and left.

Lighting: No special effects.

Sound: Traffic noises; tricycle horn.

ON CAMERA, NOAH WEBSTER!

Characters: 7 male; 5 female; 9 male or female for Chorus and Spelling Demons.

Playing Time: 15 minutes.

Costumes: Modern, everyday dress, except for Demons, who wear imp costumes and carry tridents, and Which Doctor, who wears a shaggy wig, grass skirt, and necklaces. Mother Tongue may wear long dress, shawl, mob cap, and spectacles. Penelope wears an apron.

Properties: TV camera, dictionaries, bulletin, laundry basket with crumpled paper, fresh sheet of paper, bowls, spoon, scrabble letters, pie with flags, pepper shaker.

Setting: A television studio. A large sign at the back of the stage reads: CHANNEL 26—ENTERTAINMENT AND EDUCATION FROM A TO Z. A desk and chair are down left. A table and chair are down right, with a cart holding pie, pepper shaker, and other cooking utensils nearby. A washing machine (cardboard cutout) is at center.

Sound: Teletype clicking, washing machine, as indicated in text.

Lighting: No special effects.

THE CARE AND FEEDING OF MOTHERS

Characters: 2 male; 3 female; 3 male or female for Narrator, Senior and Junior Babies.

Playing Time: 10 minutes.

Costumes: Babies wear blue and pink bathrobes or kimonos and baby caps. Senior Baby wears a mortarboard. Nurse wears uniform.

Setting: A hospital nursery. Six chairs draped with sheets to look like bassinets are placed across stage. Exit is at left.

Lighting: No special effects.

Sound: Brahms' "Lullaby" may be played in the background.

HOTEL OAK

Characters: 2 male; 19 male or female.

Playing Time: 15 minutes.

Costumes: Ax Man and Saw Man wear loggers' shirts, jeans, boots, neckerchiefs, wide belts, and hunting caps. Animals wear appropriate costumes.

Properties: Ax; saw; binoculars.

Setting: A large oak tree with branches left and right stands at center. It may have a riser in back for Caterpillar to lie on, as if on the branch, right. Low bushes stand right and left, and a small stream lined with rocks flows around the tree left, ending in a beaver dam, behind which Beaver and Fish hide. There are exits left, right, and behind tree, at rear of stage.

Lighting: No special effects.

Sound: Chopping, sawing, trees falling, thunder, as indicated in text.

THE SEARCH FOR THE SKY-BLUE PRINCESS

Characters: 10 male; 4 female; 8 or more male and female for Chorus. Two Soldiers are non-speaking parts.

Playing Time: 25 minutes.

Costumes: Dutch peasant costumes are worn by all except King, Prime Minister, Oswald, Herald and Two Soldiers, who wear appropriate court dress or uniforms.

Properties: Basket of rolls, tray of cheeses, yoke, milk pail, dipper, basket of vegetables, cabbage, spears for Oswald and Soldiers, coin, large picture of a blue tulip, bowl with dough, sugar bowl, coins, wooden boxes with peepholes, covered with thin blue paper. Bowls, spoons, honey jar, gray, purple and blue tulips in pots, two swords, rolling pin, tulips in pots for the Chorus. Note: Paste may be used to hold gray petals in place on blue tulip.

Setting: Scene 1: A street in Holland. *Scene 2:* The Van Dyke kitchen. There is a working Dutch door up center, and windows left and right of door. Dutch fireplace is at right, and left is a large cupboard. There are a kitchen table and small benches down center. *Scene 3:* Same as Scene 2, with window boxes at windows. *Scene 4:* The palace courtyard. Bare stage, except for throne at center, and picture of blue tulip hanging over throne. Brightly colored banners hang from curtain at rear.

Lighting: Blue spotlight may be used when blue tulip is shown.

Sound: Music for "Come to the Fair," as indicated in text.

NEXT STOP—SPRING!

Characters: 6 male; 15 female; 4 male or female for Riders; as many as desired for Stickball Players.

Playing Time: 25 minutes.

Costumes: Conductor, Policeman, and Ice Cream Man wear appropriate uniforms. Others wear everyday spring dress. Stickball Players have on polo shirts and jeans; Grocer wears apron; Ladies wear very fancy spring hats; Housewives have kerchiefs on their heads. At beginning of play, Riders and Boy have on heavy winter coats, which they later remove. Umbrella Man wears dark raincoat, and later appears in flowered shirt, sunglasses, and pith helmet.

Properties: Newspaper with large headlines as indicated in text, megaphone, stool, black umbrellas, flower, football, stickball bat and ball, dustcloths, large tricycle ice cream truck, cardboard popsicles, jump ropes, baby carriage, hand mirrors, watering can, small rubber ball, handball, large rubber ball, volleyball, beach ball, beach umbrella, parasols, sign reading: ON VACATION, SEE YOU IN THE FALL, and other signs, as indicated in text.

Setting: A street. Up center, there are three houses, each with a door and steps leading to sidewalk. There is a shuttered window in each house, beneath which is a flower box. The first holds a petunia, the second a geranium, and the third a large rubber plant. A grocery store is at right and a hat shop is at left. A hopscotch diagram is drawn on stage at center with chalk. Exits are at right and left and through doors of grocery store and hat shop. For subway scene before rise, appropriate subway advertisements may be hung on curtain, and a turnstile may be placed down right.

Lighting: No special effects.

Sound: Whistle, recording of polka music, as indicated in text.

WHO WILL BELL THE CAT?

Characters: 9 male. (If desired, some parts may be taken by girls.)
Playing Time: 15 minutes.
Costumes: Aesop, Greek robe, sandals. Mice, gray costumes with tails. Valiant has a cardboard sword, and has pillows stuffed under costume, which he removes, as indicated in text. Cat wears cat costume, mask with whiskers, large claws.
Properties: Scroll, cheese, baskets of grain, oversized cardboard scissors, curling iron, brushes, combs, mirrors, collar with loud bell, medals.
Setting: Mouse Town. There is a backdrop of six large mouseholes, through which characters can enter and exit. Other exits are at left and right. Four tables with vendors' wares are placed in front of mouseholes, with signs. A tree and bench are down right.
Lighting: No special effects.

PEPE AND THE CORNFIELD BANDIT

Characters: 8 male; 4 female; Sapo may be played by a girl. As many Dancers as desired.
Playing Time: 20 minutes.
Costumes: Señor Granjero, Juan, Pedro, Pepe—loose cotton tunics, cotton trousers, sandals, serapes, sombreros. Sapo—green tights, flippers, green polo shirt, green gloves with long green fingernails, knobby hood, freckles. Ixlanda—helmet with long bill, trailing multicolored feathers, long cape of many colors resembling feathers. Ixlanda's Aztec costume, short-sleeved blouse, long skirt, many necklaces and large dangling gold earrings. Chorus, Mexican costumes. Dancers, Mexican costumes.
Properties: 3 bongo drums, 3 maracas for Chorus. Comb, hand mirror, broom, rifle, feather, tortilla, extra sombrero (very large).

Setting: Backdrop with mountains, cactus, and a thatched cottage. Well with opening at the back for toad, placed down center. Three rows of corn placed down left, one without tassels.

Lighting: No special effects.

Music: Mexican folk song; Mexican Hat Dance; as indicated in text.

A SONG GOES FORTH

Characters: 3 male; 2 female; 4 male or female Narrators; as many singers as desired for Chorus.

Playing Time: 15 minutes.

Costumes: King and Queen wear crowns and robes; Susanna wears a gown and a tiara. Prince wears cape, knee breeches, hat with plume. Commentator wears cutaway and top hat, and carries a cane. Narrators and Chorus wear everyday dress.

Properties: Straw hats or stetsons for boys in Chorus; sunbonnets for girls; stick horse, pompons.

Setting: Bare stage. Chairs for Chorus are at center. Two chairs for Narrators are down left, and two are down right.

Sound: Guitar, harmonica, or accordion may accompany country-style singing. Accompaniment for other sections may be as elaborate as desired.

MELINDA'S INCREDIBLE BIRTHDAY

Characters: 7 male; 8 female; as many extras as desired for Townspeople.

Playing Time: 20 minutes.

Costumes: Melinda wears pinafore. Inspector is dressed in Sherlock Holmes outfit, and Timekeeper wears tunic and sandals, and he has a beard. Delivery Boy wears messenger's uniform and cap. Cheerleaders are dressed in pink and white outfits. Others wear everyday dress, with pink and white sashes faced in red, white and blue striped material.

Properties: Calendar with January 17th blocked out, notebooks, pencils, magnifying glass, badge, gift-wrapped packages (one of them pink and white), gold star, autograph book, pink and white key, cake, microphone, pink and white balloons, bouquet, tray with cups and saucers, red, white and blue kites.

Setting: Scene 1: The Hall of Time. A blackboard and Wheel of Time are up center, and a table marked JANUARY BIRTHDAYS is at left. At right is barrel of stars. Scene 2: An auditorium. Rostrum draped in pink and white bunting is up center, and huge banner on the backdrop reads HAPPY BIRTHDAY. Three folding chairs are in front of rostrum, and rows of chairs are at right and left. A small table is down right. Exits are at right and left.

Lighting: No special effects.

Sound: Fanfares, offstage recording of party songs to precede Scene 2.

DATE DUE

#47-0108 Peel Off Pressure Sensitive